Research on Classroom Ecologies:
Implications for Inclusion of Children
With Learning Disabilities

Research on Classroom Ecologies: Implications for Inclusion of Children With Learning Disabilities

Edited by

Deborah L. Speece
University of Maryland

and

Barbara K. Keogh
University of California

LEA LAWRENCE ERLBAUM ASSOCIATES, PUBLISHERS
1996   Mahwah, New Jersey

Lawrence Erlbaum Associates, Inc., Publishers
10 Industrial Avenue
Mahwah, New Jersey 07430

cover design by Gail Silverman

Library of Congress Cataloging-in-Publication Data

Research on classroom ecologies : implications for inclusion of children with learning
    disabilities / edited by Deborah L. Speece and Barbara K. Keogh.
        p.   cm.
      Result of a symposium held at the Mayan Ranch in Bandera, Tex., Oct. 1994.
      Includes bibliographical references and index.
      ISBN 0-8058-1896-0 (cloth : alk. paper). — ISBN 0-8058-1897-9 (pbk. : alk. paper)
        1. Learning disabled children—Education—United States—Congresses. 2. Learning dis-
    abled children—Research—United States—Congresses. 3. Mainstreaming in education—
    United States—Congresses. 4. Learning disabilities—Research—United States—Congresses.
    I. Speece, Deborah L. II. Keogh, Barbara K.
    LC4705.R486   1996   95-42599
    371.91—dc20   CIP

Books published by Lawrence Erlbaum Associates are printed on acid-free paper, and their bindings are chosen for strength and durability.

Printed in the United States of America
10   9   8   7   6   5   4   3   2   1

Contents

Epilogue

Foreword

Edward Zigler
Sterling Professor of Psychology
Yale University

The field of education has undergone major upheavals, in terms of both philosophy and practice, in recent years. Educators, and those who train and administer them, have weathered criticism, frustration, and the daunting process of reinterpretation and virtual reconstruction of their modes of practice and their proper roles in the intellectual and social development of children. As a society, we are gradually moving away from an educational paradigm in which the child is seen as the passive recipient of information imparted in a school setting insulated and separate from the other spheres of that child's life. Increasingly, educators have joined psychologists in viewing the child as a complex being whose abilities, learning capacities, and identity are influenced by many aspects of the environment, including his own experiences and actions. Part of this revised picture is the importance of the child's active participation in the learning process and the role classroom and school climate can play in fostering the acquisition of knowledge.

Such fundamental shifts in educational theory have caused tremors throughout the field, as practitioners struggle to adjust to new ways of teaching and interacting with children and with their colleagues. But, with the uncertainty of change also comes excitement and the potential for growth. Nowhere is this opportunity more apparent than in the context of educating children once placed outside the circle of general education classrooms: children with learning disabilities. As a psychologist who has seen trends in the areas of mental retardation and special education come and go, I have long been a proponent of our viewing the child with learning disabilities or other special needs as a "whole person," a full individual with social, emotional, experiential, and motivational capacities as well as cognitive ones. Thus, I can only applaud the current efforts to extend and apply this view in education research and practice.

Interwoven as this changing perception is with the widening acceptance of the ecological model of development pioneered by Urie Bronfenbrenner, we are at last able to approach an understanding of the learning process in its full richness: as a highly intricate series of reciprocal transactions between learners, teachers, and the social environments of their classrooms. From this starting point, we are able to move forward from the stagnation of a deficit model of learning disability to the more fruitful inquiries indicated by Speece and Keogh: What kinds of transactions do we want to see in classrooms and how may disabilities affect these transactions?

The appearance of this groundbreaking and immensely valuable book could not be more timely as we move somewhat haltingly from the theory and philosophy of inclusion to the actual inclusion of greater numbers of diverse learners in the nation's classrooms. Too often, the students at the extreme ends of the achievement continuum have suffered the greatest neglect when placed in general education classrooms geared to average learners. The authors of this volume, while it is impossible to summarize or characterize adequately their wisdom, insights, and various points of view, are unified in their determination to ameliorate this situation and to discover effective strategies to meet the needs of all children in a classroom.

The task undertaken by editors Speece and Keogh and their colleagues is an extremely challenging one, taken on at a critical time when the field of education as a whole and the perceived mission of the school in society is changing. Significantly, the shape of the book itself is in the form of a dialogue, a series of instructive interactions among diverse thinkers and practitioners. The resulting volume is a courageous and remarkably effective effort, and it heralds a new and hopeful era for children with learning disabilities and their teachers, classmates, and families.

Acknowledgments

This book is the result of a symposium held at the Mayan Ranch in Bandera, Texas, October, 1994, entitled *Research on Classroom Ecologies: Implications for Inclusion of Children with Learning Disabilities*. The symposium was sponsored by the Division for Learning Disabilities of the Council for Exceptional Children (DLD), the Illinois State Board of Education, the Texas State Educational Agency, the Great Lakes Regional Resource Center (GLARRC), and the South Atlantic Regional Resource Center (SARRC).

Many people deserve credit for this collaborative effort between the private and public sectors interested in the development of children with learning disabilities. Diane Davis and Larry Magliocca provided leadership for the Regional Resource Centers. LiNelle Gallagher and Connie Parr served on the planning committee as state representatives for the Learning Disabilities Association. Dan Bulara and Barbara Marshall (GLARRC) were instrumental in keeping the planning committee organized during what seemed to be interminable conference calls. Forrest Novy (Texas, DLD) and Cindy Terry (Illinois, DLD) provided the fuel to energize the relationship between DLD and RRCs. KarenSue Zoeller (Texas) was a masterful host in Bandera who handled innumerable details, solved problems, and corralled us to stay on time. In addition to the support provided by SARRC, Texas also contributed time and support related to planning and documenting the symposium. In this regard we thank Bonnie Garrington and Sherry Myer.

Daniel Hallihan (DLD) shepherded the book through the contract stages with Hollis Heimbouch, who served as our initial editor at Lawrence Erlbaum

Associates, and Ray O'Connell who completed the editorial work. We are indebted to Marcy Pruiksma, our book production editor at LEA, for her professionalism and the great care she gave this book. We thank Edward Zigler for taking time from his busy schedule to write a thoughtful Foreword. We are especially appreciative of the DLD Executive Board and the DLD Presidents who encouraged the ideas of the Research Committee and supported the work with a generous budget: Elise Blankenship, Cindy Terry, and Candace Bos. Finally, we acknowledge the 1992–93 DLD Research Committee who convened on a cold winter weekend in Reston, VA, to consider future directions for research in learning disabilities from which the idea for this conference took shape: Reid Lyon, James D. McKinney, Robin Morris, Forrest Novy, Melinda Parrill, Addison Stone, and Joseph Torgesen.

The hard work of all of these professionals is evident in the following pages. We are deeply appreciative of their time and effort.

—*Deborah Speece*
—*Barbara Keogh*

About the Contributors

Kathryn H. Au, PhD, associate professor, College of Education, University of Hawaii, 1776 University Avenue, Honolulu, HI 96822.

Dr. Au received the PhD in educational psychology from the University of Illinois at Urbana-Champaign. Her research interest is the school literacy development of students of diverse cultural and linguistic backgrounds, and she has conducted many studies in classrooms with Native Hawaiian students. Her focus in recent years has been on holistic instruction, including the process approach to writing, literature-based instruction, and portfolio assessment. She has a continuing interest in culturally responsive instruction and its relationship to students' literacy achievement.

Jacquelin Carroll, MEd, 2525 Makauli'i Place, Honolulu, HI 96816.

Ms. Carroll is a curriculum developer at Kamehameha Schools, working with elementary school teachers in the area of language arts instruction. She has taught special education classes for students in Grades 7–12. Her research interests include student goal-setting and self-evaluation, portfolio assessment, and teacher development. Ms. Carroll received her MEd in educational psychology from the University of Hawaii at Manoa.

David H. Cooper, PhD, associate professor, Department of Special Education, 1308 Benjamin Building, University of Maryland, College Park, MD 20742.

Dr. Cooper's specialty area is early childhood, with emphasis on primary-grade students who have, or are at risk for, learning and behavioral disabilities. His research focuses on instructional environments and developmental assessment of children. Currently, he directs a teacher education reform effort which aims to provide appropriate learning environments for a diverse population of children at risk.

Mark Elrich, MEd, Rolling Terrace Elementary School, Montgomery County Public Schools, 705 Bayfield Road, Takoma Park, MD 20912.

Mr. Elrich teaches fourth grade in an economically and ethically diverse school. He also serves as a member of the Takoma Park City Council. Previously, he worked as a community activist in economic development programs designed to educate people with low incomes about such issues as housing, tenant rights, and food cooperatives. As the father of four children, two of whom are foster children with Down Syndrome, he wrote an essay on diversity in the classroom that was published recently in both *The Washington Post* and *Educational Leadership*.

Frederick Erickson, PhD, GSE alumni professor of education, Graduate School of Education, University of Pennsylvania, 3700 Walnut St., #A36, Philadelphia, PA 19104.

Dr. Erickson teaches the anthropology of education and directs the Center for Urban Ethnography. In addition he convenes the *Ethnography in Education Forum*, the largest annual meeting of qualitative researchers in the field of education. His publications include two books and numerous articles including *The Counselor as Gatekeeper: Social Interaction in Interviews* and *Sights and Sounds of Life in Schools*. From 1985 to 1998 he was editor of the *Anthropology and Education Quarterly*. In 1991 he received the American Anthropological Association's George and Louise Spindler Award for outstanding scholarly contribution to educational anthropology. In 1984 he received an award for Distinguished Research on Minority Issues in Education from the American Educational Research Association. He was the R. Freeman Butts Lecturer in 1989 at the annual meeting of the American Educational Studies Association.

Lynn S. Fuchs, PhD, professor, Department of Special Education, Box 328 Peabody College, Vanderbilt University, Nashville, TN 37203.

Dr. Fuchs is codirector of the Institute on Education and Learning in The Kennedy Center of Research on Human Development at Peabody College. Having received her PhD in education psychology from the University of Minnesota in 1981, she studies alternative forms of assessment, teachers' use of those assessment methods in instructional planning, and general educators' practices in accommodating student diversity. She is the coeditor of *The Journal of Special Education*.

Ronald Gallimore, PhD, professor of psychology, Department of Psychiatry and Biobehavioral Sciences University of California, Los Angeles, 760 West-wood Plaza, Westwood, CA 90095.

After earning a PhD in clinical psychology and 2 years as an assistant professor of Psychology, Dr. Gallimore was appointed Research Psychologist at Princess Bernice Pauahi Bishop Museum. He lived and did field research for 2 years in a small Native Hawaiian community, the results of which were published by Sage in *Culture, Behavior, and Education: A Study of Hawaiian-Americans* (with J. W. Boggs & C. Jordan, 1974). This project provided the cultural data he and Roland Tharp used in 1969 to design the Kamehameha Early Education Project (KEEP), the results of which were published by Cambridge University Press in 1988 (Tharp & Gallimore, *Rousing Minds to Life: Teaching, Learning and Schooling in Social Context*). Over the past decade, Gallimore has collaborated with Claude Goldenberg in a longitudinal study of Latino families living in Southern California and on several school and teaching innovation studies.

Charles R. Greenwood, PhD, Juniper Gardens Children's Project, 1614 Washington Blvd., Kansas City, KS 66102.

Dr. Greenwood directs the Juniper Gardens Children's Project, a community-based research and development center. He is a senior scientist in the Schiefelbusch Institute for Life Span/Studies at the University of Kansas and he holds the rank of courtesy professor in the departments of Special Education and Human Development and Family Life. He is a former teacher of students with behavior disorders and emotional disturbance. His research interests include education in urban schools, classroom instruction, behavior management, behavioral assessment, social skills, and applications of computer technology. He has been the investigator or principal investigator of 25 federal grants that have supported his research, training, and service to persons with mild–moderate disabilities.

Barbara Keogh, PhD, professor emeritus of Educational Psychology, Graduate School of Education, University of California, Los Angeles, 405 Hilgard, Los Angeles, CA 90024.

Dr. Keogh has been a member of the National Advisory committee on the Handicapped and was the recipient of the 1992 Research Award of the Council for Exceptional Children. Currently she is a Research Professor in the Department of Psychiatry at UCLA. Her research activities include study of developmental problems in young children, temperament, and learning disabilities.

Reid G. Lyon, PhD, neuropsychologist and director for Extramural Research Programs in Learning Disabilities, Language Disorders, and Disorders of Attention, Human Learning and Behavior Branch, Center for Research for

Mothers and Children, National Institute of Children Health and Human Development, National Institutes of Health, 6100 Executive Blvd., #4B05D, Bethesda, MD 20892.

Dr. Lyon's primary research interests include the development and validation of classification models and systems for disorders of learning and attention. Within this context, he is particularly interested in the study of various types of educational interventions and their effects on language-based reading disorders, as well as the application of noninvasive neuroimaging methodologies to identify neurophysiological correlates of specific reading deficits.

Annemarie Sullivan Palincsar, PhD, Charles and Jean Walgreen professor of Reading and Literacy, Educational Studies, University of Michigan, 610 East University, Ann Arbor, MI 48109.

Dr. Palincsar's initial research focused on the development and investigation of reciprocal teaching, an intervention designed to enhance learning from text. Subsequent research included the design, implementation, and investigation of an early literacy curriculum, integrating oral and written literacy for students with learning difficulties. Currently, she collaborates with teachers exploring the teaching of language as a tool for making sense of and communicating one's understanding across subject matters. She teaches in a graduate program entitled Literacy, Language, and Learning Disabilities, and prepares general educators to work with diverse classrooms of learners.

Elba I. Reyes, PhD, assistant professor, Department of Special Education and Rehabilitation, College of Education, The University of Arizona, Tucson, AZ 85721.

Dr. Reyes has been in the field of education for over 15 years. She started as a teacher in general education and expanded her interests to special education classrooms as a teacher and later as a teacher trainer. Presently, her areas of research and teaching interests focus on facilitating learning environments for teachers and for students with exceptionalities as well as issues concerning the education of persons from culturally diverse backgrounds.

Janis Erhardt Sayre, MSSc, Arbor Montessori School, 2298 La Vista Road, Decatur, GA 30033.

Having completed a graduate degree in Communicative Disorders with a major in learning disabilities at Emory University in 1976, Ms. Sayre's teaching interests have remained focused on helping the broadest possible spectrum of children become empowered and motivated by their learning. After working in the field of learning disabilities for 10 years, her interest in curriculum development and child-centered models of learning drew her to Montessori education. She earned an A.M.I. elementary diploma from the Washington Montessori Institute in 1990. Her recent work has centered on the development of written language through literature and creative writing. She is also interested in the development of materials and organizational aids related to the Montessori curriculum and in the further application of the Montessori approach to children with learning disabilities.

Ann C. Schulte, PhD, associate professor, Department of Psychology, North Carolina State University, Raleigh, NC 27695-7801.

Dr. Schulte's primary research interests are learning disabilities and school consultation. As part of a research team with Susan Osborne and J. D. McKinney, she completed a three-year study of pull-out versus mainstreaming approaches for providing services for students with learning disabilities that led to the development of a collaborative teaching model, which has been used in several school districts. She is currently completing a US Department of Education grant that examines the adoption of special education innovations in schools and the impact of school restructuring initiatives on children with disabilities.

Jeanne Shay Schumm, PhD, association professor, School of Education, 312 Merrick Building, University of Miami, 5202 University Drive, Coral Gables, FL 33124.

Dr. Schumm received her PhD from the University of Miami and is presently in the university's Department of Teaching and Learning. Her primary research interests include general education teachers' planning and adaptations for reading instruction for students with learning disabilities.

Deborah L. Speece, PhD, associate professor, Department of Special Education, 1308 Benjamin Building, University of Maryland, College Park, MD 20742.

Dr. Speece received the PhD in educational psychology from the University of North Carolina at Chapel Hill. Her research interests include learning disabilities, children at risk for school failure and their learning contexts, and classification issues in special education. She currently directs the doctoral leadership training program in learning disabilities.

Addison Stone, PhD, professor and head of the Program on Learning Disabilities, Department of Communication Sciences and Disorders, Northwestern University, 2299 N. Campus Drive, Evanston, IL 60208.

Dr. Stone has general interests in the social context of cognitive and language development in normally developing and atypical children. His recent research has focused on the learning of novel linguistic and nonlinguistic symbols in preschool children, and on social forces impacting the self-perceptions of atypical children. His recent publications also include several theoretical papers on the role of adult–child interaction in the cognitive development of normal and atypical children. At Northwestern he is involved in both the clinical and researcher training of LD specialists. He teaches courses on cognitive and social development, differential diagnosis of learning problems, and research methodology.

Linda Valli, PhD, associate professor and associate dean, College of Education, 3119 Benjamin Building, University of Maryland, College Park, MD 20742.

Dr. Valli is an associate professor in the Department of Curriculum and Instruction and currently serves as associate dean for Professional Studies. Her research interests include learning to teach, cultural diversity, professional development, and school improvement. She is editor of *Reflective Teacher Education: Cases and Critiques*.

Sharon Vaughn, PhD, professor, School of Education, University of Miami, PO Box 248065, Coral Gables, FL 33124.

Dr. Vaughn received her PhD from the University of Arizona and is presently a professor in the Department of Teaching and Learning and the Department of Psychology, University of Miami. Her primary research interests are social functioning of youngsters with learning disabilities and teachers' adaptations for students with learning disabilities.

Naomi Zigmond, PhD, professor and chair, Department of Instruction and Learning, University of Pittsburgh, 5N25 Forbes Quadrangle, Pittsburgh, PA 15260.

Dr. Zigmond is responsible for overseeing all teacher preparation programs, as well as advanced degree programs, in the School of Education. She is also professor of Special Education and teaches doctoral level courses in research in special education and in issues related to educational assessment. Her major research interest is in the development and evaluation of appropriate and effective public school programs for elementary and secondary students with learning disabilities and students with emotional and behavior disorders.

1

Learning Disabilities
Within the Context of Schooling

Barbara K. Keogh
University of California, Los Angeles
Deborah L. Speece
University of Maryland at College Park

This book was written during a period of reexamination and change in the field of special education. The federal legal requirement of "least restrictive environment" for the education of children with disabilities is weathering a wave of reinterpretations including mainstreaming, the Regular Education Initiative, and inclusion. Although each interpretation has its proponents and critics, limited theory and few data are available to guide these important policy decisions. Yet, these decisions will have long-lasting impact on children with learning disabilities, and it is from this perspective that we seek better understanding of the contexts in which children receive their formal education. Although there are many important contexts for children (e.g., families, social settings, religious organizations), this volume is focused specifically on classrooms. It is our view that classrooms are the settings where educators can have the most immediate impact and where research is most needed. Our purposes in this volume are to identify major influences within classrooms and to consider the implications for children with learning disabilities. In this chapter we present some of the arguments and research that support the importance of a broader view of learning disabilities, one that includes the child in the context of the classroom. We end with an overview of the organization and scope of the volume.

HISTORICAL PERSPECTIVE

Examination of the literature on both research and practice reveals surprisingly little concern for the influence of classroom contexts on the educational competencies and problems of children with learning disabilities. Indeed, the traditional focus has been on the individual child, with a central inference that learning disabilities have a neurobiological basis. Review of the history of this field demonstrates clearly the strong neurological orientation (For comprehensive reviews, see Doris, 1986; Torgesen, 1991). The early work on "congenital work blindness" by Hinshelwood (1917), the extensive studies by Strauss and his colleagues of children with brain damage (Strauss & Kephart, 1955; Strauss & Lehtinen, 1947), and the educational applications of Cruickshank, Bentzen, Ratzeburg, and Tannhauser (1961) had in common the assumption of a neurologically based disorder. Consistent with this perspective, the definition of learning disabilities proposed by the U.S. Interagency Committee on Learning Disabilities (Kavanagh & Truss, 1986) stated that learning disabilities "are intrinsic to the individual, presumed to be due to central nervous system dysfunction . . . " (p. 550).

The concern for the neurology of learning disabilities is clearly evidenced in current research conducted through the National Institutes of Health. Important examples include work on neuro-imaging, on the evolution of language, on the search for biological markers of learning disabilities, and on major cognitive mechanisms underlying dyslexia, all supported by the National Institute of Child Health and Human Development (Lyon, 1995). Similarly, research sponsored by the National Institute of Neurological Disorders and Stroke (NICDS) on learning disabilities in children addresses questions of subtypes of reading disorders based on electrophysiological findings, of difficulties in auditory discrimination, in developmental agraphia, and in the etiologies and effects of specific neurodevelopmental syndromes (Interagency Committee on Learning Disabilities, 1987). These are important efforts that hold promise for a deeper understanding of learning disabilities, their expression, and their treatment.

We suggest, however, that understanding the neurobiological basis of the problem is only one part of the puzzle. In a seminal article, Sameroff and Chandler (1975) argued persuasively for the need to consider development within a transactional model. In their view, and we agree, development and/ or problems in development are not well explained by main-effect models, even when the main effects are neurologically or biologically based. Thus, except in extreme conditions, predicting outcomes from single conditions early on is often uncertain. We argue that understanding learning disabilities requires consideration of both neurobiological and contextual contributions to the problem. In our view, schools and classrooms represent important aspects of context, and thus deserve careful consideration in understanding the development and achievement of children with learning disabilities.

RISK AND PROTECTIVE INFLUENCES

Borrowing a page from the extensive literature on risk (Rutter, 1983; Werner,

1986), we suggest that some conditions serve to intensify vulnerability and problems and thus may be considered risk factors, whereas other influences have buffering or protective effects (Garmezy, Masten, & Tellegen, 1984; Keogh & Weisner, 1993; Rutter, 1979, 1987; Werner, 1986). Werner and Smith (1992) defined risk factors as "biological or psychosocial hazards that increase the likelihood of a negative developmental outcome . . . " (p. 3), and protective factors as those that "modify (ameliorate, buffer) a person's reaction to a situation that in ordinary circumstances leads to maladaptive outcomes" (p. 5). A number of investigators have identified child, family, and community factors that serve risk or protective functions. These include biological status, maternal mental health, family size and stability, adequacy of and access to services (Garmezy et al., 1984; Masten et al., 1988; Rutter, 1979; Werner & Smith, 1992). However, relatively little systematic research has been directed at delineating risk and protective influences within schools (Keogh, 1992). This is surprising, given the obvious importance of schooling as an influence in children's lives, and the persistent findings that children's problem behavior and performance early on in school are associated with a range of negative, and often long-term, outcomes (see Kolvin, Miller, Fleeting, & Kolvin, 1988; Robins, 1978). We suggest that it is important to identify and understand the contributions of schools and classrooms if we are to work effectively with children with learning disabilities.

LIMITATIONS OF RESEARCH ON SCHOOLING EFFECTS

Our understanding of the contribution of schooling has been limited in several ways. First, for the most part, children's performance and adjustment in school have been treated as outcome variables or as status indices. Thus, although academic scores are used to identify individuals as learning disabled (the well-known if infamous aptitude–achievement discrepancy), we have only limited insight into the mechanisms or processes that account for such discrepancies, including the possible positive or negative contributions of schools or of classroom environments. This is due, in part, to the reliance on global descriptions of schools and to the limited number of child characteristics assessed. A relationship between scores on standardized achievement tests and the economic status of schools is well documented (Nichols & Chen, 1981), yet the reasons for the relationships are not entirely clear.

In this regard Felner, Aber, Primavera, and Cauce (1985) proposed that "a clear strategy of choice would be one that focuses on the relationships between specific aspects of the school environment and specific spheres of adjustment, rather than merely on more global linkages" (p. 367). Such an approach is promising as a way of specifying the functional transactions that affect the learning and development of young pupils with problems, and, thus, may provide direction for interventions. Important working questions have to do with which aspects of schools and which indices of adjustment? Recognition of the multivariate nature of the school experience adds both conceptual and operational complexity to research efforts.

A second limitation, as noted earlier, is that the bulk of research on at-risk conditions, including children with learning disabilities, has focused on the children and, to a lesser extent, on their families. A proliferating number of tests and assessment systems presumed to have relevance for schooling are available for describing characteristics of young children. Despite giving lip service to a range of influences on readiness for learning, however, the assessment approaches are directed almost exclusively at the child, typically tapping developmental levels in domains of physical motor, language, social/emotional, and cognitive knowledge. Although data about families, home conditions, and even examiner characteristics are sometimes gathered (see McLean & McCormick, 1993, for discussion and review of guidelines for assessment), information about schools is conspicuously missing.

Exclusive focus on the child provides important but only partial information, given powerful developmental and social/cultural theories that argue for the importance of context on development and achievement (Sameroff & Chandler, 1975; Weisner, 1984). Over 10 years ago Messick (1984) argued for a two-phase assessment system: The first, involving an analysis of the context of learning, was designed to address the overrepresentation of males and ethnic minorities in special education; the second phase was focused on the individual child and his or her specific attributes and problems. Despite the seemingly sensible nature of this approach to assessment, it has yet to be adopted widely in research and practice. We emphasize that schools, as well as families, are part of the context of children's lives, yet, with a few notable exceptions (e.g., Goodlad, 1984; Rutter, Maughan, Mortimore, Ouston, & Smith, 1979), schools have rarely been studied in risk research, and, where included, too often they have been described in nonspecific, demographic terms.

Third, when schooling is taken into account, it is usually with fixed effects models that assume homogeneity of conditions within schools and similarity of relationships between intake and outcome measures across schools (Maughan, 1988). These assumptions are, of course, highly suspect, because there is clearly great variation among schools within and across school districts. Closely related, there has been almost exclusive reliance on traditional statistical techniques that are based on limited variables and aggregated data, and that yield only main effect findings addressing between-group differences (Keogh & MacMillan, 1996; Maughan, 1988). The emphasis on modal or normative findings, as well as a lack of concern for within-group variance and for interactions, have restricted our understanding of the contributions of schools to developmental and educational status.

Finally, because there have been relatively few longitudinal studies, possible long-term effects of schooling of children with learning disabilities and the impact of school at particular times are not well understood. Dunn (1988) considered children's entry into school as a normative but potentially stressful event. In their follow-up study of the Kauai sample, Werner and Smith (1992) found that certain conditions and experiences, including those related to school, were especially important at certain times or in particular developmental periods. In this regard, Jason et al. (1993) reported that transfers or transitions between schools (e.g., from elementary to middle school) can be stressful experiences that are often associated with declines in academic performance and increases in personal/social problems. The impact of changes in school context may be especially strong on vulnerable children such as those with learning disabilities. For example, longitudinal analyses of elementary school children with learning disabilities indicate a decline in performance despite special education intervention. McKinney and his colleagues documented that children identified as learning disabled in first grade became more maladaptive with respect to profiles of classroom behavior over a 3-year period (McKinney & Speece, 1986), experienced high rates of grade retention over a 5-year period, and performed significantly lower on verbal intelligence and achievement measures than did mainstreamed peers (Osborne, Schulte, & McKinney, 1991). These findings suggest there is more than individual differences at work in the performance of children with learning disabilities, and support the need to examine more closely the features of general and special education classrooms associated with academic and behavioral outcomes.

In summary, we consider schooling to be an active influence on, and contributor to, children's risk or nonrisk status and to long-term outcomes for children with learning disabilities. We argue that educational status is, in part at least, a function of "goodness of fit" between child attributes and schooling demands, noting that for some children "educational risk" changes relative to setting and to time (Keogh, 1983, 1986). We suggest that children with learning disabilities are especially vulnerable to schooling effects, including changes in instructional and curricular demands and to teachers' expectations for performance. We argue that understanding the contributions of schooling requires going beyond summarizing demographics and linear input–output "production models" to consideration of the how and why of differential outcomes.

RISK AND PROTECTIVE ASPECTS OF SCHOOLS

Although not focused on pupils with learning disabilities, important domains of schools (e.g., instructional programs, administrative practices, and school environments and climates) have been specified in a number of major studies (Goodlad, 1984; the National Education Longitudinal Study, 1988; see also Good & Brophy, 1986). These domains are consistent with the findings from the somewhat limited research base specifically addressing schooling and risk. Rutter and Madge (1976), as an example, included high teacher turnover, poor teacher attitudes, lack of incentives, low student expectations, and poor social climate in their list of school risk variables. Lerner, Lerner, and Zabski (1985) distinguished between demands related to the physical setting and organization of classrooms and to demands related to interpersonal relations, especially teachers' expectations and requirements. Krasner's (1992) review of risk and protective factors in schools identified number of students, rate of teacher turnover, number and kind of remedial and special programs, level of funding, atmosphere or climate, and physical safety. It is reasonable to hypothesize that long-term personal and educational outcomes for children, especially children with learning disabilities, are affected by curricular content and instructional techniques, by peer characteristics, and by teachers' skills, attitudes, and expectations. These influences may serve either risk or protective functions.

As a backdrop to more detailed discussion in subsequent chapters, we stress that some of the risk and protective aspects of schools are so obvious that little discussion is needed and more research is irrelevant. It is a truism that safety is important, and that quality programs require adequate materials. Yet physical safety is a major problem in many areas, and a substantial number of children, especially children from low-income communities, attend schools that lack basic instructional materials (e.g., pencils, paper, textbooks), where buildings are deteriorated and dirty, and where play space is inadequate. These conditions must be considered factors that compound the developmental and educational status of at-risk children, particularly children who are at risk for learning problems. We suggest that improving the quality of schools in this domain is not a scientific question, but rather is a matter of social/political commitment.

In contrast, the possible contributions of other aspects of schools and classrooms are not as clear, especially as they relate to children with problems. In their review of the research base on classroom contexts and achievement for young children at risk for school failure, Speece and Molloy (1995) found few studies that linked these factors. That is, although there are many studies of classrooms, there is little work that systematically examines the influence of contextual elements on children who experience learning problems. This is a critical need if we are to provide quality education for children with learning disabilities within regular education programs.

CLASSROOM ENVIRONMENTS

In this section we discuss briefly three aspects of classrooms that we argue affect students, particularly those with learning disabilities: instruction, management, and peer and teacher interactions. Each of these topics is addressed in more detail in chapters that follow.

Instruction and Curricula

It is reasonable to hypothesize that instructional demands and the content of curricula interact with children's prior experiences, interests, competencies, and limitations, in some cases leading to a good "fit," in others resulting in problems. We suggest that the well-known "cultural difference" concept is not limited to children from nonmajority backgrounds, but also applies to a broader range of children, including those with learning disabilities. Indeed, these children are likely to be especially vulnerable to the nature of instructional programs. An accumulating literature argues for the powerful effects of instructional techniques on the achievement of children traditionally viewed as at risk for school.

Goldenberg and Gallimore's (1991) ongoing studies of reading achievement of Hispanic children are illustrative. These researchers noted that statistics on reading level have consistently indicated that Hispanic students perform well below national norms and, importantly, that the gap grows from 1 year at first grade to 3 years at twelfth grade. The discrepancy from normative expectancy is commonly attributed to language differences and to home and family conditions. Consistent with national statistics, 49% of the first-grade Hispanic children in the study schools were reading in preprimers, and only 7% of the children were at grade level (Goldenberg & Gallimore, 1991). After 3 years of a different instructional program, however, these figures were reversed. Only 1% of the children were reading at the preprimer level, over half were at grade level, and nearly one fourth were reading second-grade books. Clearly, this instructional program affected the achievement of children from a group considered at risk for reading failure. In this regard it is interesting to note that in the Goodlad (1984) study, teachers reported that curricula and materials were appropriate for most students in predominantly White schools, but for only 50% of the students in predominantly Black and Hispanic schools. Given the Goldenberg and Gallimore (1991) findings we might speculate that inappropriate instructional programs, rather than inadequate learners, account for a good deal of school failures.

We suggest further that the nature of the instructional program may be especially critical for children with learning disabilities. The impact of classroom environments and instructional programs on vulnerable children are underscored by Speece (1992), who called for serious consideration of the "classroom ecology" in the study of school effects. Based on her review of research on school effects, she argued that children in the same classroom experience different educational programs, and are exposed to different content and to different instruction. In their work on subtypes of problem learners,

Cooper and Speece (1990; Speece & Cooper, 1990) documented associations between first-grade children's personal characteristics and school placement decisions. Relevant to the present discussion were findings that there were interactions between environmental (instructional) variables and problem subtypes. As an example, for children in the learning disabilities subtype, identification as needing special placement was associated with low rates of small group reading instruction. Although carried out with older students, Webb's (1982) research on grouping for mathematics instruction also documented differences in grouping effects on good and poor learners.

The importance of instructional content and method is central to the current debate about reading instruction for children with learning disabilities. The identification of phonemic awareness skills as an early risk factor for reading disability brings into sharp relief differences between code-emphasis and whole language philosophies (Pressley & Rankin, 1994). Intervention research based on phonemic awareness and sound–symbol instruction documents improved word reading performance for both normally developing children and those at risk for poor educational outcomes due to economic circumstances (see Blachman, 1994, for review). The effectiveness of these methods for children with more severe disabilities (i.e., learning disabilities) is currently under investigation (e.g., Torgesen, 1995). The point to be emphasized is that educational outcomes are a function of both child characteristics and instructional characteristics. Yet this point is frequently overlooked in the conduct of research on children with learning disabilities, and in clinical/educational decisions made about individual children.

Management

In addition to instructional variations, classrooms differ dramatically in the ways they are organized in the use of time, space, and resources. In his comprehensive chapter on classroom management, Doyle (1986) noted that management and instructional issues are closely intertwined as "some minimal level of orderliness is necessary for instruction to occur and lessons must be sufficiently well constructed to capture and sustain student attention" (p. 394). Doyle made clear that management is not just maintaining discipline, but rather includes the amount and organization of physical space, the number and arrangement of individuals in that space, the materials and resources available, the organization of learning activities within the classroom, and time and duration of instructional components. Loughlin (1992) suggested that the organization of space and the arrangement of materials within the classroom are associated with characteristics of pupils' behavior, because they influence traffic patterns, the use of materials, and the amount of time spent in particular activities. The importance of the structural aspect of the classroom environment is illustrated by a study by Nordquist, Twardosz, and

McEvoy (1991), who documented improvement in compliant behavior and in the use of materials by young autistic children when the physical organization of their classrooms was changed. In addition to differences in children's behaviors, these investigators also reported increases in teachers' positive behaviors as a function of classroom reorganization.

We suggest that consideration of these broad aspects of management becomes especially important as inclusion policies result in greater numbers of children with learning disabilities being instructed in regular classrooms. The mere physical placement within a regular class is not the goal of inclusion for children with learning problems. Rather, as argued in the recent policy statement from the Orton Dyslexia Society (1994), inclusion describes "the opportunity for all students with disabilities to have access to and to participate in all activities of the school environment" (p. 1). This, of course, means careful consideration of the organization and delivery of all aspects of the school program. Doyle (1986) concluded: "From this perspective, management effectiveness cannot be defined solely in terms of rules for behavior. Effectiveness must also include such cognitive dimensions as comprehension and interpretation, skills which are necessary for recognizing when to act and how to improve classroom events to meet immediate circumstances" (p. 424).

Interactions of Teachers and Peers

A large amount of the literature demonstrates that there are major teacher effects on students' achievement (Brophy & Good, 1986), and that effective instruction involves teachers' decisions about how classrooms are organized, how instruction is presented, and goals and expectations for performance. Clearly there are differences among teachers in their knowledge of subject matter, in the adequacy and appropriateness of their instructional practices, in the ways they organize classrooms and programs, and in their personal attributes and competencies. These differences might be viewed as protective or risk influences, because some teachers mitigate and buffer children's problems, whereas others enhance and exacerbate the risks in schooling. Important influences also are found in teachers' beliefs, attitudes, and expectancies and in the attributions that they make about children's behaviors and achievements, because teachers' behaviors are linked to teachers' thoughts (see Clark & Peterson, 1986, for discussion).

The expectation and attribution literature is particularly relevant for understanding the school experiences of at-risk children. As shown in a number of observational studies carried out at UCLA (Burstein & Keogh, 1988; Siegel, 1992; Wilcoxen, 1984), instructional time is not evenly divided among children in a classroom. The frequency of interactions between teacher and student, and the nature of that interaction, is in part related to teachers' beliefs about children's potential for achievement. Whole groups of children may be at increased risk because teachers have low expectations for performance because of ethnic or cultural factors. Individual children may be at increased risk because their personal characteristics and behavioral styles are discrepant from teachers' beliefs and expectations. Teachers' views of pupils influence their instructional and management decisions, so that differential interactions are the mode, not the exception, in most classrooms.

Finally, although not as well studied, there appear to be clear risk and protective factors related to peers. Maughan (1988) suggested that the composition of pupil groups (i.e., the proportion of advantaged or disadvantaged peers) is associated with effects beyond those explained by characteristics of individual pupils. These considerations become especially important when the majority of children with learning disabilities are now in regular education classrooms.

CONCLUSIONS AND IMPLICATIONS FOR RESEARCH

Schools and classrooms are not just buildings and play yards, but rather are complex social systems. We underscore the enormous variation among schools and within schools and classrooms. Some schools and classrooms are safe havens for children from disrupted or threatening homes and communities. Indeed, the social and intellectual experiences of schooling can be active, facilitating, protective influences for many children with developmental or learning problems. In contrast, other schools may intensify problems and increase the vulnerability of already vulnerable children. Thus, a major implication is that to understand the long-term outcomes for children with learning disabilities our research efforts must take into account the nature of schools. As noted earlier, most assessment approaches focus exclusively on the individual child with learning disabilities, with little (if any) attention paid to the characteristics of classrooms. Yet children spend the largest part of the their school time in classrooms, and it is in classrooms that major social and educational experiences occur. Classroom experiences are powerful contributors to the success or failure of children with learning disabilities. Thus, we suggest that the study of schools and classrooms is a necessary, even critical, area of research.

It is clear, too, that we must go beyond the usual quantitative, summarizing descriptors (e.g., class size, SES) to get a more complete picture of what actually happens in school classrooms. Goodlad (1984) distinguished between ideal and formal aspects of curricula and the operational curriculum, emphasizing the distinction between what should be done and what actually occurs. The operational and the ideal or formal curricula often differ dramatically. Even within schools with a common philosophy or formal curriculum, programs vary by classroom. Thus, to understand the impact of a program on a child's school experience, it is necessary to know the instructional program and the classroom environment at the operational level. This requires more powerful and more sensitive techniques for assessing classrooms and schools, and a willingness to carry out research "where the action occurs," that is, in the classroom.

ORGANIZATION OF THE VOLUME

The goals of this volume are (a) to establish what is known about classroom ecologies from both general and special education perspectives, (b) to integrate the perspectives of researchers and practitioners, and (c) to chart directions for further research specifically related to children with learning disabilities. To accomplish these goals, researchers and practitioners representing a variety of theoretical and methodological perspectives were invited to prepare chapters or responses in their area of expertise. To make the task manageable, the construct of classroom ecology was defined as three interrelated domains: instruction, teacher and peer interaction, and organization and management. This scheme provides the structure for the book. The overlapping nature of these domains is evident in the chapters that follow.

Each of the first three sections of the book contains chapters by an educational researcher outside the field of special education and an educational researcher with expertise in special education and learning disabilities. Two response chapters follow. The first is by a general or special education teacher noted for his or her expertise with children, and the second is by a researcher in the field of learning disabilities. The response chapters are designed to reflect the content of the first two chapters and to chart new directions based on this knowledge. The final section, Research Methodology, contains two chapters reflecting differing views of appropriate questions and their study, and one response chapter. In the Epilogue, we identify themes from the volume and consider implications for research on learning disabilities.

The authors who have contributed to this volume have provided an enormous service to the field of education. Their clear thinking and cogent analyses have identified important issues and problems for us to consider as we tackle the difficult task of making classrooms places where all children with learning disabilities thrive. Taken as a whole, the content of the chapters underscores the limits of our current knowledge, while at the same time providing directions for needed changes in both research and practice. The nascent nature of our knowledge of classroom effects on learning is hardly surprising given the traditional emphasis on the child rather than the child in context. We hope this volume will broaden our views and improve the educational experiences of children with learning disabilities.

REFERENCES

Blachman, B. (1994). Early literacy acquisition: The role of phonological awareness. In G. P. Wallach & K. G. Butler (Eds.), *Language learning disabilities in school-age children and adolescents* (pp. 253–274). New York: Macmillan.

Brophy J., & Good, T. L. (1986). Teacher behavior and student achievement. In M. C. Wittrock (Ed.), *Handbook of research on teaching,* 3rd ed. (pp. 328–375). New York: MacMillan.

Burstein, N. D., & Keogh, B. K. (1988). Relationship of temperament to preschool children's interactions with peers and teachers. *Exceptional Children, 54*(5), 456–461.

Clark, C. M., & Peterson, P. L. (1986). Teachers' thought processes. In M. C. Wittrock (Ed.), *Handbook of research on teaching,* 3rd ed. (pp. 255–296). New York: MacMillan.

Cooper, D. H., & Speece, D. L. (1990). Maintaining at-risk children in regular education settings: Initial effects of individual differences and classroom environments. *Exceptional Children, 57,* 117–126.

Cruickshank, W. M., Bentzen, F. A., Ratzeburg, F. H., & Tannhauser, M. T. (1961). *A teaching method for brain-injured and hyperactive children.* Syracuse, NY: Syracuse University Press.

Doris, J. (1986). Learning disabilities. In S. T. Ceci (Ed.), *Handbook of cognitive, social, and neurological aspects of learning disabilities* (Vol. 1, pp. 3–53). Hillsdale, NJ: Lawrence Erlbaum Associates.

Doyle, W. (1986). Classroom organization and management. In M. C. Wittrock (Ed.), *Handbook of research on teaching* (pp. 392–431). New York: Macmillan.

Dunn, J. (1988). Normative life events as risk factors in childhood. In M. Rutter (Ed.), *Studies in psychosocial risk: The power of longitudinal data* (pp. 227–244). Cambridge, England: Cambridge University Press.

Felner, R. D., Aber, M. S., Primavera, J., & Cauce, A. M. (1985). Adaptation and vulnerability in high-risk adolescents: An examination of environmental mediators. *American Journal of Community Psychology, 13*(4), 365–379.

Garrmezy, L., Masten, A., & Tellegen, A. (1984). The study of stress and competence in children: A building block for developmental psychopathology. *Child Development, 55,* 97–111.

Goldenberg, C., & Gallimore, R. (1991). Local knowledge, research knowledge, and educational change: A case study of early Spanish reading improvement. *Educational Researcher, 20*(8), 2–14.

Good, T. L., & Brophy, J. E. (1986). School effects. In *Handbook of research on teaching,* 3rd ed. (pp. 570–602). New York: Macmillan.

Goodlad, J. (1984). *A place called school.* New York: McGraw-Hill.

Hinshelwood, J. (1917). *Congenital word blindness.* London: H. R. Lewis.

Jason, L., Weine, A. M., Johnson, J. H., Danner, K. E., Kurasaki, K. S., & Warren-Sohlberg, L. (1993). The school transition project: A comprehensive prevention intervention. *Journal of Emotional and Behavioral Disorders, 1*(1), 65–70.

Kavanagh, J. F., & Truss, T. J., Jr. (Eds.). (1986). *U.S. Interagency Committee on Learning Disabilities: Proceedings of a national conference.* Parkton, MD: York Press.

Keogh, B. K. (1983). Individual differences in temperament: A contribution of the personal, social, and educational competence of learning disabled children. In J. D. McKinney & L. Feagens (Eds.), *Current topics in learning disabilities* (pp. 33–55). Norwood, NJ: Ablex.

Keogh, B. K. (1986). Temperament and schooling: What is the meaning of goodness of fit? In J. V. Lerner & R. M. Lerner (Eds.), *New directions in child development: Temperament and social interaction during infancy and childhood* (pp. 89–108). San Francisco, CA: Jossey-Bass.

Keogh, B. K. (1992). Learning disabilities in preschool children. In F. R. Brown III, E. H. Aylward, & B. K. Keogh (Eds.), *Diagnosis and management of learning disabilities: An interdisciplinary lifespan approach.* San Diego, CA: Singular Press.

Keogh, B. K., & MacMillan, D. L. (1996). Exceptionality. In D. Berliner & R. Calfee (Eds.), *Handbook of Educational Psychology*. Washington, DC: American Psychological Association.

Keogh, B. K., & Weisner, T. S. (1993). An ecocultural perspective on risk and protective factors in children's development: Implications for learning disabilities. *Learning Disabilities Research and Practice, 8*(1), 3–10.

Kolvin, I., Miller, F. J. W., Fleeting, M., & Kolvin, P. A. (1988). Risk/protective factors for offending with particular reference to deprivation. In M. Rutter (Ed.), *Studies of psychosocial risk: The power of longitudinal data* (pp. 77–95). Cambridge, England: Cambridge University Press.

Krasner, D. (1992). *A study of risk and protective factors and achievement of children at risk.* Unpublished doctoral dissertation, University of California, Los Angeles.

Lerner, J. V., Lerner, R. M., & Zabski. (1985). Temperaments and elementary school children's actual and rated academic performance: A test of a "goodness of fit" model. *Journal of Child Psychology and Psychiatry, 26,* 125–136.

Loughlin, C. E. (1992). Classroom physical environment. in M. Alkin (Ed.), *Encyclopedia of educational research,* 6th ed. (pp. 161–164). New York: Macmillan.

Lyon, G. R. (1995). Research initiatives in learning disabilities: Contributions from scientists supported by the National Institute of Child Health and Human Development. *Journal of Child Neurology, 10,* Supplement Number 1, S120–S126.

Masten, A. S., Garmezy, N., Tellegen, A., Pellegrini, D. S., Larkin, K., & Larsen, A. (1988). Competence and stress in school children: The moderating effects of individual and family qualities. *Journal of Child Psychology and Psychiatry, 29,* 745–764.

Maughan, B. (1988). School experiences as risk/protective factors. In M. Rutter (Ed.), *Studies of psychosocial risk: The power of longitudinal data* (pp. 200–220). Cambridge, England: Cambridge University Press.

McKinney, J. D., & Speece, D. L. (1986). Academic consequences and longitudinal stability of behavioral subtypes of learning disabled children. *Journal of Educational Psychology, 78*(5), 365–372.

McLean, M., & McCormick, K. (1993). Assessment and evaluation in early intervention. In W. Brown, S. K. Thurrman, & L. F. Pearl (Eds.), *Family-centered early intervention with infants and toddlers* (pp. 43–79). Baltimore, MD: Paul Brookes.

Messick, S. (1984). Assessment in context: Appraising student performance in relation to instructional quality. *Educational Researcher, 13*(3), 3–8.

National Educational Longitudinal Study (NELS) (1988). U.S. Department of Education National Center for Educational Statistics, Washington, DC.

Nichols, P. L., & Chen, T.-C. (1981). *Minimal brain dysfunction: A prospective study.* Hillsdale, NJ: Lawrence Erlbaum Associates.

Nordquist, V. M., Twardosz, S., & McEvoy, M. A. (1991). Effects of environmental reorganization in classrooms for children with autism. *Journal of Early Intervention, 15*(2), 135–152.

Orton Dyslexia Society (1994). *Special issue: Perspectives on inclusion, 20*(4), 1–16.

Osborne, S. S., Schulte, A. C., & McKinney, J. D. (1991). A longitudinal study of students with learning disabilities in mainstream and resource programs. *Exceptionality, 2,* 81–95.

Pressley, M., & Rankin, J. (1994). More about whole language methods of reading instruction for students at risk for early reading failure. *Learning Disabilities Research & Practice, 9,* 157–168.

Robins, N. L. (1978). Study of childhood predictors of adult outcome: Replication from longitudinal studies. *Psychological Medicine, 8,* 611–622.

Rutter, M. (1979). Protective factors in children's response to stress and disadvantage. in J. W. Kent & J. E. Rolf (Eds.), *Primary prevention of psychopathology, Vol. 111, Social Competence in Children* (pp. 49–72). Hanover, NH: University Press of New England.

Rutter, M. (1983). Stress, coping, and development: Some issues and some questions. In N. Garmezy & M. Rutter (Eds.), *Stress, coping, and development in children* (pp. 1–41). New York: McGraw-Hill.

Rutter, M. (1987). Psychosocial resilience and protective mechanisms. *American Journal of Orthopsychiatry, 57*(3), 316–331.

Rutter, M., & Madge, N. (1976). *Cycles of disadvantage: A review of research.* London: Heinemann.

Rutter, M., Maughan, B., Mortimore, P., Ouston, J., & Smith, A. (1979). *Fifteen thousand hours: Secondary schools and their effects on children.* London: Open Books.

Sameroff, A., & Chandler, M. (1975). Reproductive risk and the continuum of caretaking casualty. In F. D. Horowitz (Ed.), *Review of child development research* (Vol. 4, pp. 187–244). Chicago: University of Chicago Press.

Siegel, J. (1992). *Regular education teachers' attitudes and behaviors toward their mainstreamed learning handicapped students.* Unpublished doctoral dissertation, University of California, Los Angeles.

Speece, D. (1992, February). *An examination of the contribution of the classroom environment to the development of learning disabilities.* Paper presented at the third annual meeting of the International Association for Cognitive Education, Riverside, CA.

Speece, D. L., & Cooper, D. H. (1990). Ontogeny of school failure: Classification of first-grade children. *American Educational Research Journal, 27,* 119–140.

Speece, D. L., & Molloy, D. E. (1995). *How does context connect with achievement for young children with learning problems?* Manuscript in review.

Strauss, A. A., & Kephart, N. C. (1955). *Psychology and education of the brain injured child: Progress in theory and clinic* (Vol. 2). New York: Grune and Stratton.

Strauss, A. A., & Lehtinen, L. E. (1947). *Psychology and education of the brain injured child.* New York: Grune & Stratton.

Torgesen, J. K. (1991). Learning disabilities: Historical and conceptual issues. In B. Y. L. Wong (Ed.), *Learning about learning disabilities* (pp. 3–37). San Diego, CA: Academic Press.

Torgesen, J. K. (1995, February). *Phonological reading disability: Developmental and educational perspectives.* Presentation to the Doctoral Leadership Program in Learning Disabilities, Department of Special Education, University of Maryland, College Park.

Webb, N. (1982). Student interaction and learning in small groups. *Review of Educational Research, 52,* 421–445.

Weisner, T. S. (1984). Ecocultural niches of middle childhood: A cross-cultural perspective. In W. A. Collins (Ed.), *Development during middle childhood: The years from six to twelve* (pp. 338–368). Washington, DC: National Academy of Sciences Press.

Werner, E. E. (1986). The concept of risk from a developmental perspective. In B. K. Keogh (Ed.), *Advances in special education vol. 4; Developmental problems in infancy and the preschool years* (pp. 1–24). Greenwich, CT: JAI Press.

Werner, E. E., & Smith, R. (1992). *Overcoming the odds. High risk children from birth to adulthood.* Ithaca, New York: Cornell University Press.

Wilcoxen, A. G. (1984). *Relationships among teacher attitudes and teacher–pupil interactions in special classes.* Unpublished doctoral dissertation, University of California, Los Angeles.

PART I

Classroom Instruction

Current Research on Classroom Instruction: Goals, Teachers' Actions, and Assessment

Kathryn H. Au
Jacquelin H. Carroll
University of Hawaii at Manoa

In the broadest sense, classroom instruction includes any activities and experiences organized to encourage student learning. Instruction generally occurs as part of a cycle of teaching and learning. Although its phases overlap and are interrelated, we can think of the cycle as beginning with an understanding of the goals of instruction, proceeding through a vision of classrooms and teachers' instructional actions, and moving to assessment. In practice, phases of teaching and assessment are closely linked and may be indistinguishable from one another.

CHANGING VIEWS OF INSTRUCTION

New ideas about classroom instruction are perhaps best understood against the backdrop of the paradigm shift taking place in educational psychology, as research perspectives have changed from behaviorism to cognitive science to social constructivism (Hiebert & Raphael, in press). In the behaviorist and cognitive science perspectives, instruction is seen as a process of transmission from teacher to student, and the guiding metaphor is that of the conduit (cf. Wertsch, 1991). In the conduit metaphor, the teacher sends or transmits a signal that is received by the student. The signals are unidirectional, implying that instruction is monologic. The sender, or teacher, is assumed to be active, whereas the receiver, or student, is seen as passive. The receiver's job is to extract the meaning from the signal, to get the intended meaning into his or her own mind. The task of extraction is assumed to be simple, so the role of the reader or listener is trivial in comparison to that of the writer or speaker.

From a social constructivist perspective, instruction is seen as a process of transaction between teacher and student, and the guiding metaphor is that of the conversation. The teacher and student exchange ideas for the purpose of generating new knowledge. The conversation metaphor assumes that signals flow in both directions, so instruction is dialogic. Both teacher and student are active in the process of knowledge construction and in seeking to understand one another's thinking. The task of knowledge construction is assumed to be complex and to involve learning by both the teacher and student.

Although the conduit and conversation metaphors are useful heuristic devices, processes of transmission and transaction are not mutually exclusive, in either theory or practice. A given instructional event might have elements of both transmission and transaction. For example, the transmission model often includes students' responses, and a teacher's actions may be changed as a result of what students say or do. The transaction model often includes an element of transmission, because it sometimes makes sense to teach students a skill directly. Furthermore, one may use a transaction model to teach strategies (e.g., Englert, Raphael, & Anderson, 1992; Palincsar & Brown, 1984).

Behaviorist and Cognitive Science Perspectives

Transmission views of instruction found support in the work of Bloom (1976) and other behaviorists, who see the goals of instruction in terms of clearly specified skills. Through direct instruction, teachers explain and demonstrate skills, and students practice skills, usually on worksheets. Students' mastery of skills is assessed through criterion-referenced testing. Process–product research consistent with this perspective on instruction was reviewed by Brophy and Good (1992).

For today's educators, the legacy of mastery learning, direct instruction, and related approaches may be less in the specific instructional technology proposed than in the vision toward which this technology was aimed. Bloom and others argued that the purpose of education is not the selection of talent, but the development of talent. Previously, success was generally assumed to be highly related to, or even predetermined by, native intelligence. The purpose of behavioral objectives, direct instruction, and criterion-referenced testing is to make it possible for all students to succeed in school. With the behaviorist movement, success is connected to such variables as time allocated for instruction and student engagement in instructional activities; in other words, factors that educators can influence.

The cognitive science perspective was built on the foundation provided by behaviorism, while seeking to correct weaknesses evident in the earlier approach (Hiebert & Raphael, in press). One weakness is that skills are taught and learned in isolation, with little attention paid to teaching students when they should apply these skills. To remedy this problem, cognitive science approaches make strategies, rather than skills, the goal of instruction. When teaching strategies, teachers seek to impart to students what they will be learning, when the strategy should be used, why it is important, and how it should be carried out (Roehler, Duffy, & Meloth, 1986). Often, assessment examines not only students' use of strategies but also their metacognitive awareness of the strategies. Reading research consistent with this perspective on instruction was reviewed by Roehler and Duffy (1991).

The behaviorist and cognitive science perspectives share certain assumptions consistent with positivism and postpositivism (for characterizations of these paradigms, refer to Guba & Lincoln, 1994). One assumption, as seen in the conduit metaphor, is that knowledge can be transmitted from the teacher (the expert) to the student (the novice) (cf. Hiebert & Raphael, in press). Another assumption is that complex processes such as reading and writing are best taught by moving from part to whole. That is, teachers teach skills or steps that, when put together, enable students to read and write. This assumption means that initial learning is often separated from doing, or carrying out the full processes of reading and writing. This bottom-up transmission model of instruction is consistent with an ontology of realism, or the belief in an apprehendable reality (Guba & Lincoln, 1994).

Constructivist and Social Constructivist Perspectives

The constructivist and social constructivist perspectives cast new light on issues of classroom instruction (for a history of constructivism, refer to Schwandt, 1994). The central concern of constructivism is lived experience, or the world as it is felt and understood by social actors. The realism of positivism and postpositivism is replaced by relativism, the belief that there are multiple intangible realities formulated by groups and individuals (Guba & Lincoln, 1994). If knowledge is created, not discovered, then in some sense it must always be constructed or reconstructed by the knower. Instruction cannot be seen purely as a process of transmission, because the learner must be actively involved in creating his or her own knowledge.

Within psychology and educational psychology, earlier views of constructivism centered on the personal, subjective nature of knowledge construction. For example, this view is seen in the whole language movement, which draws on the work of Piaget in stressing the meaning-making abilities of the individual child. Newer views of constructivism, known as *social constructivism,* focus on the social, intersubjective nature of knowledge construction (Mehan, 1981). Social constructivism is based on the idea that both social and cognitive structures are created and situated in interactions among people. Social constructivists argue that the very terms by which people perceive and describe the world, including language, are social artifacts (Schwandt, 1994). Because they believe reality to be created through processes of social exchange, social constructivists are interested in the collective generation of meaning among people. As is evident in the metaphor of the conversation, instruction is seen as a process of the joint construction of meaning by social actors.

From a social constructivist perspective, the starting point for instruction is students' interest in and involvement with an authentic activity (Au, 1993a). The teacher's first task is to motivate students to become involved in the activity. Once students are engaged, the teacher provides them with the support needed to complete the activity successfully. In other words, instruction starts with interest and follows with skills. In contrast, in the behaviorist and cognitive science perspectives, instruction tends to start with skills. Interest is generally assumed to develop as a consequence of students' proficiency in skills and strategies. Behaviorist approaches have been criticized for leading to an overemphasis on skill instruction, for example, in remedial reading programs (Allington, 1991), which generally result in students becoming neither proficient nor interested in reading.

Although there is considerable documentation of the limitations of transmission instruction, there is as yet little documentation, beyond considerable anecdotal evidence, of the promise of transaction instruction. There is considerable debate about whether traditional measures of students' learning can or should be applied to transaction instruction, and, if not, what types of measures if any might be appropriate (McKenna, Stahl, & Reinking, 1994).

From the perspective of our own research with transaction instruction, as well as related studies, we will discuss three topics: goals for instruction, teachers' instructional actions, and assessment. Our research with transaction instruction was conducted at the Kamehameha Elementary Education Program (KEEP), a 24-year research and development effort to improve the literacy achievement of elementary school students of Native Hawaiian ancestry. From 1989 to 1994, KEEP's work centered on the implementation of a whole literacy curriculum, including portfolio assessment (for details, refer to Au & Asam, 1994).

GOALS FOR INSTRUCTION

Changes in the way many researchers currently think about instructional goals reflect the shifting paradigms. In the field of literacy, for example, earlier experiments by behaviorists and cognitive scientists, largely conducted with adults, led researchers to analyze reading into an elaborate set of skills (e.g., Gough, 1972). Instruction was seen as a matter of teaching these skills.

From a social constructivist perspective, studies in emergent literacy conducted with young children in homes and schools led to a different set of conclusions. Researchers discovered that children actively construct their own understandings about the functions of literacy before they learn about its forms, such as letters and sounds (Taylor, 1983). For example, children scribble lists or phone messages, showing that they understand the use of writing as an aid to memory, before they can actually use letters to spell words. Regardless of cultural background or socioeconomic status, all children in literate societies such as the United States have considerable experience with literacy prior to entering kindergarten (Taylor & Dorsey-Gaines, 1988), although the nature of this experience varies considerably.

When literacy is seen from a social constructivist perspective, the goals of instruction are quite different. Skills (such as using knowledge of beginning sounds or understanding the sequence of events in a story) may still be present, but objectives are stated in more global terms and oriented toward full processes and thoughtful, purposeful use. Value is attached to students' knowledge of the functions of literacy and construction of their own understandings, including personal interpretations.

An example of a constructivist approach to goals for instruction is seen in the whole literacy curriculum developed to guide instruction at KEEP (Asam et al., 1993). This curriculum replaced an earlier one that emphasized reading comprehension. The whole literacy curriculum addressed six aspects of literacy: ownership, the writing process, reading comprehension, word reading strategies and spelling, language and vocabulary knowledge, and voluntary reading.

The first aspect of literacy, ownership, was also the overarching goal of the curriculum. Ownership has to do with students valuing their own ability to read and write. Students who have ownership of literacy have a positive attitude toward reading and writing and routinely use literacy in their everyday lives. The next aspect of literacy is the writing process. Writing is seen as dynamic and nonlinear, including such activities as planning, drafting, revising, editing, and publishing (Graves, 1983). Reading comprehension, the third aspect, involves a complex interaction among the reader, the text, and the social situation or context in which reading takes place (Wixson, Peters, Weber, & Roeber, 1987).

The fourth aspect of literacy, word reading strategies and spelling, centers on Clay's (1985) notion that effective word identification requires the simultaneous use of information from different cue systems. Children must learn to take a problem-solving approach, cross-checking their responses with information available from meaning (i.e., passage and sentence context), structural, and visual cues.

Language and vocabulary knowledge, the fifth aspect of literacy, involves the ability to understand and use appropriate terms and structures in both spoken and printed English. It includes the ability to derive the meanings of new words while reading. The whole literacy curriculum followed an approach to vocabulary consistent with the knowledge hypothesis (Mezynski, 1983), the idea that vocabulary represents a person's knowledge of particular topics as opposed to dictionary-style definitions. In voluntary reading, the final aspect of literacy, students select the materials they wish to read, either for information or for pleasure. Ideally, students also choose the times when they will read (Spiegel, 1981).

The shift in paradigms is evident in several features of this curriculum framework. The first and sixth aspects of literacy are affective ones, which would not have been included in a skills-oriented curriculum. In these earlier curricula, proficiency was seen as the ultimate goal. When ownership is the goal, instruction must go beyond proficiency and deal with the issue of whether students value literacy enough to make it part of their everyday lives.

In addition, the relationship among affective and cognitive aspects of literacy is different from that hypothesized in a skills curriculum, which assumes that mastery of skills comes first. Instead, ownership is seen as both a mediating factor and an outcome. Ownership of literacy may increase students' motivation to read and write, prompting attention to the learning of skills. Of course, an ability to apply skills may make reading and writing easier, so that they are undertaken and enjoyed more often.

The writing process and reading comprehension are considered to be equally important, in contrast to earlier approaches at the elementary level that emphasized reading. Writing was downplayed because composition was assumed to be too difficult for children in kindergarten and first grade. Writing, we now know, is as important as reading in young children's literacy development (Shanahan, 1990). The whole literacy curriculum highlights the writing process to foreground students' active efforts to construct meaning from text. Vocabulary and word reading strategies, areas advocated by those concerned with basic skills, also are seen in terms of students' efforts at meaning-making. Skills are subsumed under strategies, and strategies are related to the larger processes of reading comprehension and writing.

The KEEP whole literacy curriculum went a step further than most holistic, constructivist curricula in translating the aspects of literacy into grade-level benchmarks or performance standards. The purpose of the benchmarks was to provide goals specific enough to guide teachers' instructional actions. The challenge in formulating grade-level benchmarks was to make them concrete yet holistic enough to be true to a constructivist perspective.

In the previous KEEP curriculum, objectives were stated in behavioral terms and assessment took place through conventional criterion-referenced tests. For example, one of the objectives for reading comprehension read as follows: The child will read a narrative story and answer written, multiple-choice, or sentence completion items.

The questions assess five levels of comprehension:

(1) association (details)
(2) classification (categorization)
(3) seriation (cause and effect, sequence)
(4) integration (main idea, major problem)
(5) extension (application of understanding beyond immediate story structure).

The following sample benchmarks for reading comprehension illustrate the new approach:

- Reads and comprehends text at grade level
- Writes personal responses to literature
- Makes connections among different works of literature
- Writes summary that includes story elements

Following Rosenblatt (1978) and others who explored reader response theory, the benchmarks require students to take both aesthetic and efferent stances toward literature, that is, to read for the personal experience of reading, as well as to read to extract information from the text. The personal responses of one student may differ from those of another, so the emphasis is less on a single correct answer and more on the process of text interpretation. The notion of having students deal with increasingly difficult text is conveyed in the requirement that students must be reading material at grade level. In short, research taking a holistic, socially contextualized view of literacy led to dramatic changes in instructional goals.

TEACHERS' INSTRUCTIONAL ACTIONS

As the field moves toward process-oriented goals for students' meaning-making in social contexts, teachers' instructional actions must follow different models. Because learning is not seen as the acquisition of a discrete set of skills or strategies, teaching is not conducted as a discrete set of actions. Instead, teachers consider the full processes of reading and writing as they plan their instruction.

Classroom organization and transaction instruction can be highly complex. However, research at KEEP suggests that it is possible to specify the features of this instructional model. KEEP did this by creating a checklist to guide staff development. (See Table 2.1 for examples of checklist items.) Teachers used the checklist to identify features of instruction already implemented in their classrooms. Then they set goals for their own staff development by identifying features they wanted to implement next and worked to make the necessary changes.

The checklist was divided into three areas: classroom organization, the teacher's role, and the student's role. We discuss these areas by contrasting

TABLE 2.1
Selected Classroom Implementation Checklist Items
for the Writers' Workshop

Classroom Organization	Teacher's mini-lessons:
Frequency (average 4–5 times per week)	Audience: whole class, small group,
Length (minimum 45 minutes per day)	individual
Workshop rules and procedures:	Type: classroom procedures, author's
Collaborative decisions	craft, mechanics
Clarity and consistency	Teacher/student conferences:
Student portfolios:	Procedures
Contents: writing samples, record-	Content
keeping forms	*Student Opportunities*
Meetings with teacher	Ownership of process:
Teacher monitoring student work:	Enjoy writing
Systematic data collection:	Show confidence/pride
Status of the class	Have a sense of audience
Portfolios	Knowledge of process:
Other forms	Select own topics
Data informs instruction	Plan
Teacher Participation	Draft
Teacher as a writer:	Revise
Demonstrations	Edit
Member of writing community:	Publish
Writes with students	Share
Shares own writing	Confer
Shares experiences with writing	Understand reasons behind process
process	Knowledge of grade level benchmarks
	Independence as writer

the transaction model of instruction growing from the constructivist perspective with the transmission model of instruction growing from the behaviorist and cognitive science perspective.

Classroom Organization

When teachers plan instruction based on the transmission of knowledge, classrooms are organized so that students operate under the watchful eye of the teacher. Writing instruction is most often directed at the whole class, where it is easier for the teacher to observe and monitor behavior. Reading instruction is often done in teacher-assigned small groups, where the teacher may listen to children's one-by-one oral reading, or teach skills or strategies from a reading series teacher's guide, while those in other groups do individual seatwork activities. The teacher maintains control over the resources of the classroom and the movement of the students from activity to activity.

In one such classroom, a writing lesson was observed. The teacher told her third graders that they would be writing poems about Christmas. She suggested several topics: what they wanted for Christmas, what they liked about Christmas, or what they did to celebrate Christmas in their own homes. She explained that poems didn't have to rhyme, although they could. Then she passed out lined paper and the students began writing. When one child whispered to another, the teacher reminded the class, "No talking. Just do your own work." The children brought their drafts to her, and she corrected spelling and punctuation, pointing out each error and explaining why it needed correction. Finally, the children were given clean sheets of paper for their final copies. One child was nominated to pass out paper for the poem covers, and each child chose either red or green.

Teachers who follow a transaction model of instruction set up their classrooms so that students are joint participants in decision making and are allowed to make choices in how they use their time to work at literacy tasks. Resources and materials are readily available and not controlled by the teacher. Access to peers and to the teacher is under joint control. Classrooms are organized to accommodate multiple activities occurring at the same time. Activities are "authentic," that is, an effort is made to have activities resemble those in the world outside the classroom.

One structure used to involve students in the full processes of reading and writing is the workshop, most often expressed as a writers' workshop or a readers' workshop. The workshop metaphor evolved from the domain of artists or craftspeople, who may come together to work on individual pieces at different paces and in different stages, even though they operate in the same physical area, may share tools and techniques, and have the common purpose of artistic creation. Graves (1983) described how students operated in a workshop setting as they moved through the writing process. Other educators such as Calkins (1986), Hansen (1987), and Atwell (1987) elaborated on the writing workshop and applied the workshop metaphor to the operation of a readers' workshop.

After the change to the whole literacy curriculum, KEEP classrooms were organized around writers' and readers' workshops in a transaction model. The contrast with the transmission classroom described earlier is quite striking, as can be seen in the following observation of a KEEP writers' workshop at second grade.

Instead of controlling the distribution of supplies, the teacher in this classroom set up a table giving students easy access to different types of paper, pencils, scissors, staplers, and other materials. A nearby bookcase held various dictionaries, thesauruses, informational books, and magazines. Rather than curtailing interaction, the teacher encouraged students to talk together and use each other as resources. Several students who were beginning new pieces sat together on the carpet to discuss their ideas. The teacher did not assign topics or set a standard length. The students were expected to choose their own individual topics and determine the length of their pieces. Later they would decide whether to publish that particular piece and, if so, in what format. Other students who were drafting, revising, editing, or publishing moved among areas designated for quiet writing, peer conferences, teacher conferences, and publishing, according to their needs.

The teacher began the workshop with a mini-lesson and ended with whole-class sharing, but in between students made choices and decisions about how to use their time. Because of the high degree of organization, the students knew how to move through the workshop and where to get information when they needed it. A bulletin board display served as a reminder, and the teacher often pointed students to it when they forgot where they were in the writing process and what their future options were. Sign-up sheets gave students access to their teacher or peers when they needed help.

The Role of the Teacher and the Student

The teacher's role in a transmission model is to convey information. The most efficient way to accomplish this is to conduct whole-class lessons by teaching facts or skills, asking questions that narrow the range of expected answers, calling on one student at a time, and reinforcing correct responses. Even with strategy training, which may involve small-group instruction and more of an interactive style (Roehler & Duffy, 1991), the teacher is the repository of knowledge and the authority on success and failure.

Students in a transmission model are expected to watch, listen, and respond according to the dictates of the teacher. The strongest image of students in this type of a classroom is that of rows of desks facing the front of the room, with students sitting still, looking straight ahead, and listening quietly. For most activities, there are right or wrong answers, and students are expected to learn the right answers and avoid making mistakes. Even in small-group discussions, students expect to be led by the teacher, often through participation structures that involve a sequence such as teacher initiation, student response, and teacher evaluation (Mehan, 1979).

In contrast, the transaction model requires the teacher to define his or her role within a dialogic process. As a member of the classroom community, he or she is learner as well as teacher. In the writers' workshop, the teacher writes with the students about topics of importance to him or her and shares that writing with the class. The teacher also examines his or her own experiences with the writing process, using these incidents to explore strategies and skills with the students. In the readers' workshop, the teacher reads when the students read, shares his or her books with the class, and talks about his or her experiences with the reading process. This goes beyond demonstrating or modeling; although the teacher uses his or her own writing and reading as models, the primary purpose is to show students that writing and reading are processes that the teacher and other adults engage in and enjoy. Needless to say, a teacher such as this is an active reader and writer.

For example, a KEEP first-grade teacher read aloud *Noisy Nora* (Wells, 1973) and talked about how the character reminded her of when her son was young and did naughty things to distract his mother from taking care of the new baby. The teacher then invited students to share things the story made them think of. She showed the class a webbing she had created as a plan for a story about her son and daughter, who were now in high school. She shared the beginning of her story and explained how she wanted to write about this time so she wouldn't forget what her children had been like. When she invited comments, the students told her what they liked and what they thought she needed to add or change. As the students were dismissed to their seats, the teacher said, "You may want to write about your brothers and sisters or your family too. Or you may want to write about something else. This is just one idea."

In a transaction model of instruction, knowledge and understanding grow from discussion, shared ideas, and interaction, so the student's role is to contribute to the conversation. Students' ideas matter because without their active thinking and participation, the level of knowledge remains static. The teacher supports students through scaffolding, enabling them to carry out tasks too difficult for them to do independently, and gradually releases responsibility to the students (Pearson, 1985). Instruction occurs in what Vygotsky (1987) called the *zone of proximal development*. In group literature discussions, for example, the teacher may provide scaffolding to assist students in carrying on conversations about books (see Eeds & Wells, 1989; Short & Pierce, 1990).

In a KEEP fourth-grade classroom during a readers' workshop, the teacher was sitting with a group of students discussing the novel *On My Honor* (Bauer, 1986). The students knew their teacher was participating as a member of the group, not as the source of all answers. The group was deeply engaged in conversation about the first few chapters. Keith's comment about Tony (one of the characters in the book) jumping into the river sparked discussion. "I think it was dumb," Jessie declared.

"Why?" the teacher asked him. Several students chimed in to say that Tony couldn't swim. "How do you know that?" the teacher asked, and she began flipping through the pages of her book to look for verification of this point.

Sheena located a passage and read it aloud. "It says right here, 'He never noticed before what a poor swimmer Tony was,' " she explained.

"Yeah," agreed Keith. As he mimed Tony's poor swimming style, he remarked, "He didn't even know how to breathe right."

"Tony was acting brave," Dustin thought.

Keith disagreed. "He's just showing off." Several students agreed. The teacher asked if other information in the story matched this behavior. Keith and Kawika both had examples of other reckless behavior by Tony. "Why do students do that, I wonder?" the teacher mused. The discussion continued with students giving examples of their own bravado.

Later, the teacher showed the students how she had written to one of the characters in her reading response log because she was so distressed at his behavior. When the discussion finished, she told the group, "Please feel free to write in your reading response logs about anything that bothers you or grabs you. Put your thoughts on paper. Don't wait for me to tell you."

Peer interactions can also provide a type of scaffolding by allowing students to help each other work through a process they cannot yet manage independently. Peer writing conferences are good examples of how students can support each other in thinking through a writing piece. In a first-grade KEEP writers' workshop, Joseph and Kale were sitting on the floor for a writing conference on Kale's piece. Joseph listened as Kale read his piece, and then Joseph commented that Kale's drawing looked like Christopher Reeves. "Come on," Kale urged, and Joseph began to ask questions about the piece, an imaginative adventure story. "How come the helicopter was picking up the lady?" Joseph wanted to know. Kale explained it was because the ambulance had run out of gas. "Well, why did they have to take her? How come you never save her?" Joseph queried. Kale tried to clarify the events of his story further.

"You gotta ask me more questions and sign your name," Kale then told Joseph. Joseph signed his name on Kale's draft to indicate that they had conferred. He looked at the class chart on conference procedures for additional questions to ask Kale. When he finished, they walked to a nearby table and looked at the draft again together before Joseph returned to his own piece.

As these observations show, transaction instruction gives students excellent learning opportunities but can be quite challenging for teachers. To date, very little research exists linking transaction instruction to improvements in student achievement. In research at KEEP, we attempted to establish a link. In classrooms where teachers had implemented about 90% of the features of the whole literacy curriculum, we found that dramatic improvements occurred in students' literacy achievement, as measured by portfolio assessment, which is discussed in more detail later in the chapter.

ASSESSMENT

Assessment is an integral part of the instructional cycle. Assessment completes the loop as teachers move from instructional goals to classroom practices to evaluation of those practices, in order to determine whether and how well teachers and students have met their goals. Assessment feeds back to changes in instructional actions, revision of goals, and the setting of new goals. In the move from transmission to transaction models, teachers and other educators have searched for types of assessment that reflect the new focuses of instruction. Assessment has moved away from norm-referenced and criterion-referenced testing to performance assessment.

Norm-Referenced Testing

In transmission models of instruction, assessment tends to center on the use of norm-referenced or standardized testing. Norm-referenced tests fit with the behaviorist perspective that knowledge is a set of one-way signals imparted to students; therefore, learning can be evaluated in terms of how well students have received and remembered those signals.

Test items do not provide an adequate representation of any curricular domain; they are selected for the purpose of spreading students along the normal curve. However, test items are sometimes treated as if they constituted a curriculum. In settings with high-stakes testing (often those with many low-income students of diverse cultural and linguistic backgrounds), teachers come to feel they must teach to the test in order to raise scores (Smith, 1991). Standardized tests contribute to a narrowing of the curriculum, because time spent drilling students on tested skills detracts from students' opportunities to engage in the full processes of reading and writing and to construct their own interpretations.

Criterion-Referenced Testing

Like norm-referenced testing, criterion-referenced testing, such as that associated with the earlier KEEP curriculum, treats reading and writing as sets of discrete skills. Criterion-referenced testing has the advantage of reflecting an entire domain of skills from a behaviorist perspective. Unlike standardized testing, criterion-referenced testing is designed to drive instruction. If teachers provide direct instruction in skills, students' performance should improve. As mentioned earlier, criterion-referenced testing of the type advocated by Bloom (Bloom, Madaus, & Hastings, 1981) and others lends support to the idea that achievement can be seen as a function of time spent learning, rather than innate ability. Criterion-referenced testing also has the advantage of making the goals of instruction explicit for teachers and students. But although criterion-referenced tests seem an improvement over norm-referenced tests, teachers in transaction models still find that they are not able to assess student performance in the full processes of reading and writing.

Performance Assessment

Performance assessment requires students to show their competence or knowledge by creating a product or response (Hiebert, Valencia, & Afflerbach, 1994). Performance assessment fits with the social constructivist perspective that knowledge is jointly created. Therefore, learning can and should be evaluated in terms of how well students have constructed and can express their own understandings.

Interest in performance assessment has been heightened by the standards movement. The term *standards* has various meanings in current educational debates (Pearson, 1993). Content standards define the particular domain of knowledge, whereas performance standards refer to the degree of proficiency students must show and the manner in which it will be demonstrated. In a sense, standards are intended to serve the same purpose as behavioral objectives: Both are intended to improve instruction and student achievement by making instructional goals explicit. However, in most cases standards are stated more broadly, reflecting a constructivist perspective on the nature of learning.

Portfolio assessment is a particular kind of performance assessment involving individual collections of student work gathered over time (Valencia, 1990). Portfolios offer a means of evaluating a student's progress and current levels of performance in ways that tests cannot. Test results are often likened to a snapshot—a picture of a student's performance on a given task at a particular time in a single setting. Portfolios are more like a photo album—they illustrate a collection of performances on a variety of tasks in a number of different settings.

Portfolios do not narrow the domain of literacy in the way that tests do. Portfolios may contain evidence of students' participation in teacher and peer conferences, literature discussions, and other classroom events. In this way they provide information not only about students' progress, but also about the type of instruction and social situations that supported learning. Portfolios enable both the teacher and the student to participate in the evaluation process. In addition, students' own metacognitive knowledge (i.e., knowing what they know and don't know, how they learn best, and what to do to help themselves learn better) can be included in their portfolios through written reflections.

Research on Portfolio Assessment

Can the use of portfolio assessment, in conjunction with standards or benchmarks, improve students' achievement? This question was explored in a 2-year study at KEEP. In the first year the study involved 13 teachers; in the second year, 29 teachers. Teachers were observed monthly to monitor their level of implementation of the whole literacy curriculum, including portfolio assessment. Observations based on the checklist mentioned earlier indicated that teachers had achieved high levels of implementation, averaging 92% of the features at the end of the first year and 93% of features at the end of the second year.

Portfolio assessment was used to monitor student progress and was tied to the grade-level benchmarks described earlier. The portfolio assessment system was designed primarily for purposes of program evaluation. It allowed data to be aggregated across classrooms to determine the percentage of students achieving above, at, and below grade level with respect to the benchmarks (for further information about the portfolio assessment system, refer to Au, 1994).

At the start of the study, none of the teachers placed a high value on portfolio assessment or benchmarks, and none was particularly knowledgeable about them (Au, 1993b). With support from KEEP staff members, the teachers learned to collect portfolio evidence, including anecdotal notes, in an ongoing manner. They became thoroughly familiar with the benchmarks for their grade level and took steps to acquaint students with the benchmarks. In most cases, benchmarks were prominently posted in the classroom for students' reference.

The greatest challenge the teachers faced was involving students in the assessment process. A feature of the KEEP portfolio assessment system was student goal setting and monitoring of their own progress in meeting the benchmarks. For example, students in the writers' workshop kept a list of writing skills they had acquired, a log of their published pieces, a file of pieces they had abandoned but might want to go back to, and a list of personal writing goals. The teacher recorded a daily status of the class, wrote observational notes, reviewed students' writing folders and portfolios, and charted benchmarks of individual growth. During portfolio conferences, the teacher and student looked at the student's progress and discussed goals for reading and writing, referring to evidence they each had gathered. Eventually, the teachers succeeded in teaching students as early as second grade to keep their own records, chart their progress, and set goals.

In the KEEP portfolio assessment system, there had to be evidence that the student had met each and every benchmark before the student was considered to be at grade level for any given aspect of literacy. Any reasonable evidence could be presented, and students as well as teachers used their judgment in determining what would go into the portfolios.

Results reported for each classroom were subject to an audit, in which the portfolios of two randomly selected students were checked for the accuracy of ratings, benchmark by benchmark. Teachers became highly aware of the benchmarks and of documenting students' progress systematically, in part because of accountability pressures. As a group, teachers reported that working with the benchmarks and portfolio assessment, along with transaction instruction, enabled them to bring their students to higher levels of achievement than ever before (Oshiro, 1994).

An overview of three years of achievement results, as shown through portfolio assessment, is presented in Fig. 2.1. In the study, teachers were given a

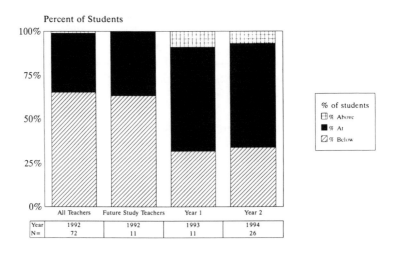

FIG. 2.1.   KEEP portfolio assessment results for the writing process.

choice of focusing on reading or writing. In the first year of the study, 11 of
the 13 teachers chose to focus on writing; in the second year 26 of the 29
teachers made this same choice. As indicated in the first column of Fig. 2.1,
in the year before the study began only about one third of the KEEP students
were achieving at grade level in the writing process, with two thirds below
grade level and none above grade level. Even those teachers who would be in
the study the following year did not show a different pattern of results (column 2). Poor results were obtained despite evidence that students had developed positive attitudes toward literacy and had spent considerable class
time engaged in the full processes of reading and writing. Changes in students' attitudes were easier to obtain than were changes in aspects of literacy
such as the writing process, which require the application of complex forms
of thinking (Au, 1994).

In the first year of the study, the teachers were able to reverse the pattern
described previously, improving on the results they had obtained the year before. For the writing process, 9% of students were above grade level, 59% at
grade level, and only 32% below grade level (column 3). Similar results were
obtained by the larger group of teachers during the second year of the study
(column 4). Improved achievement was also seen in the classes where teachers chose to focus on reading. However, because of the small number of
classes, less confidence can be placed in these results.

With typical instruction, few students from the population served by KEEP
achieve at grade level (Kamehameha Schools, 1993). In the study, we were
able to reduce by half the number of students rated as below grade level in lit-

eracy achievement. The results indicate that portfolio assessment, tied to grade level benchmarks or standards, can make a difference in improving students' achievement. In the case of KEEP, portfolio assessment and benchmarks raised the expectations for students' literacy achievement. Classroom observations indicate that teachers responded by providing students with systematic instruction aimed at developing the knowledge and strategies needed to meet the benchmarks.

As the experiences of these teachers suggest, portfolios and benchmarks are difficult to integrate into ongoing classroom instruction (Au, 1993b). Extensive staff development was required before teachers felt they could manage portfolio assessment. Although the audit was an unpopular idea, accountability requirements undoubtedly motivated both teachers and KEEP staff members to attend closely to the benchmarks, portfolio data, and progress of individual students. We believe that portfolio assessment must be rigorous, tied to benchmarks or standards with requirements for evidence, if it is to be effective in improving student achievement.

A concern with goals, benchmarks, standards, or outcomes, within a constructivist perspective, is seen in other successful portfolio projects as well. The Bellevue Literacy Assessment Project began with a constructivist philosophy of teaching and learning and was guided by the district's six student learning outcomes (Valencia & Place, 1994). These outcomes were broader than were the KEEP benchmarks, making the gathering of evidence and scoring of portfolios less cumbersome. Bellevue teachers decided to use "common tools" or specific forms of assessment to be administered two or three times per year. For example, written or oral retellings served as the common tool for the outcome "interacts with text." The Bellevue project places a high value on students' reflections on their own progress. There are entry slips indicating the significance of most items in the portfolios, often prepared by the students rather than the teacher.

Unlike standardized tests, portfolios can support the broad instructional goals of constructivist curricula. Portfolios can be integrated into ongoing instruction in a manner that is meaningful to students. Portfolios may also serve purposes of program evaluation, showing students' growth as learners within a whole literacy curriculum. In short, portfolio assessment appears to be an important component of transaction models of instruction.

CONCLUSIONS

The paradigm shift from the behaviorist and cognitive science perspectives to the constructivist perspective has led to dramatic changes in views of classroom instruction. These changes are highlighted in the metaphors of the conduit and the conversation, one conveying the idea of the straightforward transmission of knowledge, the other the idea of the dynamic construction of knowledge.

Goals of instruction have changed, as the emphasis has shifted from proficiency in skills and strategies to ownership and application of processes in social contexts. Educators have come to see that students should learn actively to construct meaning through conversation rather than passively to receive knowledge through a conduit. Teachers' instructional actions changed from a transmission to a transaction model in response to this more complex view of goals. Forms of classroom organization became more flexible, with students engaged in a variety of activities in a workshop atmosphere. Teachers involved students in discussions much more like everyday conversations than like conventional classroom recitation. Students took an active role in contributing their own thinking to literature discussions. In writing, students decided on their own topics, organized ideas, revised, and chose the form in which their work would be published.

Major changes occurred in assessment, with a shift from norm- and criterion-referenced testing to performance assessment, including portfolios. Multiple-choice and short-answer tests had worked well to assess specific skills and factual knowledge, but proved too limited to assess full processes and interpretations. These tests were replaced by tasks requiring students to demonstrate the application of full processes, for example, by reading a story and writing a summary. With portfolio assessment, as in the KEEP system, teachers did not have to administer separate tests at all but could guide students in collecting samples of their work to show their growth as learners and current level of achievement. Portfolio assessment could be conversational and interactive in ways that testing was not. Students discussed their work with teachers and peers, evaluated their own progress, and set their own goals.

In terms of practical implications, we believe that improved achievement can occur only when educators look at goals, teachers' instructional actions, and assessment as interrelated components within a system. Clearly stated goals are required to guide both instructional actions and assessment. Instructional actions are required to improve students' learning, or assessment will not show gains. Assessment is required to show how students are progressing and to determine whether goals are achievable. Improvements in student achievement will not come about unless there is change in all three components, not just one or two.

To make the shift to the new paradigm, teachers need consistent, long-term support. Support might begin with discussions of the philosophy underlying transaction instruction. It would include meetings providing teachers with information about new forms of classroom organization and instruction, such as the readers' and writers' workshops, and follow-up discussions that allow teachers to share their struggles and successes. In our view, it makes sense to introduce changes in assessment only after teachers have begun to change instruction. Our experience suggests that the change from transmission to transaction views of instruction, including portfolio assessment, should probably be seen as requiring a period of 5 years or more.

In terms of research, we believe that the key questions have to do with the development of entire systems—including goals, instructional actions, and assessment—that will work in classrooms. Research on entire systems seems to represent a greater need than does research on individual components, such as assessment. Researchers may collaborate with teachers in creating these systems. They can begin by working with teachers and students to define instructional goals based on a philosophy of learning. From there, researchers may assist teachers through classroom observations, interviews of students, and discussions that promote teacher and student reflection on ways of improving instructional actions and learning opportunities. Researchers' support may be especially helpful in the design of portfolio and other assessment systems, including opportunities for student involvement in data gathering and evaluation. New knowledge grows through a collaboration in which the researcher is involved as a participant in the changing social context of the school and classroom. It would seem, then, that the metaphor of the conversation can be extended to the research process, as well as to the process of instruction.

REFERENCES

Allington, R. L. (1991). Children who find learning to read difficult: School responses to diversity. In E. H. Hiebert (Ed.), *Literacy for a diverse society: Perspectives, practices, and policies* (pp. 237–252). New York: Teachers College Press.

Asam, C., Au, K. H., Blake, K., Carroll, J., Jacobson, H., & Scheu, J. (1993). *Literacy curriculum guide.* Honolulu, HI: Kamehameha Elementary Education Program, Kamehameha Schools/Bernice Pauahi Bishop Estate, Early Education Division.

Atwell, N. (1987). *In the middle: Writing, reading, and learning with adolescents.* Portsmouth, NH: Boynton/Cook.

Au, K. H. (1993a). *Literacy instruction in multicultural settings.* Fort Worth, TX: Harcourt Brace Jovanovich.

Au, K. H. (1993b, December). *Implementing a portfolio assessment system: Relationships to students' literacy learning.* Paper presented at the annual meeting of the National Reading Conference, Charleston, SC.

Au, K. H. (1994). Portfolio assessment: Experiences at the Kamehameha Elementary Education Program. In S. W. Valencia, E. H. Hiebert, & P. P. Afflerbach (Eds.), *Authentic reading assessment: Practices and possibilities* (pp. 103–126). Newark, DE: International Reading Association.

Au, K. H., & Asam, C. L. (1994, October). *Improving the achievement of students of diverse backgrounds: Changes in curriculum, assessment, and teacher development.* Paper presented at the Inaugural Guy Bond Commemorative Reading Conference, Minneapolis, MN.

Bauer, M. (1986). *On my honor.* New York: Houghton Mifflin.

Bloom, B. S. (1976). *Human characteristics and school learning.* New York: McGraw-Hill.

Bloom, B. S., Madaus, G. F., & Hastings, J. T. (1981). *Evaluation to improve learning.* New York: McGraw-Hill.

Brophy, J. E., & Good, T. L. (1992). Teacher behavior and student achievement. In M. C. Wittrock (Ed.), *Handbook of research on teaching* (pp. 328–375). New York: Macmillan.

Calkins, L. M. (1986). *The art of teaching writing.* Portsmouth, NH: Heinemann.

Clay, M. M. (1985). *The early detection of reading difficulties* (3rd ed.). Auckland, New Zealand: Heinemann.

Eeds, M., & Wells, D. (1989). Grand conversations: An exploration of meaning construction in literature study groups. *Research in the Teaching of English, 23,* 4–29.

Englert, C. S., Raphael, T. E., & Anderson, L. M. (1992). Socially mediated instruction: Improving students' knowledge and talk about writing. *Elementary School Journal, 92,* 412–465.

Gough, P. B. (1972). One second of reading. In J. F. Kavanaugh & I. G. Mattingly (Eds.), *Language by eye and by ear* (pp. 331–358). Cambridge, MA: MIT Press.

Graves, D. (1983). *Writing: Teachers and children at work.* Exeter, NH: Heinemann.

Guba, E. G., & Lincoln, Y. S. (1994). Competing paradigms in qualitative research. In N. K. Denzin & Y. S. Lincoln (Eds.), *Handbook of qualitative research* (pp. 105–117). Thousand Oaks, CA: Sage.

Hansen, J. (1987). *When writers read.* Portsmouth, NH: Heinemann.

Hiebert, E. H., & Raphael, T. E. (in press). Perspectives from educational psychology in literacy and literacy learning and their extensions to school practice. In R. Calfee (Ed.), *Handbook of Educational Psychology.*

Hiebert, E. H., Valencia, S. W., & Afflerbach, P. P. (1994). Definitions and perspectives. In S. W. Valencia, E. H. Hiebert, & P. P. Afflerbach (Eds.), *Authentic reading assessment: Practices and possibilities* (pp. 6–21). Newark, DE: International Reading Association.

Kamehameha Schools. (1993). *Native Hawaiian educational assessment.* Honolulu, HI: Kamehameha Schools, Office of Program Evaluation and Planning.

McKenna, M. C., Stahl, S. A., & Reinking, D. (1994). A critical commentary on research, politics, and whole language. *Journal of Reading Behavior, 26,* 211–233.

Mehan, H. (1979). *Learning lessons.* Cambridge, MA: Harvard University Press.

Mehan, H. (1981). Social constructivism in psychology and sociology. *The Quarterly Newsletter of the Laboratory of Comparative Human Cognition, 3*(4), 71–77.

Mezynski, K. (1983). Issues concerning the acquisition of knowledge: Effects of vocabulary training on reading comprehension. *Review of Educational Research, 53,* 253–279.

Oshiro, G. (1994). *Experiences of first and second year teachers in the KEEP demonstration classroom project: Spring 1994.* Unpublished manuscript, Kamehameha Schools Bishop Estate, Early Education Division, Evaluation Department, Honolulu, HI.

Palincsar, A. S., & Brown, A. L. (1984). Reciprocal teaching of comprehension-fostering and comprehension-monitoring activities. *Cognition and Instruction, 2,* 117–175.

Pearson, P. D. (1985). Changing the face of reading comprehension instruction. *The Reading Teacher, 38,* 724–738.

Pearson, P. D. (1993). Standards for the English language arts: A policy perspective. *JRB: A journal of literacy, 25,* 457–475.

Roehler, L. R., & Duffy, G. G. (1991). Teachers' instructional actions. In R. Barr, M. L. Kamil, P. Mosenthal, & P. D. Pearson (Eds.), *Handbook of reading research* (Vol. 2, pp. 861–883). New York: Longman.

Roehler, L. R., Duffy, G. G., & Meloth, M. (1986). What to be direct about in direct instruction in reading. In T. Raphael (Ed.), *Contexts of school-based literacy* (pp. 79–96). New York: Random House.

Rosenblatt, L. (1978). *The reader, the text, the poem: The transactional theory of the literary work.* Carbondale, IL: Southern Illinois University Press.

Schwandt, T. A. (1994). Constructivist, interpretivist approaches to human inquiry. In N. K. Denzin & Y. S. Lincoln (Eds.), *Handbook of qualitative research* (pp. 118–137). Thousand Oaks, CA: Sage.

Shanahan, T. (Ed.) (1990). *Reading and writing together: New perspectives for the classroom.* Norwood, MA: Christopher-Gordon.

Short, K. G., & Pierce, K. M. (Eds.). (1990). *Talking about books: Creating literate communities.* Portsmouth, NH: Heinemann.

Smith, M. L. (1991). Put to the test: The effects of external testing on teachers. *Educational Researcher, 20*(5), 8–11.

Spiegel, D. L. (1981). *Reading for pleasure: Guidelines.* Newark, DE: International Reading Association.

Taylor, D. (1983). *Family literacy: Young children learning to read and write.* Portsmouth, NH: Heinemann.

Taylor, D., & Dorsey-Gaines, C. (1988). *Growing up literate: Learning from inner-city families.* Portsmouth, NH: Heinemann.

Valencia, S. (1990). A portfolio approach to classroom reading assessment: The whys, whats, and hows. *The Reading Teacher, 43,* 338–340.

Valencia, S. W., & Place, N. A. (1994). Literacy portfolios for teaching, learning, and accountability: The Bellevue Literacy Assessment Project. In S. W. Valencia, E. H. Hiebert, & P. P. Afflerbach (Eds.), *Authentic reading assessment: Practices and possibilities* (pp. 134–156). Newark, DE: International Reading Association.

Vygotsky, L. S. (1987). Thinking and speech. In R. W. Rieber & A. S. Carton (Eds.), *The collected works of L. S. Vygotsky, Volume 1, Problems of general psychology* (pp. 37–285). New York: Plenum.

Wells, R. (1973). *Noisy Nora.* New York: Dial Press.

Wertsch, J. V. (1991). *Voices of the mind: A sociocultural approach to mediated action.* Cambridge, MA: Harvard University Press.

Wixson, K. K., Peters, C. W., Weber, E. M., & Roeber, E. D. (1987). New directions in statewide reading assessment. *The Reading Teacher, 40,* 749–754.

3

Research on the Practices and Behavior of Effective Teachers at the Juniper Gardens Children's Project: Implications for the Education of Diverse Learners

Charles R. Greenwood
Juniper Gardens Children's Project
University of Kansas

My program of research of the last 16 years and that of my colleagues at the Children's Project, past and present, have focused on improving the literacy and social outcomes of children attending inner-city schools. Of interest have been students who are at risk because they are poor and culturally diverse and who have disabilities (Greenwood, Carta, Hart, et al., 1992; Hall, Schiefelbusch, Hoyt, & Greenwood, 1989). The Children's Project takes its name from the Juniper Gardens Public Housing Project located in Northeast Kansas City, Kansas, a historically African American, low-income neighborhood. The Children's Project was founded in 1964. To this day, it represents a collaboration between residents of the community and faculty of the University of Kansas. The Project's mission is to "to develop and test interventions that improve the developmental experiences and the academic and social achievements of children and youth, within the context of their family, school, community, and friends" (Bureau of Child Research, Planning Document, 1964).

The outcomes and lessons learned from this research on improving the instruction in inner-city schools are the topics of this chapter. First, we discuss issues of theory and the constructs and components found important in the analysis of classroom instruction. Second, we review work designed to improve instruction and student achievement across four areas: (a) procedure building; (b) implementation variation; (c) longitudinal prevention/intervention; and (d) identification, translation, and promotion of practices used by effective teachers. Concluding the chapter is a discussion of implications for classroom application and future research.

A THEORETICAL FRAMEWORK FOR INSTRUCTIONAL CLASSROOM ECOLOGY

From the beginning, work addressed the persistent, lower academic performance of disadvantaged students by focusing on alterable instructional variables and their effects on growth in individual achievement (Hall et al., 1989). Initial studies applied the behavioral approach and its principles of motivation, context, and personal history as causes of past and present performance. These principles asserted that behavior was a function of its immediate consequences (motivation), in specific situations (contexts), and one's cumulative history of these situation-behavior-consequence interactions. Thus, differences in the academic performance of diverse learners and the characteristically lower performance of children with LD could be explained in these terms: "The interaction between the child and the environment is continuous, reciprocal, and interdependent. We cannot analyze a child without reference to an environment, nor is it possible to analyze an environment without reference to a child. *The two form an inseparable unit consisting of an interrelated set of variables, or an interactional field*" (Bijou & Baer, 1978, p. 29; emphasis added).

As did Bijou and Baer, behaviorists working in education recognized early on that influencing student learning in the classroom had to be a matter of changing the classroom environment in certain, specific ways, and that understanding how to improve students' academic performance and growth in achievement had to be a matter of understanding how changing the environment led to changed student behavior (Skinner, 1968).

Applications in classrooms focused on demonstrating these behavior principles. For example, Hall, Lund, and Jackson (1968) improved students' attention using reinforcing consequences in the form of teacher praise and point systems. It was demonstrated repeatedly that classroom behaviors improved when they were reinforced and declined when they were not. Subsequent studies focused on altering behavioral antecedents as well as consequences (Delquadri, Greenwood, Stretton, & Hall, 1983), and it was demonstrated that classroom behaviors improved when students experienced increased opportunities to respond, when response opportunities were presented in gradations of difficulty (i.e., easy to difficult), and when these responses were reinforced. Thereby students' classroom behavior and academic accomplishments were increased. The special contribution of this research was its focus on the functional relations children had with their environment. Because these techniques led to measurable changes in student behavior and identified the variables responsible for that change, they were useful to researchers, teachers, and parents, and this knowledge led to further development.

Models based on these techniques emerged for organizing daycare programs (O'Brien, Porterfield, Herbert-Jackson, & Risley, 1979) and for the teaching of specific subject matter (Engelmann, Becker, Carnine, & Gersten, 1988) among many others. Unlike earlier work that had focused primarily on individuals and individual behaviors, this work was applied to the teaching of multiple skills and subject matter to the entire class or schoolwide for significant periods of time per day. This effort involved restructuring of the instructional ecology and classroom climate in ways that also produced functional changes in students' behavior. The success of this work, however, depended increasingly on information on the behavior of teachers as well as students, and it also required information on the arrangement of instructional situations (e.g., lessons, materials, grouping, scheduling; see Greenwood, Carta, et al., 1992). The extension of applied behavior analysis to include formal study of the ecology of behavior, was eventually termed "ecobehavioral assessment and analysis" (Morris & Midgley, 1990). With ecobehavioral assessment came the lens needed to examine how instruction regulated interactions between persons and between persons and the classroom environment in ways that, for some students, either accelerated or decelerated their opportunity to respond and to learn academic subject matter (Greenwood, Carta, & Atwater, 1991).

Component Constructs of Classroom Instruction: Ecology, Teacher, and Student

As early as 1978, it was clear that we needed a better means of assessing instruction and its effects on students in order to guide research on restructuring. To our already well-practiced set of behavioral observation instruments, we expanded the existing taxonomies to include: ecological, teacher, as well as student events in classrooms (Hall, Delquadri, Greenwood, & Thurston, 1982). We did so because these events were implicated by the conceptual and empirical knowledge of that time and our own practical experiences in classrooms (Hall et al., 1982). We needed a better means of directly assessing the form and function of classroom instruction. Direct assessment was needed because teachers' schedules and estimates of teaching time were often inaccurate when compared to what was actually implemented, because anecdotal observations suggested that the lowest reading groups actually met the least, because instructional methods appeared to promote low rather than high levels of engagement in academic responding (i.e., reading, writing, discussing, questioning), and because there appeared to be few salient differences between the instruction provided students in special as compared to regular education classrooms.

What emerged eventually became a family of "ecobehavioral" observational assessment instruments (Greenwood, Carta, Kamps, Terry, & Delquadri, 1994; see Table 3.1). The goal of ecobehavioral assessment/analysis is to display the interactions and covariations among ecological, teacher, and student behavior events, and, like behavior analysis, determination of functional relationships between and among these variables (Morris & Midgley, 1990).

These instruments were capable of generating the usual displays of individual behaviors and behavioral profiles expected in a behavioral assessment (Greenwood, Carta, Kamps, & Arreaga-Mayer, 1990). However, ecobehavioral instruments also provided analyses of environmental (e.g., settings, subject matter, or materials), and teacher variables (see Table 3.1). Because of the sampling patterns employed, it also was possible to display ecobehavioral relationships as conditional probabilities, for example, the probability of reading behavior given a teacher engaged in teaching behavior during reading period, leading to the identification of specific situational factors that either accelerated or decelerated the probability of the occurrence of specific academic behaviors during instruction (Greenwood, Delquadri, Stanley, Terry, & Hall, 1985, 1986). Thus, analyses of instruction as ecobehavioral profiles, trends over time, normative peer comparisons, sequential ecobehavioral relations, and functional changes over time were obtained and used to guide the selection and development of effective instruction (Greenwood, Carta, Kamps, et al., 1994).

Effective Ecobehavioral Components

Forms of evidence emerged that illustrated the components' (i.e., ecology, teacher, and student variables) sensitivity to students' growth in academic achievement and to differences in instructional practice. Of primary importance was the role of students' academic responding as the proximal product of daily instruction. Correlational studies indicated that academic responding, a composite of seven individual academic responses,[1] were positive correlates of standardized achievement (Greenwood, Delquadri, & Hall, 1984; Greenwood et al., 1981), whereas task management behaviors were not, and competing, inappropriate classroom behaviors were negatively correlated. Descriptive studies indicated that students' levels of academic responding varied widely among: (a) children in regular and special education classrooms, (b) variations in classroom context, (c) young children referred and nonreferred for special services, and (d) students in Chapter 1 versus non-

---

[1]Academic responding in CISSAR is a composite of the percentage occurrence of writing, academic game play, reading aloud, silent reading, academic talk, asking, and answering question behaviors.

TABLE 3.1

Comparison of CISSAR, MS-CISSAR, and ESCAPE Taxonomies by
Ecological, Teacher, and Student Constructs and Components

Components	Description	Instrument		
		CISSAR	MS-CISSAR	ESCAPE
Ecology Construct				
Setting	Service delivery settings	0	11	0
Activity	Subject of instruction	12	20	13
Activity structure	Degree of teacher direction	0	0	5
Task material	Curriculum situation	8	9	13
Location	Classroom location	0	0	9
Physical location	Seating arrangement	3	3	5
Instructional Grouping	Instructional pattern	0	5	0
Disability Composition	Degree of integration	0	0	7
Teacher Construct				
Definition	Person teaching student	0	9	8
Location	Position relative to student	6	5	0
Focus	Recipient of teacher behavior	0	4	5
Behavior	Teacher response	5	11	15
Student Construct				
Academic response	Engagement	7	6	10
Task management	Enabling behavior	5	7	0
Inappropriate Response	Competing behavior	7	8	6
Talk	Verbalizations	0	0	5
Summary				
	Total events	53	99	101
	Subcategories	9	13	12
	Categories	3	3	3

Adapted from Greenwood, Carta, Kamps, and Arreaga-Mayer, 1990, p. 39. Abbreviations are
as follows: CISSAR = Code for Instructional Structure and Student Academic Response (Stanley & Greenwood, 1981); MS-CISSAR = Mainstream Version of CISSAR (Carta, Greenwood,
Schulte, Arreaga-Mayer, & Terry, 1987); ESCAPE = Ecobehavioral System for Complex Assessment of Preschool Environments (Carta, Greenwood, & Atwater, 1985).

Chapter 1 school classrooms (e.g., Cooper & Speece, 1990a, 1990b; Greenwood, Delquadri, & Hall, 1984; Greenwood, Delquadri, et al., 1985; Thurlow, Ysseldyke, Graden, & Algozzine, 1984). This work refined the earlier knowledge of the importance of on-task and attention as indices of classroom academic behavior (Greenwood, Delquadri, & Hall, 1989; Hoge, 1985) in that it was now possible to separate out specific academic responses along with their relevant instructional contexts.

A typical pattern of momentary variation in engagement in academic responding is provided in Fig. 3.1. These data reflect a continuous observation during prime time subject matter instruction for a single student in first grade (top panel) and again 2 years later in third grade (bottom panel). Although changes in instructional ecology (e.g., subject matter, materials, etc.) and teacher behavior are not depicted in each graph, they covaried with these momentary fluctuations in academic behaviors. Striking in each graph is the moment-to-moment fluctuation in engagement and the growth in engagement level for this student between first and third grades. These level changes reflect the development of this student's expanded academic repertoire with more time spent engaged in reading, writing, and academic talk in third grade, as well as her increased capacity to be engaged.

In addition to its sensitivity to development, engagement in academic responding has also been accelerated with changes from conventional practice to interventions like ClassWide Peer Tutoring (CWPT) (e.g., Greenwood, 1991a) as we cover in detail in the next section. Ecobehavioral descriptions of instructional practices have also produced distinctive ecological "footprints" in terms of materials used, teacher location, and teacher behaviors that have covaried with student's academic responding (Greenwood, 1994, October). And support for the importance of these components and growth in achievement has come from a recent effort to fit alternative instructional models to longitudinal data (Greenwood, Terry, Marquis, & Walker, 1994). We examined the fit between: (a) a direct effects instructional model, where exposure (time taught a subject), task quality (materials), and student engagement all had direct influence on achievement; (b) a model in which instruction (defined by exposure and task quality) and engagement were hypothesized to have direct effects on achievement; and (c) a model in which engagement mediated the effect of instruction on achievement. The best fit was obtained by the model mediated by engagement [Comparative Fit Index $= .93$, $\chi^2(54) = 70.1$, $p < .07$, $R^2 = 27\%$].

Summary. Behavioral approaches to instruction have been supported and guided by observational measures of ecological, teacher, and student component constructs. These constructs have been shown be sensitive to differences in age, socioeconomic status, schools, subject matter, materials, teacher behaviors, and students' academic achievement. Engagement in aca-

First Grade

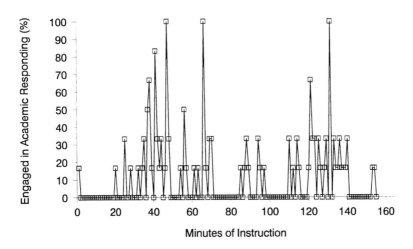

Third Grade

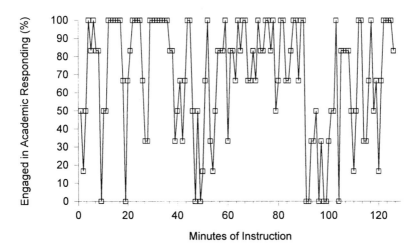

FIG. 3.1. Consecutive minutes of engagement in academic responding during prime time daily instruction for one student observed in first and third grades using the CISSAR.

demic responding also was shown sensitive to these variables and it appears to be a proximal indicator of effective instruction and as well as a cumulative product of past and present instructional history (Greenwood, Hart, Walker, & Risley, 1994). All are constructs helpful in explaining differential rates of academic progress, as we see in the next section.

RESEARCH ON IMPROVING THE INSTRUCTION OF AT-RISK STUDENTS AND STUDENTS WITH LD

Procedure Building

From the very beginning, we were struck with how conventional teaching failed to engage the active participation of all students in inner-city classrooms. In observations, we found statistically lower daily levels of academic responding between inner-city versus suburban children in the same grades on the order 12 minutes per day (Greenwood, Delquadri, & Hall, 1984; Stanley & Greenwood, 1983) or a cumulative total of 365 hours by middle school (Greenwood, Hart, et al., 1994). Surprisingly, we documented more instances of down time, lack of materials, infrequent opportunities to respond to the curriculum, and lowered levels of motivation than instances of misbehavior or of behavior problems in inner-city classrooms (see Greenwood, Delquadri, & Hall, 1984). Thus, the lower achievement of at-risk, inner-city children soon became a hypothesis implicating conventional instructions' general failure to accelerate and sustain academic responding. And, for children labeled LD, the ecobehavioral hypothesis was extended to self-contained special education programs (e.g., Thurlow et al., 1984; Ysseldyke, Christenson, Thurlow, & Bakewell, 1989; Ysseldyke, Thurlow, Christenson, & Weiss, 1987).

Our first goal was to restructure instructional procedures in ways that increased active academic responding and that were acceptable to teachers, did not dramatically alter the curriculum content to be taught, and were effective for all students. We were seeking effective methods of improving instruction that would appeal to teachers but not unduly increase workload or exceed existing cost parameters. As reported by Delquadri, Greenwood, Stretton, and Hall (1983), a form of CWPT emerged with initially positive results.

Over the course of many studies, CWPT evolved as a system in which class members, organized as tutor–tutee pairs, work together on teams (Greenwood, Delquadri, & Carta, 1988). At the beginning of each week, all students in a class are paired for tutoring, and these tutor–tutee pairs are then assigned to one of two teams. The teams compete for the winning total score determined daily and weekly. Tutees earn points for their team by responding to the tasks presented to them by their tutors. Tutor and tutee roles are highly structured to ensure that tutees receive frequent, distributed response trials in a consistent format and that a standard error correction procedure is applied (e.g., Greenwood, Carta, & Hall, 1988; Greenwood, Terry, Delquadri, & Elliott, in press). Tutoring is reciprocal. Halfway through the session students switch roles; the tutor becomes the tutee, the tutee becomes the tutor. Teachers organize the academic content to be tutored into weekly units and prepare materials to be used daily within the CWPT format. In summary, CWPT core procedures are:

1. Review and introduction of new material to be learned.
2. Unit content materials to be tutored (e.g., reading passages, spelling word lists, or math fact lists).
3. New partners each week.
4. Partner pairing strategies.
5. Reciprocal roles in each session.
6. Teams competing for the highest team point total.
7. Contingent individual tutee point earning.
8. Tutors providing immediate error correction.
9. Public posting of individual and team scores.
10. Social reward for the winning team.

Added to these core procedures are subject-matter-specific procedures designed to support peer teaching (Greenwood, Delquadri, & Carta, 1988). For example, when applied to passage reading, a tutee reads brief passages from the curriculum to his or her tutor. The tutor provides points for correctly read sentences (2 points) and error correction (1 point). Teachers assess the fluency of the students' reading using oral reading rate measures. When applied to reading comprehension, the tutee responds to who, what, when, where, and why questions concerning the passage provided by the tutor. The tutor corrects responses and provides feedback. When applied to spelling, the tutee writes and spells words orally. The tutor dictates the words from a list to the tutee and then checks tutee performance. Similar variations are applied to vocabulary, mathematics, silent reading, as well as seat work, at the elementary level; and to social studies (Maheady, Sacca, & Harper, 1988) and history (Bell, Young, Blair, & Nelson, 1990) at the secondary level.

CWPT Components.   The CWPT was based on a combination of previously validated instructional procedures. Based on his earlier uses of tutoring, Delquadri (1978) had been struck by the sizable progress that low-functioning students made when taught one on one by an adult, as compared to when they were taught in the regular classroom by the teacher. A design challenge became one of how to reap the advantages of individually tutoring within a classwide, same-aged peer, teaching format so that an effective and efficient form of tutoring could be developed.

Based on our earlier successes with individual and group-oriented reinforcement contingencies, we had a second set of validated procedures for use in general education classrooms. These forms of reinforcement had been successfully used in consultant-mediated intervention packages for students who acted out (CLASS: Hops et al., 1978), who were not engaged (PASS: Greenwood, Hops, et al., 1979), who were socially withdrawn (PEERS: Hops, Walker, & Greenwood, 1979), and who were aggressive (RECESS: Walker, Hops, & Greenwood, 1981). These contingencies had produced increased attention, participation, task completion, cooperation, peer social interaction, and achievement, and because they involved *all* students in a class, they were appropriate for the general education classroom. Based on a third line of work on tutoring error correction procedures (Delquadri, 1978; Harris, 1982), we had a third set of procedures that could be used by peer tutors. Thus, CWPT became a merger of these validated components. Other investigators contributed substantially by adapting, innovating, and testing these and other new components in independent replications in which achievement was improved compared to conventional instruction (e.g., The Tutor Huddle: Heward, Heron, & Cooke, 1986; Fredonia CWPT: Maheady & Harper, 1987; Reciprocal Peer Tutoring: Fantuzzo, King, & Heller, 1992; Peabody CWPT: Mathes, Fuchs, Fuchs, Henley, & Sanders, 1994; Supplementary Practice Activities: Kohler, Ezell, Hoel, & Strain, 1994).

Supports for Inclusion.   CWPT incorporated a number of features that made it inclusive of diverse learners and for schoolwide application. First, CWPT was used with the general education curriculum, either teacher or commercially prepared materials. Second, tutoring was reciprocal in that each student functioned as the tutor and the tutee. Third, it rewarded individual students based on their own performance as well as the performance of their partner and their team. Such contingencies of reinforcement promoted peer teaching and motivated peer help (Greenwood & Hops, 1981). Fourth, changing tutor–tutee roles (daily) and changing partners (weekly) prevented boredom and kept children motivated. Fifth, all learners were included in the formative measurement system that was used to evaluate CWPT effects and guide decisions about change in instruction.

Accommodating Ethnic Diversity.   For many ethnically diverse learners, CWPT has been described as including components (oral tradition, peer learning, reciprocal teaching) that matched alternative learning styles (e.g., Garcia, 1992; Harper, Maheady, Mallette, & Karnes, in press). Additionally, a number of studies demonstrated improvements in the oral reading rates of students with learning disabilities, the majority of whom were African American (e.g., Greenwood, Delquadri, & Hall, 1984). Madrid and his colleagues reported that CWPT was more effective than was conventional teacher-mediated instruction with Hispanic, bilingual students with academic delays (Madrid, Canas, & Watson, 1993). Achi-Dror (1991) translated the procedures to Hebrew, and taught them to teachers who applied them to the improvement of reading and spelling in five schools in Israel.

Extensions to Mild-Moderate Disabilities. Harper, Mallette, and their colleagues demonstrated improvements in spelling accuracy for students with mild retardation including retention over time (e.g., Harper et al., in press). Additionally important, they reported that words learned during CWPT spelling instruction generalized to story-writing tasks in the absence of specific training (Harper, Mallette, Maheady, Parkes, & Moore, 1993). Sideridis (1995) demonstrated improvements in students' weekly spelling accuracy, time engaged, and increased peer social interaction when using CWPT with students with LD and EMR included in the general education classroom. DuPaul and Henningson (1993) demonstrated that CWPT was effective for one student with ADHD in a regular classroom, and Bell et al. (1990) developed an application of CWPT to a general education history class with students with behavioral disorders included.

Summary. Across a line of small-scale, experimental intervention studies spanning various subject matter, ages, settings, and student characteristics in the general education classroom, CWPT has been shown superior to conventional instruction in increasing indices of literacy and social competence (Greenwood, Carta, & Kamps, 1990). In the majority of studies, students with LD or other mild disabilities have improved when analyzed individually or as a group, as have the non-LD, nondisabled learners in the classroom. And, in some instances, they have performed equally well (e.g., Delquadri et al., 1983; Sideridis, 1995). Through the restructuring of the classroom ecology and teacher–student interactions provided by CWPT, a combination of reciprocal, same-age, peer tutoring; individual and group-oriented contingencies; and modeling error correction overcame some traditional challenges to the instruction of diverse learners in the general education classroom and, as a result, instruction became more inclusive with better outcomes.

Implementation Variation and CWPT

An outgrowth of this work in the school and classroom was research on factors affecting implementation of CWPT at the system, classroom, and tutor levels. In some cases, these factors prevented high-quality, sustained implementation of CWPT (Greenwood, Terry, Arreaga-Mayer, & Finney, 1992), and thus, were barriers to scaling up the potential impact on student learning. In other cases, the untrained tutoring behaviors that some tutors brought to CWPT were found to improve tutee performance.

System Restructuring.   We encountered a number of system problems. For example, we had a curriculum supervisor cancel a CWPT program in progress because "it wasn't consistent with district goals," although it had been approved and adopted by the principal and the classroom teacher. To address system problems such as this, we developed and tested an administrative-adoption model for CWPT designed to address system level issues (Delquadri & Elliott, 1990). The model put in place procedures that addressed:

1. Formal acceptance of CWPT as a practice for use within and across both the special and general education programs.
2. Formal certification of CWPT as an approved procedure for use within students' IEPs.
3. Orientation and training of multiple staff concerning the program.
4. Identification of persons on-site with sufficient expertise to become local CWPT experts and to address teachers' questions about CWPT implementation.
5. Promotion of multiple sources of teacher contact and reinforcement concerning the program and its effects.
6. Administrative-level as well as classroom-level formative evaluation procedures.
7. Formal integration of both special and general education students in the CWPT program (e.g., Delquadri & Elliott, 1990; Delquadri, Flanagan, & Greenwood, 1987).

We evaluated the effect of the model on the measured quality of CWPT implementation and its continued use by teachers 1 year later. Training and implementation of the model eventually involved 516 regular and special education teachers, and over 10,000 students in 42 schools in 20 school districts and 11 special education cooperatives. Overall results indicated that implementation quality increased from 88% to 94% between Year 1 and Year 2 with use of the model, and that the percentage of teachers using CWPT actually increased from 78% in Year 1 to 82% in Year 2. Individual schools varied one year to the next, but each maintained very high levels of teacher participation and CWPT implementation quality. Additional indices of change indicated improvement in the frequencies of contacts between and among CWPT teachers and coordinators, inclusion of special education students in the program, students' academic engagement, and reading achievement (Delquadri, Elliott, Hughes, & Porter, 1990a, 1990b, 1990c). In these schools and districts, CWPT has since become a basic element in their restructuring for inclusion of children with mild disabilities.

Classroom Implementation.   We received reports and observed examples of individual classroom implementation difficulties, including point cheating by students, too few weekly tutoring sessions, teachers not monitoring tutors, and use of unchallenging materials. This stimulated research on CWPT implementation requirements and variations (Greenwood, Terry, Utley, Montagna, & Walker, 1993; Maheady, Harper, Mallette, & Winstanley, 1991), and on the failure of some students to make progress in the program (Greenwood, Dinwiddie, et al., 1987). To address classroom problems such as these, we sought to provide individual teachers with feedback on their program and its effects on students' achievement. To provide this feedback, roles were restructured creating a CWPT Building Representative and CWPT Teacher Partnerships among faculty so that sources of checking program implementation, student outcomes, and providing feedback on improvements in implementation could be linked. We also sought to improve diagnosis of common implementation problems by linking them to observed patterns in weekly student outcomes and provision of advice and appropriate procedures. This information was included in computer software designed to provide individual teachers with advice they could use in their weekly planning, daily implementation, and monitoring of progress (Greenwood, Finney, et al., 1993).

Effective Peer Teaching Behaviors. We observed that some tutors produced better performances by their tutees than others, even though they were taught the same scripted teaching sequence. The peer tutoring literature has long supported the view that tutors trained in specific peer teaching skills produce better results than those left on their own (e.g., Niedermeyer, 1970). In addition to what we taught them, some tutors prompted their tutees to respond more quickly instead of waiting long periods for a response. Some tutors provided assistance to promote tutee success and more rapid responding and content coverage (Kohler & Greenwood, 1990). In other cases, children encouraged their team members to perform well, and they provided positive social consequences to individuals who met or exceeded standards of performance (Kohler, Richardson, Mina, Dinwiddie, & Greenwood, 1985). These tutoring behaviors appeared to be functional because they increased individual points earned and team success.

We followed these informal observations with a study designed to test the function of such skills when taught to other tutors. We taught go-faster prompts, praise for responding, and specific forms of help. When incorporated into tutors' core CWPT teaching skills, the effect was higher rates of spelling words practiced and corrected during tutoring, and increased spelling accuracy on weekly tests. These findings were replicated across four low-achieving tutees (Kohler & Greenwood, 1990).

Summary. Beyond the initial development and validation of CWPT, research on factors affecting its use in local schools at the system, classroom, and peer interaction levels of analysis improved our knowledge of how implementation moderated the potential outcomes of CWPT and how implementation quality could be maintained and improved. Demonstrated were procedures for improving the system-level context for CWPT and creation of roles within local schools for supporting and monitoring implementation quality. This led to analyses of implementation requirements and methods of assessment for use in teacher training. By studying specific instances of students failing to learn in CWPT, variations in teacher and tutor implementation of core procedures were identified and methods of assessing and remediating them developed. And, by studying the peer teaching behaviors naturally contributed by some tutors, their addition to the core procedures led to further improvement in outcomes for tutees.

Longitudinal Prevention/Intervention Research

Having developed CWPT and achieved an improved understanding of its components, our knowledge of its academic benefits remained limited to short-term studies of 1 year duration or less. Thus, the next objective was to assess the cumulative benefit to a group of at-risk first graders. This effort became a 4-year-long exposure to CWPT in reading, spelling, and math in first through fourth grades, followed by an 8-year follow-along investigation of effects. Compared in this longitudinal study were an at-risk Experimental Group receiving CWPT, and two additional groups, one an equally at-risk Control Group; the other a nonrisk Index Group (Greenwood, Delquadri, & Hall, 1989). Both of these no-treatment groups received conventional instruction. Based on earlier findings, the hypothesis tested was that CWPT would increase at-risk students' academic responding during instruction, and weekly curriculum-based measures compared to the Control and Index Groups and that the cumulative effect of greater daily academic responding would significantly influence their growth in standardized measures of academic achievement and thereby reduce the incidence of early school failure.

Results for First through Fourth Grades. Results reported for first, second, and third grades (Greenwood, 1991a) and first through fourth grades (Greenwood, 1991b; Greenwood, Delquadri, & Hall, 1989) supported this hypothesis. Levels of student engagement were significantly increased in the Experimental Group with the onset of CWPT and thereafter, compared to the other two groups. The CWPT Group exceeded the Control Group but not the Index Group. After controlling for initial first-grade differences in measured IQ and achievement, the means of the CWPT group on the Metropolitan Achievement Test at the end of second, third, and fourth grades exceeded to a statistically significant degree those of the Control Group. Fourth-grade effect sizes were 0.37, 0.57, and 0.60 for arithmetic, reading, and language subscales. The means of the Index Group also exceeded those of the Control Groups, with effect sizes of 0.59, 0.93 and 0.90 for arithmetic, reading, and language subscales. However, the differences between the CWPT and Index Groups were not statistically different (Greenwood, Delquadri, & Hall, 1989, p. 379).

Follow-Along Results at Middle and High School.   We also reported the longer-term benefits of the use of CWPT in elementary school, at middle school, and high school in terms of standardized achievement, special education services received (e.g., LD, EMR, etc.), and early school dropout. Overall, analyses of services received through sixth grade by 90 students who had received some form of special services favored the at-risk CWPT group (Greenwood, Terry, Utley, et al., 1993). Statistically fewer CWPT students had received special services and, of those who had, proportionally more had received less restrictive services compared to the Control Group. We reported that more of the CWPT special education students had received their services from itinerant teachers or in the mainstream, compared to the Controls who were served more often in the special classroom or resource room. By 11th grade, it was evident that dropout rates also favored the CWPT and the Index Groups over the Control Group (Greenwood, 1994, February). The relative risk of dropout for the three groups was 13.4%, 7.4%, 9.3%, respectively for the Control, CWPT, and Index Groups.

Summary.   Sustained early use of CWPT in elementary school produced significant and practical long-term benefits to students in middle school and high school in terms of higher achievement, reduced special education services, less restrictive services, and lower dropout. Based collectively on these results and those of prior studies, we know that restructuring instruction in specific ways as reflected in CWPT increased students' daily academic responding and their weekly and annual growth in academic achievement.

Important to obtaining a quality, sustained implementation of these procedures was objective assessment of implementation quality and feedback to teachers and retraining when needed in order to improve and maintain quality. Yet, even with these procedures, a complete implementation of CWPT in subject areas in all years was not achieved for all students (Greenwood, Delquadri, & Hall, 1989). Important, however, was the fact that these improved outcomes were obtained even in the face of only partial implementation of CWPT. Thus, the current findings should be viewed as conservative, with even better outcomes attainable given complete implementation (Greenwood, Delquadri, & Hall, 1989). Based on these and prior findings, another line of work emerged that sought to identify the behaviors of effective teachers and promote these behaviors among other, less effective teachers.

Studies of What Effective Teachers Do
as Validated in Applications by Other Teachers

Although the prior work revealed much about the importance of implementation quality, the classroom processes of CWPT, the behaviors of teachers and students that made a difference in the growth of student achievement, and long-term benefit, it become increasingly important to identify other practices used naturally by classroom teachers that orchestrated the same and similar processes and that also led to similar academic outcomes. For this purpose, 65 students with LD and their teachers (regular and special education) in two school districts were assessed and screened using product (pre- and posttest gains on the Metropolitan Achievement Test) and process observation measures (MS-CISSAR: Greenwood, Carta, Arreaga-Mayer, & Rager, 1991). We observed the total daily instruction of these students who were receiving some varying degrees of mainstreaming. Based on prior findings with these measures, we expected student groups who differed significantly in their annual growth in achievement also to differ in daily mean levels of academic responding.

This hypothesis was supported. Low- versus high-growth student groups on achievement test measures also differed by 9% in their mean level of daily academic responding measured on the MS-CISSAR observation instrument. The majority of this difference was explained by significantly lower levels of engagement in academic talk by students in the low-growth group. Ecological and teacher behavior differences also distinguished low- from high-growth groups of students. Low-gaining students with LD spent more time in music instruction, in small rather than large instructional groups, in instruction provided by a special rather than a regular education teacher, and in instruction with the teacher focused more often on other students than on the target student with LD.

Although these analyses confirmed the relationship between growth in achievement and student's academic engagement and localized differences in the instructional ecology of low- versus high-growth students, the effects of specific instructional practices presumed effective for individual high-growth students remained unknown. Thus, the next step sought to identify these instructional practices of the most effective teachers.

For these teachers and subject areas, information obtained from interviews and informal observations of their teaching were used to form concise statements of their teaching procedures (see Table 3.2). For example, most effective teachers provided direct instruction, wherein students knew what to do, experienced specific organized activities, fast pacing, group responding, response opportunities, and feedback in multiple forms including teacher verbalizations, stickers, points, and posted charts. Very ineffective teachers provided lecture and discussion, and students often engaged in seatwork. Pacing was slow and at times students waited. Students were questioned and prompted by the teacher who called on volunteers. Feedback tended to follow incorrect responses only, and it sometimes included physical contact.

To demonstrate that these practices of effective teachers would lead to improved achievement when used by other teachers and their students, we studied their use by other teachers. For example, with assistance of project staff,

TABLE 3.2
Characteristics of the Most Effective and Ineffective LD Teachers

Instructional Components	Effective Teachers		Ineffective Teachers	
	ID	Attribute	ID	Attribute
Method	1	Direct instruction	8	Lecture and discussion
	2	Direct instruction	9	Lecture and discussion
	4	Direct instruction	10	Discussion, teacher prompting
	7	Structured drill practice		
Orchestration	1	Students know what to do	11	Lecture and questions
	4	Six sets of activities	8	Lecture and questions
			9	Lecture, teacher prompts for correction of concepts, review, independent seatwork
			11	Lecture, questions, and seatwork
Pace	1	Fast-paced	8	Slow-paced
	2	Quick verbal prompts	10	Delay getting started
	6	Fast paced	11	Put entire list on board, asked class to copy as study guide
Monitoring	2	Group responding using hand signal or flashcards, and students justifying their answers	8	Prompted students to give correct response
	3	Asked students one at a time to provide examples of concept	9	Prompted students' responses in unison with correction
			10	Prompted students to provide examples
			11	Called on volunteers
Feedback	2	Immediate feedback using stickers, posted charts, reviewed individual progress	8	Immediate feedback for incorrect response
	4	Recorded points for on-task behavior	11	Circulated among students and patted those who were correct
	5	Conducted conferences with individual students		
	6	Received points for accuracy, did timed readings, recorded total points earned, received stickers for good behavior		
	7	Teacher circulated and checked students' work		

Adapted from Greenwood, Arreaga-Mayer, & Carta (1994, p. 147).

an identified effective resource room teacher taught one of the ineffective resource room teachers to employ her procedure. Results indicated that the ineffective teacher learned and implemented the new procedure to a high level
of fidelity and that, compared to her own procedure as baseline, students reduced the number of written errors on weekly writing samples and increased
levels of mastery on weekly content tests (Greenwood, Carta, Arreaga-Mayer,
& Rager, 1991). These superior effects were repeated in a replication of these
same procedures with other students, further supporting the functional relationship between the effective method and growth in students' writing fluency
and weekly content achievement. Other studies extended these findings into a
general education classroom setting when used by a regular education teacher
for both writing and reading instruction (Greenwood, Carta, Arreaga-Mayer,
& Rager, 1991; Greenwood, Delquadri, & Bulgren, 1993; Terry & Arreaga-
Mayer, 1993).

Summary. The practices of teachers whose students made the largest
gains in achievement and who had engaged in the highest levels of academic
responding during instruction were found effective when applied by other,
less effective teachers as evidenced by growth in the achievement of their students. This work extended the prior process–product research on the benefits of CWPT to include the analysis of teacher-developed practices, and it has
subsequently been applied to the improvement of the instruction and outcomes of students with autism and developmental disabilities (Kamps, Leonard, Dugan, Boland, & Greenwood, 1991). Like the earlier CWPT work, this
analysis of effective teachers shared several important commonalties, including (a) the link between increased levels of daily academic responding
and growth in content achievement, and (b) fidelity of implementation. This
work also extended the earlier work of Good and Grouws (1979) in that the
inclusion of ecological and process data appeared to strengthen the accuracy
of procedural identification and its translation for use by others.

For example, the ecobehavioral approach focused on what individual effective teachers did as opposed to groups of teachers, making it suitable for
individual classroom as well as building-based studies of instructional improvement. This approach focused on time spent learning a subject matter
and the organization of classroom instruction in terms of materials, grouping, teacher location, focus, and behavior such that objective procedural
protocols could be developed as a basis for training others. Although this
represented an important advance in knowledge of the form and function
of effective teaching, the work remains limited by only a few replications
to date. Additional research is needed to more fully validate these methods,
validate practices derived from it, and extend its application to schoolwide
improvement.

DOES THE EVIDENCE WARRANT APPLICATION IN CLASSROOMS? HOW AMENABLE ARE THE COMPONENTS TO INTERVENTION OR CHANGE?

The ecobehavioral approach and the practices/behavior of effective teachers have strong implications for classroom application in three areas: basic knowledge of academic learning processes, specific practices, and guides for instructional improvement efforts.

Basic Academic Learning Processes

One of the barriers to major improvements in the quality of the national education product has been the failure of educational research to provide insight on classroom learning processes that may be used to guide efforts to improve instructional practice (e.g., Kaestle, 1993). In contrast, the work reviewed based on an ecobehavioral perspective provides a framework for understanding academic learning as change in classroom behavior due to change in instruction. As an operational model, it has led directly to designs and methods of assessment for investigating teaching and classroom learning. Additionally, results have been useful in the form of new findings, forms of instruction, and replications. Because these findings demonstrated measurable improvements in students' learning as a function of changes in instructional ecology and process, they have led to additional studies that have tested other components and have increased the generality of the model.

Instructional practices that orchestrated and sustained low versus high levels of academic responding during instruction led to differentially higher rates of growth on weekly content taught (e.g., CBM, portfolios, etc.) and annual measures of standardized achievement (e.g., achievement tests). How instruction is planned, organized, and implemented is primarily important in terms of how it affects students' academic responding, moment to moment, week to week, month to month. Of secondary importance is the nature of the curriculum, because it affects what is to be learned and the contexts created for teaching.

Asserting that curriculum is necessary but not sufficient is in contrast to most views of classroom teaching and learning (see Au and Carroll, chap. 2, in this volume). Supporting this view is the work with CWPT where it has been used repeatedly to enhance students' outcomes across a range of subject matter and curricula designed from any number of conceptual frameworks. Additionally, the lesson learned in the past decade is that curriculum reforms traditionally fail to address the critical issue of active student responding and its promotion during classroom lessons. Evidence for this is the absence of systematic strategies for engaging students in active responding as either individuals or as groups, and the very wide ranges in engagement and participation that are typical of students within traditional forms of instruction. Thus, the risk of early academic failure is elevated for many students experiencing these practices. The failure to control for differential levels of student engagement in the curriculum is also a confounding variable in much of traditional educational research on alternative instructional practices. In contrast, effective instruction practices ensure that students' engagement in academic responding is promoted, monitored, and maintained over time, and curricula are designed and integrated with this principle in mind. The basic knowledge provided by the work reviewed is that the management and supervision of student academic responding is critical to the rate of present and future academic learning.

Specific Instructional Strategies

CWPT is one strategy that provides many of the features of effective instruction (see Berliner, 1988) and that may be adapted to or integrated with existing curricula. Because it is a classwide system of reciprocal peer tutoring, it can have a powerful effect on the participation of *all* students, and it promotes academic responding in multiple forms (written, text, verbal) across both tutee and tutor roles. This stands in stark contrast to many traditional forms of teacher lecture/discussion where attention is promoted combined with intermittent responses to teacher questions from individual students, followed by time devoted to seatwork where individual responding is paced by each individual student resulting in a wide range of attention and participation. The contribution of the work reviewed has been documentation of the fact that students learn less in these traditional forms of instruction, particularly students who are culturally diverse, have limited proficiency at English, are at risk, or who have LD or other disabilities.

Also supported in the work reviewed is the fact that even CWPT will produce less than optimum results given that is only partially implemented or if the quality of its implementation drifts from the original protocol. In these instances, students have received reduced time to learn and, because the quality of peer tutoring is reduced, so too are students' opportunities to respond to the curriculum and to be reinforced and to be corrected. The development and promotion of the practices of effective teachers provided additional support to the assertion that academic learning is a function of classroom academic responding. Although in need of addition work and replication, the strategy used to identify, translate, and promote effective practices in the teaching of others clearly is a promising one for local efforts to improve instruction and academic outcomes.

Guiding Improvement Efforts

The work reviewed also demonstrates the importance and utility of ecobehavioral assessment information (e.g., CISSAR, MS-CISSAR, ESCAPE) to the validation of effective instruction. The availability of these instruments in practitioner-friendly forms (Greenwood, Carta, Kamps, Terry, & Delquadri, 1994) provides the capability of extending the current research findings to local reform efforts. Anecdotal observations of school districts and schools that have implemented ecobehavioral assessments as part of either their school psychology services or evaluation of school reform/inclusion efforts have indicated several important outcomes.

The instrument taxonomy (i.e., MS-CISSAR) has quickly become a common language for discussing and thinking about instructional intervention. Interventions are discussed in terms of their potential or known effects on increasing students' academic responding, or reducing competing behaviors. When used in data sharing meetings with the school's principal, inclusion coordinators, and classroom teachers, all of whom have learned the taxonomy, inquiry is focused on change goals and the effects of change in these terms. For example, previous progress implementing particular strategies may be discussed in terms of what has changed, what might change, and plans set for what is to be tried next. Additionally, ecobehavioral data have been joined with curriculum-based measures as part of school improvement plans, converting from traditional psychometric testing to performance-based assessment. The complementary relation between ecobehavioral assessment and CBM as process and product of instruction is important. Ecobehavioral assessment describes instruction and its effects on student behavior, whereas CBM describes the outcome of instruction in terms of change in fluency and mastery. Thus, together these measures provide information and analyses that potentially inform the following areas of programming: intervention development and validation, inclusion, prereferral intervention, and transition programming, among others.

WHERE DO WE GO FROM HERE?

Described in this chapter has been systematic research on the behavior and practices of effective teachers. The work was based on the ecobehavioral approach with its emphasis on direct observational assessment of instruction, functional relationships between instruction and change in student performance, and behavioral development within longitudinal designs. There are several implications of this approach for the education and treatment of children with LD.

First, the approach explains why improving student learning is not simply a matter of changing or reforming what is taught or how it is taught, that is, the curricula. This is because learning is a product of one's history of interactions in which situations and behavior are functionally interrelated through consequences (i.e., the principle of reinforcement). Thus, in situations where behavior is expected but not observed to occur, its future occurrence may be influenced by providing reinforcement or by altering the situation in ways known to evoke a response already learned. Thus, learning of subject matter at its root is a function of managing the details involved in the daily interactions of students, teachers, and curriculum materials. Therefore, learning is inherently individualistic because even the interactions of teachers and students in the same lessons are unique. That is why teaching that seeks to be uniform for all will only succeed with some, and not all, students.

Second, the approach validates the saliency of engagement in academic responding as both the immediate outcome and as process in the path from instruction to academic achievement. As noted in the prior point, unless instructional reform leads to improvements in one's daily and cumulative minutes of academic responding, subject matter achievement will not likely follow, nor will gaps in achievement levels between types of learners be closed.

Third, the approach demonstrates the possibility of preventing LD in some segment of the population, and the futility of remediation. For example, third grade is simply too late to act with LD services to close the gap in achievement (Greenwood, Hart, et al., 1994). This is because overcoming the cumulative deficit in lost hours of engagement in academic responding in past years, one's personal history with the subject matter, cannot be accomplished in the time remaining in subsequent grades given the intensity of current instructional technology. Most remediational efforts can, at best, produce only localized effects that are short-lived. Thus, prevention of small cumulative histories of engagement with academic subject matter in the lives of diverse learners based on observational measures beginning in kindergarten or earlier (Hart & Risley, 1992, 1995; Walker, Greenwood, Hart, & Carta, 1994) is needed.

Fourth, the approach is applicable to a range of subject matter and traditions of instruction. Whether or not instruction is guided by the behavioral approach, an essential question addressed with ecobehavioral analysis is how ongoing instruction is influencing students' current and cumulative engagement in academic responding. Another essential question concerns how instruction might change to improve students' engagement, and, therefore, improve formative measures of achievement. It is through this improvement that change in academic achievement, whether measured by curriculum-based measurement, portfolios, or standardized tests, will be influenced to an important degree.

Future work is needed in several areas in which students with LD are integrated. Research designed to explore the relevance of academic responding in other instructional formats, such as the various forms of cooperative learning, is needed. Perhaps least addressed in these popular forms of instruction is exactly how academic responding is promoted and how it may be related to students' rates of academic growth, as in the case of CWPT. Similar studies of still other instructional forms such as "whole language" or those based on the social constructivist approach (see Au and Carroll, chap. 2, this volume) may be highly profitable in identifying where, when, and how academic responding is achieved, the range in individual variation reduced, and learning most facilitated as a consequence.

Research in local school buildings is needed designed to further demonstrate the benefits of identifying, translating, and promoting the practices of effective teachers. The work described provides a model capable of application to individual teachers, and, thus, its implications for building-based applications seems highly feasible. The approach is also timely, because many schools are seeking the means of identifying and keeping what works as opposed to entirely reinventing their programs every 5 or so years. Needed are collaborative studies in which the model is used and the benefits at the levels of individual students, teachers, and buildings over time assessed.

The role of ecobehavioral assessment in the validation of instruction deserves continued attention. As a research and development tool, ecobehavioral assessment has grown in its range of applications in special and general education research and it is beginning to see applications by practitioners in local schools. Because of the number of studies, replications and variations of the approach across populations, settings, and behaviors in the last 16 years, the approach is now much more than just a theoretical framework: It is an approach tempered by instruments, data, application, practices, and hypotheses tested. The variety of analyses and knowledge of effective components based on it has grown, and new applications continue to be developed. This progress represents our growing understanding of how classroom instruction acts to change student performance and growth in subject matter achievement.

At the level of research, more work is needed in refining and extending the use of ecobehavioral instruments and approaches that we have illustrated. For example, other areas of educational practice stand to benefit from similar research (e.g., bilingual special education), and progress has been made in developing instruments (Arreaga-Mayer, Carta, & Tapia, 1994). Similar work for younger children in the home and older youth in the work environment also has seen progress but remains in need of continued research. Experimental validation of effective practices in these and other areas remain to be completed.

Lastly, perhaps the greatest need for future research is in terms of controlled, developmental studies of students at risk and with LD who receive improved instructional interventions and strategies. Perhaps least addressed in the current literature is our ability to demonstrate prevention, particularly of the early failure to learn to read and its implications on later educational success. Longitudinal studies offer perhaps the only means of demonstrating, with certainty, that early efforts have affected later educational outcomes and services. In the past, all too often we have had short-term studies and cross-sectional designs that have provided opportunities to examine only localized effects of interventions. We don't know the later life benefits of these efforts. We need this information if we are to improve our programs in ways that are truly effective.

ACKNOWLEDGMENT

Preparation of this manuscript was supported by grant H023A40040 from the Office of Special Education Research and Rehabilitative Services, U.S. Department of Education, with additional support from the Kansas Mental Retardation Research Center. The opinions presented in this chapter are those of the author and no endorsement by the agency is intended or implied. This work is dedicated to the students, families, teachers, and schools of the Kansas City Public Schools in Kansas. Additional information may be obtained from Dr. Charles R. Greenwood, Director, Juniper Gardens Children's Project, University of Kansas, 1614 Washington Blvd., Kansas City, KS 66102.

REFERENCES

Achi-Dror, N. (1991). *Field replication of classwide peer tutoring in Israel.* Unpublished master's thesis, Department of Human Development and Family Life, University of Kansas, Lawrence.

Arreaga-Mayer, C., Carta, J. J., & Tapia, Y. (1994). Ecobehavioral assessment of bilingual special education settings: The opportunity to respond revisited. In R. Gardner III, D. Sainato, J. Cooper, T. Heron, W. Heward, J. Eskleman, & T. Grossi (Eds.), *Behavior analysis in education: Focus on measurably superior instruction* (pp. 225–240). Pacific Grove, CA: Brooks/Cole.

Bell, K., Young, K. R., Blair, M., & Nelson, R. (1990). Facilitating mainstreaming of students with behavioral disorders using CWPT. *School Psychology Review, 19,* 564–573.

Berliner, D. C. (1988). The half-full glass: A review of research on teaching. E. L. Meyen, G. A. Vergason, & R. J. Whelan (Eds.), *Effective instructional strategies for exceptional children* (pp. 7–341). Denver, CO: Love.

Bijou, S. W., & Baer, D. M. (1978). *Behavior analysis of child development.* Englewood Cliffs, NJ: Prentice-Hall.

Bureau of Child Research (1964). *The Juniper Gardens' planning document.* Lawrence, KS: University of Kansas.

Carta, J. J., Greenwood, C. R., & Atwater, J. (1985). *Ecobehavioral system for complex as-*

sessments of preschool environments (ESCAPE). Kansas City, KS: Juniper Gardens Children's Project, Bureau of Child Research, University of Kansas.

Carta, J. J., Greenwood, C. R., Schulte, D., Arreaga-Mayer, C., & Terry, B. (1987). The mainstream code for instructional structure and student academic response (MS-CISSAR): Observer training manual. Kansas City, KS: Juniper Gardens Children's Project, Bureau of Child Research, University of Kansas.

Cooper, D. H., & Speece, D. L. (1990a). Instructional correlates of students' academic responses: Comparisons between at-risk and control students. Early Education and Development, 1, 279–300.

Cooper, D. H., & Speece, D. L. (1990b). Maintaining at risk children in regular education settings: Initial effects of individual differences and classroom environments. Exceptional Children, 57, 117–127.

Delquadri, J. (1978). An analysis of the generalization effects of four tutoring procedures on oral reading responses of eight learning disability children. Unpublished doctoral dissertation, Department of Human Development and Family Life, University of Kansas, Lawrence.

Delquadri, J. C., & Elliott, M. (1990, May). The effect of an administrative component on large-scale implementation of Classwide Peer Tutoring. Paper presented at the 16th Annual Convention of the Association for Behavior Analysis, Nashville, TN.

Delquadri, J. C., Elliott, M., Hughes, V., & Porter, M. (1990a). An administrative model for implementing effective instructional procedures in the regular classroom: Teaching and mainstreaming learning disabled and low achieving students. Kansas City, KS: Juniper Gardens Children's Project, University of Kansas.

Delquadri, J. C., Elliott, M., Hughes, V., & Porter, M. (1990b). Classwide peer tutoring for reading and comprehension: A manual of procedures for teachers and special education consultants. Kansas City, KS: Juniper Gardens Children's Project, University of Kansas.

Delquadri, J. C., Elliott, M., Hughes, V., & Porter, M. (1990c). The effects of an administrative model for school principals on the effectiveness and maintenance of the reading classwide peer tutoring program. Kansas City, KS: Juniper Gardens Children's Project, University of Kansas.

Delquadri, J., Flanagan, P., & Greenwood, C. R. (1987). The pyramid administrative model for classwide peer tutoring. Kansas City, KS: The Juniper Gardens Children's Project, University of Kansas.

Delquadri, J., Greenwood, C. R., Stretton, K., & Hall, R. V. (1983). The peer tutoring game: A classroom procedure for increasing opportunity to respond and spelling performance. Education and Treatment of Children, 6, 225–239.

DuPaul, G. J., & Henningson, P. N. (1993). Peer tutoring effects on the classroom performance of children with attention deficit hyperactivity disorder. School Psychology Review, 22, 134–142.

Englemann, S., Becker, W. C., Carnine, D., & Gersten, R. (1988). The Direct Instruction follow-through model: Design and outcomes. Education and Treatment of Children, 11, 303–317.

Fantuzzo, J. W., King, J. A., & Heller, L. R. (1992). Effects of reciprocal peer tutoring on mathematics and school adjustment: A component analysis. Journal of Educational Psychology, 84, 331–339.

Garcia, E. E. (1992). Linguistically and culturally diverse children: Effective instructional practices and related policy issues. In H. C. Waxman, J. W. deFelix, J. E. Anderson, & H. P. Baptiste, Jr. (Eds.), Students at risk in at-risk schools: Improving environments for learning (pp. 65–86). Newbury Park, CA: Sage.

Good, T. L., & Grouws, D. A. (1979). The Missouri mathematics effectiveness project: An experimental study in fourth-grade classrooms. Journal of Educational Psychology, 71, 355–362.

Greenwood, C. R. (1991a). A longitudinal analysis of time, engagement, and academic achievement in at-risk vs. non-risk students. *Exceptional Children, 57,* 521–535.

Greenwood, C. R. (1991b). Classwide peer tutoring: Longitudinal effects on the reading, language, and mathematics achievement of at-risk students. *Reading, Writing, and Learning Disabilities International, 7,* 105–124.

Greenwood, C. R. (1994, February). *ClassWide Peer Tutoring and inclusion.* Paper presented at the second annual meeting of the Pacific Coast Research Conference, La Jolla, CA.

Greenwood, C. R. (1994, October). The ecobehavioral analysis of classroom instruction: The path from interaction to achievement. In B. K. Keogh & D. L. Speece (Co-chairs), *Conference on research on classroom ecologies: Implications for inclusion of children with disabilities.* San Antonio, TX.

Greenwood, C., Arreaga-Mayer, C., & Carta, J. (1994). Identification and translation of effective teacher-developed instructional procedures for general practice. *Journal of Remedial and Special Education, 15*(3), 140–151.

Greenwood, C. R., Carta, J. J., Arreaga-Mayer, C., & Rager, A. (1991). The behavior analyst consulting model: Identifying and validating naturally effective instructional procedures. *Journal of Behavioral Education, 1,* 165–191.

Greenwood, C. R., Carta, J. J., & Atwater, J. B. (1991). Ecobehavioral analysis in the classroom. *Journal of Behavioral Education, 1,* 59–77.

Greenwood, C. R., Carta, J. J., & Hall, R. V. (1988). The use of classwide peer tutoring strategies in classroom management and instruction. *School Psychology Review, 17,* 258–275.

Greenwood, C. R., Carta, J. J., Hart, B., Kamps, D., Terry, B., Arreaga-Mayer, C., Atwater, J., Walker, D., Risley, T., & Delquadri, J. C. (1992). Out of the laboratory and into the community: 26 years of applied behavior analysis at the Juniper Gardens Children's Project. *American Psychologist, 47,* 1464–1474.

Greenwood, C. R., Carta, J. J., & Kamps, D. (1990). Teacher versus peer-mediated instruction. In H. Foot, M. Morgan, & R. Shute (Eds.), *Children helping children* (pp. 177–206). Chichester, England: John Wiley.

Greenwood, C. R., Carta, J. J., Kamps, D., & Arreaga-Mayer, C. (1990). Ecobehavioral analysis of classroom instruction. In S. R. Schroeder (Ed.), *Ecobehavioral analysis and developmental disabilities: The twenty-first century* (pp. 33–63). New York: Springer-Verlag.

Greenwood, C. R., Carta, J. J., Kamps, D., Terry, B., & Delquadri, J. (1994). Development and validation of standard classroom observation systems for school practitioners: Ecobehavioral assessment systems software (EBASS). *Exceptional Children, 61,* 197–210.

Greenwood, C. R., Delquadri, J., & Bulgren, J. (1993). Current challenges to behavioral technology in the reform of schooling: Large-scale, high-quality implementation and sustained use of effective educational practices. *Education and Treatment of Children, 16,* 401–440.

Greenwood, C. R., Delquadri, J., & Carta, J. J. (1988). *Classwide peer tutoring.* Seattle, WA: Educational Achievement Systems.

Greenwood, C. R., Delquadri, J., & Hall, R. V. (1984). Opportunity to respond and student academic performance. In W. Heward, T. Heron, D. Hill, & J. Trap-Porter (Eds.), *Behavior analysis in education* (pp. 58–88). Columbus, OH: Merrill.

Greenwood, C. R., Delquadri, J. C., & Hall, R. V. (1989). Longitudinal effects of classwide peer tutoring. *Journal of Educational Psychology, 81,* 371–383.

Greenwood, C. R., Delquadri, J. C., Stanley, S. O., Sasso, G., Whorton, D., & Schulte, D. (1981). Allocating opportunity to learn as a basis for academic remediation: A developing model for teaching. *Monograph in Behavior Disorders* (Summer), 22–33.

Greenwood, C. R., Delquadri, J., Stanley, S. O., Terry, B., & Hall, R. V. (1985). Assessment of ecobehavioral interaction in school settings. *Behavioral Assessment, 7,* 331–347.

Greenwood, C. R., Delquadri, J., Stanley, S., Terry, B., & Hall, R. V. (1986). Observational assessment of ecobehavioral interaction during academic instruction. In S. E. Newstead, S. H.

Irvine, & P. D. Dan (Eds.), *Human assessment: Cognition and motivation* (pp. 319–340). Dordrecht, The Netherlands: Nijhoff Press.

Greenwood, C. R., Dinwiddie, G., Bailey, V., Carta, J. J., Dorsey, D., Kohler, F. W., Nelson, C., Rotholz, D., & Schulte, D. (1987). Field replication of classwide peer tutoring. *Journal of Applied Behavior Analysis, 20,* 151–160.

Greenwood, C. R., Finney, R., Terry, B., Arreaga-Mayer, C., Carta, J. J., Delquadri, J., Walker, D., Innocenti, M., Lignugaris-Kraft, J., Harper, G. F., & Clifton, R. (1993). Monitoring, improving, and maintaining quality implementation of the ClassWide Peer Tutoring Program using behavioral and computer technology. *Education and Treatment of Children, 16,* 19–47.

Greenwood, C. R., Hart, B., Walker, D., & Risley, T. R. (1994). The opportunity to respond revisited: A behavioral theory of developmental retardation and its prevention. In R. Gardner III, D. M. Sainato, J. O. Cooper, T. E. Heron, W. L. Heward, J. W. Eshleman, & T. A. Grossi (Eds.), *Behavior analysis in education: Focus on measurably superior instruction* (pp. 213–223). Pacific Grove, CA: Brooks/Cole.

Greenwood, C. R., & Hops, H. (1981). Group contingencies and peer behavior change. In P. Strain (Ed.), *The utilization of classroom peers as behavior change agents* (pp. 189–259). New York: Plenum.

Greenwood, C. R., Hops, H., Walker, H. M., Guild, J. J., Stokes, J., Young, K. R., Keleman, K. S., & Willardson, M. (1979). Standardized classroom behavior management program (PASS): Social validation and replication studies in Utah and Oregon. *Journal of Applied Behavior Analysis, 12,* 255–271.

Greenwood, C. R., Terry, B., Arreaga-Mayer, C., & Finney, D. (1992). The classwide peer tutoring program: Implementation factors that moderate students' achievement. *Journal of Applied Behavior Analysis, 25,* 101–116.

Greenwood, C. R., Terry, B., Delquadri, J., & Elliott, M. (in press). *ClassWide Peer Tutoring: Research review.* Longmont, CO: Sopris West.

Greenwood, C. R., Terry, B., Marquis, J., & Walker, D. (1994). Confirming a performance-based instructional model. *School Psychology Review, 23,* 652–668.

Greenwood, C. R., Terry, B., Utley, C. A., Montagna, D., & Walker, D. (1993). Achievement, placement, and services: Middle school benefits of ClassWide Peer Tutoring used at the elementary school. *School Psychology Review, 22*(3), 497–516.

Hall, R. V., Delquadri, J., Greenwood, C. R., & Thurston, L. (1982). The importance of opportunity to respond in children's academic success. In E. D. Edgar, N. Haring, J. R. Jenkins, & C. Pious (Eds.), *Serving young handicapped children: Issues and research* (pp. 107–149). Austin, TX: Pro-Ed.

Hall, R. V., Lund, D., & Jackson, D. (1968). Effects of teacher attention on study behavior. *Journal of Applied Behavior Analysis, 1,* 1–12.

Hall, R. V., Schiefelbusch, R. L., Hoyt, R. K., Jr., & Greenwood, C. R. (1989). History, mission, and organization of the Juniper Gardens Children's Project. *Education and Treatment of Children, 12,* 301–329.

Harper, G. F., Maheady, L., Mallette, B., & Karnes, M. (in press). Peer tutoring and the minority child with disabilities. In L. Meyers & C. Utley (Eds.), *School reform and multicultural special education: Implementing effective instructional practices.* Baltimore, MD: Brookes.

Harper, G., Mallette, B., Maheady, L., Parkes, V., & Moore, J. (1993). Retention, and generalization of spelling words acquired using a peer-mediated instructional procedure by children with mild handicapping conditions. *Journal of Behavioral Education, 3,* 26–35.

Harris, J. W. (1982). *A comparison of out-of-class tutoring formats on the in-class oral reading performance of learning disabled students.* Unpublished doctoral dissertation, Department of Human Development and Family Life, University of Kansas, Lawrence.

Hart, B., & Risley, T. R. (1992). American parenting of language-learning children: Persisting differences in family–child interactions observed in natural home environments. *Developmental Psychology, 28,* 1096–1105.

Hart, B., & Risley, T. R. (1995). *Meaningful differences in the everyday experience of young American children.* Baltimore, MD: Paul H. Brookes.

Heward, W. L., Heron, T. E., & Cooke, N. L. (1986). Tutor huddle: Key element in a classwide peer tutoring system. *The Elementary School Journal, 8,* 115–123.

Hoge, R. D. (1985). The validity of direct observation measures of pupil classroom behavior. *Review of Educational Research, 55,* 469–483.

Hops, H., Walker, H. M., Fleischman, D. H., Nagoshi, J. T., Omura, R. T., Skindrud, K., & Taylor, J. (1978). CLASS: A standardized in-class program for acting-out children. II. Field test evaluations. *Journal of Educational Psychology, 70,* 636–644.

Hops, H., Walker, H. M., & Greenwood, C. R. (1979). PEERS: A program for remediating social withdrawal in the school setting: Aspects of a research and development process. In L. A. Hamerlynck (Ed.), *Behavioral system for the developmentally disabled: I. School and environments* (pp. 48–86). New York: Bruner/Mazel.

Kaestle, C. F. (1993, January–February). Research news and comment: The awful reputation of education research. *Educational Researcher,* pp. 23–31.

Kamps, D., Leonard, B. R., Dugan, E. P., Boland, B., & Greenwood, C. R. (1991). The use of eco-behavioral assessment to identify naturally occurring effective procedures in classrooms serving students with autism and developmental disabilities. *Journal of Behavioral Education, 4,* 367–397.

Kohler, F. W., Ezell, H., Hoel, K., & Strain, P. S. (1994). Supplemental practice in a first-grade math class: Effects on teacher behavior and five low-achievers' academic responding and acquisition of content. *The Elementary School Journal, 94,* 389–403.

Kohler, F. W., & Greenwood, C. R. (1990). Effects of collateral peer supportive behaviors within the classwide peer tutoring program. *Journal of Applied Behavior Analysis, 23,* 307–322.

Kohler, F. W., Richardson, T., Mina, C., Dinwiddie, G., & Greenwood, C. R. (1985). Establishing cooperative peer relations in the classroom. *The Pointer, 29,* 12–16.

Madrid, D., Canas, M., & Watson, D. (1993). Spelling instruction for Hispanic bilingual children: A case for passive peer tutoring. Pueblo, CO: Department of Psychology, Southern Colorado State College.

Maheady, L., & Harper, G. (1987). A classwide peer tutoring program to improve the spelling performance of low-income, third-, and fourth-grade students. *Education and Treatment of Children, 10,* 120–133.

Maheady, L., Harper, G., Mallette, B., & Winstanley, N. (1991). Training and implementation requirements associated with the use of a classwide peer tutoring system. *Education and Treatment of Children, 14,* 177–198.

Maheady, L., Sacca, M. K., & Harper, G. F. (1988). Classwide peer tutoring program on the academic performance of mildly handicapped students. *Exceptional Children, 55,* 52–59.

Mathes, P. G., Fuchs, D., Fuchs, L. S., Henley, A. M., & Sanders, A. (1994). Increasing strategic reading practice with Peabody Classwide Peer Tutoring. *Learning Disabilities Research and Practice, 9,* 44–48.

Morris, E. K., & Midgley, B. D. (1990). Some historical and conceptual foundations of eco-behavioral analysis. In S. Schroeder (Ed.), *Ecobehavioral analysis and developmental disabilities: The twenty-first century* (pp. 1–32). New York: Springer-Verlag.

Niedermeyer, F. C. (1970). Effects of training on the instructional behaviors of student tutors. *Elementary School Journal, 64,* 119–123.

O'Brien, M., Porterfield, J., Herbert-Jackson, E., & Risley, T. R. (1979). *The toddler center: A practical guide to day care for one- and two-year-olds.* Baltimore, MD: University Park Press.

Sideridis, G. (1995). *The academic and social effects CWPT on students with LD and EMR in-*

cluded in the general education classroom for instruction. Unpublished doctoral dissertation, Department of Human Development and Family Life, University of Kansas, Lawrence.

Skinner, B. F. (1968). The technology of teaching. New York: Meredith.

Stanley, S. O., & Greenwood, C. R. (1981). Code for instructional structure and student academic response: CISSAR. Kansas City, KS: Juniper Gardens Children's Project, Bureau of Child Research, University of Kansas.

Stanley, S. O., & Greenwood, C. R. (1983). Assessing opportunity to respond in classroom environments: How much opportunity to respond does the minority, disadvantaged student receive in school? Exceptional Children, 49, 370–373.

Terry, B., & Arreaga-Mayer, C. (1993). ClassWide Responsive Teaching (CWRT): Manual for teachers. Kansas City, KS: Juniper Gardens Children's Project, University of Kansas.

Thurlow, M. L., Ysseldyke, J. E., Graden, J., & Algozzine, B. (1984). Opportunity to learn for LD students receiving different levels of special education services. Learning Disabilities Quarterly, 7, 55–67.

Walker, D., Greenwood, C. R., Hart, B., & Carta, J. (1994). Prediction of school outcomes based on early language production and socioeconomic factors. Child Development, 65, 606–621.

Walker, H. M., Hops, H., & Greenwood, C. R. (1981). RECESS: Research and development of a behavior management package for remediating social aggression in the school setting. In P. Strain (Ed.), The utilization of classroom peers as behavior change agents (pp. 261–303). New York: Plenum.

Ysseldyke, J. E., Christenson, S. L., Thurlow, M. L., & Bakewell, D. (1989). Are different kinds of instructional tasks used by different categories of students in different settings. School Psychology Review, 18, 98–111.

Ysseldyke, J. E., Thurlow, M. L., Christenson, S. L., & Weiss, J. (1987). Time allocated to instruction of mentally retarded, learning disabled, emotionally disturbed, and nonhandicapped elementary students. Journal of Special Education, 21, 43–55.

4

The View From a Montessori Classroom: A Response to Au & Carroll and Greenwood

Janis Erhardt Sayre
Arbor Montessori School
Decatur, Georgia

The previous two chapters raised important questions and offer new directions for the field of learning disabilities. Kathryn Au and Jacquelin Carroll's contribution directed us to look at the newer theoretical constructs (i.e. social constructivism) in education. Their work should focus those in the field of learning disabilities on questions related to how the needs of children with learning disabilities can be met in educational environments that are structured on the basis of these interpretations of learning. Charles Greenwood's work emphasized the application of a model called Classwide Peer Tutoring (CWPT) and the identification of the methods used by effective teachers within a framework in which there are multiple influences on learning.

Although differing, at the core there is much in the work of both researchers that is consonant. Both seem to define a successful learning environment as one in which the child's attention to and interaction with relevant learning tasks is maximized by educational designs that focus on stimulating, child-centered activities that build skill and literacy. Writing and reading workshops insert the learning of details into the practice of broader literary functions. Classwide Peer Tutoring focuses on the rehearsal of skills, and finds its success in the increase in academic responding that the model engenders. The constructivist-designed classrooms use the "natural" reinforcers of self-expression, peer communication, and authentic tasks. The classrooms using CWPT are designed such that there are social rewards to building skills, and these classrooms use the increased participation of the children and individual and group contingencies to achieve them. Both seem to acknowledge that learning is a social endeavor that best succeeds in classrooms where children help each other. The framework and goals are structured by the adult teacher, and it is everyone's responsibility and reward to teach. Although stemming from different theoretical bases, both approaches highlight valid parameters of real and broadly applicable learning.

I have acquired half of my teaching experience in classrooms where learning takes place in a milieu that, I believe, accords with Au and Carroll's description of social constructivism. In these Montessori classrooms there is ownership of literacy, and peer teaching is ongoing. Children and teachers set goals together. Learning tasks are sometimes initiated by the teacher and other times by the children, both individually and in various groups. With guidance, children are free to make many decisions about the use of their time. All materials are available for the children to select and use as they have been shown by a teacher or another student. Ownership by the child of all aspects of learning and interaction is a key organizing principle in these classrooms.

There are approximately 250 students in the private Montessori school where I have worked for the past 9 years. The children are grouped in multiage classrooms. Each primary classroom is for a group of children who range in age from 2½ to 6 years. Each lower elementary classroom has children between the ages of 6 and 9 whereas each upper elementary classroom is designed to meet the needs of a group of 9- to 12-year-olds. The majority of these children are more than well provided for by families that are primarily middle or upper middle class. In many of these families, one or both parents are working professionals. Culturally, the student body is fairly heterogeneous, although there are only a small number of African American students. In most cases, our students have been immersed in literacy of the highest quality since a very early age.

Despite the advantages they bring to their school experience, some of these children encounter difficulties learning. In some cases, they are diagnosed as learning disabled. In most cases, those who continue their enrollment through the elementary school years have mild disabilities. They are usually not children who would be described as dyslexic, nor are they children who have serious attention problems. In addition to the learning that generates from the classroom, the educational progress of the children with learning disabilities or difficulties may be supplemented by the services of a privately engaged tutor.

LEARNING AS DIALOGUE

From the basis of my experience both as a teacher of children with learning disabilities and as a Montessori teacher, I believe teaching that is flexible enough to adapt to a range of learners has as its fulcrum the concept of learning as a process of engaging in dialogue. This learning dialogue is most successful when the teacher and the student connect well emotionally and cognitively. In an instructional dialogue with an individual child, the interaction proceeds something like the following example. In the context of a mutual endeavor, the teacher informs, listens, watches, and asks questions (not always in this order). The child responds by listening, watching, asking questions, and taking mutually agreed-on actions. The teacher may then offer a strategy, a sequence, or a small challenge for the child to attempt, according to the skills and understanding brought to the task. If the teacher's judgment has been sound and what was offered as the next step for the child to take was appropriate, then the child's trial is successful. The child and the teacher are pleased and share the feelings this success has engendered. New or additional interest is fostered by this shared experience so that the child is interested in attempting the task again.

But what if the child's attempt was unsuccessful? The teacher's close observation of the nature of the child's difficulty usually provides some clue about what is now needed. Optimally this can be provided during the ongoing dialogue by altering the nature of the task a bit or by inserting a quick verbal or visual reminder. Then the teacher and the student can go at the task with this adjusted approach. Either of these would be a successful dialogue. Within this dialogue there is an exchange of strategies. The child shows or tells how he or she works, and the teacher responds by modeling a different approach, adding some refinement or redirection to the series of skills the child is already using.

SCAFFOLDS AND LADDERS

For me, the effective teaching scaffold is largely built by helping the child become aware of, and able to use, strategies that will generalize. However, children with learning disabilities usually need more follow-up on what is discovered in the teaching dialogue. The scaffold analogy (Au & Carroll, chap. 2, this volume; Stone & Reid, 1994) is powerfully descriptive of the natural process of teaching and learning. Yet, for children with learning disabilities, I think the scaffold or the way it is constructed must differ somewhat. If the metaphor is changed a bit and the scaffold is referred to instead as a ladder, the metaphor can be extended. Through the process of scaffolding, we may be able to take a child with learning disabilities to the point of carrying out more difficult tasks than he or she was able to accomplish at the outset. However, in our dialogue the scaffold (or ladder) at times may need to be built with more closely spaced rungs of simpler sentences. Perhaps more frequent and repeated responses from the child are necessary to show that a particular element of the process can be accomplished with understanding and consistency. Sometimes the larger process needs to be set aside for more work at a particular rung.

The work of teaching through a dialogue goes on in group settings by directing different questions to different students; by taking the children's questions and comments and adjusting what is done in response to them; and by actively supervising work among the children, stopping to work with individuals as needed. The children pursue at least some of their work at their own pace in many learning environments. For example, in open-ended work periods the children can choose to pursue different tasks individually, in pairs, or in small groups. In such learning environments, a teacher can follow up with more individualized dialogues with particular children.

THE WRITING WORKSHOP

The model known as a *writing workshop* discussed in Au and Carroll's chapter of this book has been a component of my teaching for the past 2 years. It suits the scope of abilities in our multi-age classroom and has been flexible enough to address some of the other learning differences among the students. I believe there is rich potential for application of this model to teaching that is inclusive of children with learning disabilities. Twice weekly, for approximately an hour at a time, the classroom operates much as any number of those described in the work of Lucy Calkins (1986).

In my opinion, a large part of the power of the writing workshop model emanates from the fact that the majority of the work the teacher and child engage in together happens at the point of intersection of oral and written language. As the child's manuscript is taken through each phase of development toward a final written product, writing as a communication of experience is emphasized. At meetings with individual children, the teacher hears the child's story and, through questioning, expressing genuine interest in the story, and engaging in dialogue, elicits an elaboration. Together, the child and the teacher come to an agreement about what will be added, changed, or rearranged to fulfill the child's communicative intent. As a product of this transaction, the written story is enhanced. This meeting is a time when the teacher can work individually with children who may have expressive language problems, helping them to find ways to tell their stories with different words or in a different sequence. It occurs while the other children write independently or meet with each other to accomplish these same sequences of goals.

BENEFITS FOR CHILDREN
WITH LEARNING PROBLEMS

The workshop is a potentially powerful tool for an inclusion classroom, in part because of the individualization inherent in the conference structure. Additionally, because the teaching dialogue occurs through the medium of a product the child has created, it is always initiated at a level appropriate for that child. When an individual child's learning differences are known, these differences can be specifically addressed at the conference between the teacher and the child. Even those children with decoding problems can read the stories they write if given the chance to do so soon after composing them. In this model, encoding difficulties are set aside to be dealt with at a later editing stage, so that the child with written language problems is not discouraged from developing a story by focusing too soon on the rules of the written language code. During a conference with a child who has memory problems, the teacher can jot down notes about the ideas that were mutually generated. The child uses these notes to aid the further development of his or her story. The writing workshop is also a powerful diagnostic tool. When work begins directly with the child's unassisted written product, testament is given to the written language skills the child has or has not incorporated. This information can be used to plan other appropriate teaching and learning interactions.

I support the learning environment designed according to a social-constructivist model, as described by Au and Carroll (chap. 2, this volume). I believe it to be both effective and worth further study as the potential foundation on which to design inclusion classrooms. It is my experience that internal motivation is created by the children's interest in the tasks they have had a part in developing. Self-esteem is enhanced when children are provided with the opportunity to make a contribution that is shared with their peers. Under these conditions the child puts more effort and attention to the task. In the writing workshop, children with oral or written language problems may produce fewer stories than the other children, take longer to get them on paper, and require a lot more work at the editing phase. Children with attention problems may spend inappropriately lengthy periods of time conferencing with anybody and everybody in the area of the classroom specified for that activity. They may take more time to finish a story or may produce many very short stories, and resist second drafts or embellishment. However, if children with these or other learning difficulties are provided with the support necessary for them to produce a story that the other children enjoy, they will write more stories and build language skills in the process.

In the writing workshop each story is read to the whole group, where its author hears what the other children like about it, what they are curious about, and what they would like to understand better. The interest in the child author that is thus demonstrated is exceptionally affirming, acknowledging the child's membership in the social group. These are benefits available to every child who participates. Because children with learning disabilities must put forth a greater effort for their work to come to the same or similar qualitative level as the work of others, these are particularly powerful and meaningful social motivators and rewards. These benefits, I believe, result from the affective rewards for learning built into a classroom that is social-constructivist in nature. Similar natural motivators can also be built into other aspects of a curriculum that is transactional.

UNANSWERED QUESTIONS

In my experience, the social-constructivist model of learning is entirely descriptive of the process of teaching all children. Yet the teaching demands are complex when there is a broad range of children in a class and when they need a broad range of types of scaffolds. The teacher is required to be both very skilled in quickly constructing the dialogue necessary for each child and capable of responding flexibly to the changes this individualization requires. The question that comes up for me is how are we to develop and support the teacher's acquisition and use of these skills? What class or school structure will facilitate the application of these skills? I have found that the multi-age classroom affords the teacher enough time to become acquainted with individuals. Over a 2- to 3-year span this knowledge can be used to explore different dialogues, try different teaching strategies, and communicate with care what a child's needs are to the family. Can multi-age classroom designs better accommodate, diagnose, remediate, and challenge the breadth of learning abilities that includes the learning disabled?

The general structure of the writing workshop, with mini-lessons at the outset of each, is flexible enough to accommodate the learning of children who have no language or learning disabilities. However, in my experience, children with written language problems will need more in the way of helping them acquire the mechanical skills that pertain to the editing dimension of writing. How is this need to be met in classrooms where children with learning disabilities are to learn among others whose learning needs may not be so specific? Perhaps incorporating a form of Classwide Peer Tutoring offers a way to provide the skills that children who are at-risk or learning disabled need.

PEER TEACHING

Peer teaching is a significant and powerful tool to be explored in the quest for successful learning environments for children with learning disabilities. It is an organizing principle and an ongoing activity in our classroom. When children are able to share their knowledge, expertise, and achievement with other children, their learning has an immediate social and personal usefulness that can raise their prestige in the community of the classroom. It has been my experience that when peer teaching is the right and responsibility of all the children, learning has the natural consequence of enabling the child teacher to take on a leadership role among the other children. It becomes the adult teacher's task in such a network of teachers and learners to find opportunities for all the children to experience these social rewards. When particular skills or knowledge are brought to a level at which the child is prepared to help others, it is the adult's task to steer the child to an application that has usefulness within the social context of the class or the school. One such application is to supervise, teach, or check another child's use of these same skills. Greenwood's work in this area substantiates my experience as to the effectiveness of peer teaching (although, in a multi-age classroom, peers are more broadly defined).

I have found keys to the success of peer teaching that are consistent with some of the contingencies Greenwood identified. In our classroom, individual partnerships and the tasks that partners are to accomplish together are varied, in recognition of the motivational benefits this derives. In my experience, the more specific guidance the children are given with regard to their joint task, the more successfully they achieve it. Can constructivist classrooms use CWPT to meet the needs that casting the broad net of inclusion requires? Greenwood's description of CWPT as an approach that can be used with either commercial or teacher-prepared materials clearly enhanced its potential in this regard. For both constructivist and CWPT models to contribute to improved environments for all children's achievement, work on identifying effective teacher practices needs to extend to an analysis of academic responding in the constructivist classroom. In my observation, these are environments wherein peer teaching thrives with somewhat less teacher orchestration. How does this affect academic responding? If, as Greenwood stated, CWPT can be used "across a range of subject matter and curricula designed from any number of conceptual frameworks" (this volume, p. 57), there would seem to be no real barrier to adopting CWPT within the context of constructivist classrooms.

Although at theoretical variance from behaviorism, Montessori learning environments (which are constructivist in nature) have used peer tutoring to create somewhat inclusive classrooms for a very long time. Yet, I have watched children who struggle to understand social cues or who have behavior difficulties or receptive language problems sometimes find the experience of learning complex tasks from a peer to be frustrating. When the child who takes on the role of the peer tutor has good communication skills and an ability to stay on task, understands and can execute a specified tutorial role and has personal qualities that allow him or her to be supportive to the tutee, then peer teaching can achieve certain goals in relation to the learning needs of children whose patterns, rates, strengths, and weaknesses in learning may vary from the norm. This personal observation is consistent with Greenwood's finding that "go faster" prompts, praise, and help were spontaneously offered by some peer tutors with good results. It is encouraging to see that Greenwood's findings support the responsiveness of children to learning effective peer teaching practices (a finding that is consonant with my experience). In addition to the objective, quantifiable increase in academic responding that peer teaching engenders, are there other benefits it offers and other ways it facilitates student progress? I believe that there is an increase in motivation, that sequential memory can be supported by the peer tutor's cues, and that the child with learning differences may feel less "on the spot" and, consequently, more willing to take risks when partnered with an effective peer. Questions, however, remain. What are the demands made on specific kinds of processing difficulties when one child attempts to teach another? Are there limits to the complexity of tasks that children can teach each other? What kinds of additional adult structuring may more complex tasks require for peer tutoring to be beneficial?

A TEACHING EXAMPLE:
TRANSMISSION TO TRANSACTION

In reading with the children I teach, I have observed qualitative improvements in both the children's work and their enjoyment and involvement as a function of engaging in dialogue with them. One component of our reading instruction is group novel reading. Approximately 8 to 10 children and an adult share this experience. Meanwhile, the rest of the class works in small, peer-composed groups at specified tasks related to the Montessori curriculum, under the supervision and assistance of the second adult in the class.

At first, in an effort to work on comprehension, our format might have been considered more consistent with the transmission model described by Au and Carroll. After we read a chapter together, the children were given comprehension questions for independent response. Even when these questions were specifically worded to elicit an opinion, the children usually thought there was a specific and correct answer to be found somewhere and that someone else knew it. There was little elaboration in any of the children's written responses. Gradually, this approach shifted to one more consistent with the transactional, constructivist model. As in the writing workshop, this modified approach keeps us working closer to the juncture of spoken and written language. Now the time we share reading together is also used to process what we've read. Reading is no longer segmented from its discussion or from the oral structuring and rehearsal of the work that will follow.

Before beginning a chapter, we discuss some of the vocabulary to be encountered. We do this to share our knowledge and contribute potentially relevant experiences. This exploration may involve using the children's current level of familiarity with morphological aspects of word structure as well as parts of speech. The goal is to broaden their understanding of how these words will be used in the text. All contributions are pooled and recorded for us all to use. We then read together, stopping along the way to react to different aspects of the story, to share our emotional responses and our understandings of phrases, expressions, and idioms. We talk about how a character's words reflect his or her feelings and motivations. With guidance, even the very youngest children integrate story elements and personal experience into these discussions, coming to conclusions about inferred relationships and responding with appropriate insight to ideas embedded in the text.

Following the reading we might share predictions, respond to each other's questions and observations, or fill in missing parts of the plot with our own creations. This is done together, in discussion, prior to the children's making independent responses in writing. In this approach the teacher is brought closer to all components of how the child processes what is read. By engaging in dialogue while reading together, an understanding of the story is constructed that incorporates the teacher's and the children's individual perspectives and understanding. In this way an authentic purpose of literature would seem to be fulfilled. We have connected meaningfully with each other through the medium of the text. When our communication over the reading is not distanced by time and by the artificiality of using only the questions preselected by another set of readers, it seems that our learning is fulfilling a natural, social function: the sharing of experience and understanding. The written responses that follow this kind of oral work together are more thorough and embellished than was the work the children previously produced when the less interactive model was used. It has also been more satisfying to the children. Analyzing our work from Greenwood's perspective, I presume that engaging in dialogue has created multiple, fast-paced opportunities for academic responding that ecobehavioral observation would assess as effective teaching.

IMPLICATIONS FOR CHILDREN
WITH LEARNING DISABILITIES

Children with many kinds of learning differences can have their needs specifically addressed within this format. Discussion can target questions that help assess and address a child's need for clarification. The teacher or the other children can explain complexities that might be potentially confusing for the child with a receptive language problem. Reading strategies can be modeled for those who have difficulty decoding. However, for a child with more extensive difficulties in either decoding or understanding, this kind of reading instruction may be appropriate only when there is a group of children whose needs are similar and when it is supplemented with separate and additional work to build necessary skills and generalizations. Greenwood's work highlights the need all children have for the opportunity to respond academically. Underpinning this must be specific awareness of the nature of the child's learning needs such that strengths are used, weaknesses are remediated, and teaching occurs at levels appropriate to the difficulties a child is encountering.

The integrated group reading process just described would not, I believe, provide all that children with dyslexia need by way of an effective learning scaffold. These children need the process of decoding itself to be scaffolded for them. According to a constructivist model, the teaching goal is to design tasks that are both authentic and purposeful and that also address these learning needs. For inclusion classrooms I believe such tasks should target the processing and skill content needs of children with, or at risk for, learning disabilities. Greenwood's work also directs the task designs to maximize academic responding. How might we provide learning environments that have the overall framework of a transactional model, but that also have an infrastructure of tasks or systems that can support children who have a variety of learning differences? For me, the major question remains of how the instructional practices Au and Carroll describe can be applied in classrooms so that children with learning disabilities progress.

The ecobehavioral tools described by Greenwood seem particularly suited to assessing the way a child with learning disabilities functions in a transactional learning environment. Ecobehavioral instruments could help us identify which teacher practices most increase engagement, participation, ownership, and success in constructivist learning environments. A most important use of any instrument or process in evaluating the effectiveness of classroom practices should be to continually assess the outcome of the inclusion of children with learning disabilities in particular programs. Greenwood's report of the progress children with learning disabilities made in classrooms using CWPT suggested the appropriateness of including carefully structured peer tutoring programs in inclusion classrooms. Observational tools help us understand what conditions exist in classrooms where a teacher is able to successfully modify practices such that children with learning disabilities progress. Are there factors such as class size or organizational frameworks that support the teaching flexibility that diversity requires? Further questions include: How successful is the inclusion of children with particular kinds of learning disabilities in particular kinds of classrooms? What additional supportive services increase learning? How successful is this inclusion when additional support services are not offered? What models bringing support services into the classroom are most effective?

All day, every day, I observe different students having different experiences in different segments of the overall opportunities in one classroom. At times, for some individuals, academic responding seems maximal. At other times I see children watching and waiting. Are these differences natural, beneficial, and to be sustained? Does the dynamic nature of a transactional classroom magnify or minimize this? If children with learning disabilities are to be included all day, every day, in learning environments that fully use the transactional model, we will need careful and accurate assessments of what such children experience, accomplish, and learn in these environments. The incremental progress that occurs in the teaching dialogue can be very difficult to see and to trust. For this model of a teaching/learning environment to be used in more classrooms inclusive of children with diverse learning needs, it will be important to continue and evaluate work in the area of performance assessment.

As a teacher attempting on a daily basis to implement and coordinate the multiple demands of a transactional classroom that includes children with a variety of learning needs, I believe teachers feel particular need for assistance in the area of realistic, objective assessment that is not overwhelmingly time consuming. Such assessment must preserve the teacher's ability to be flexible and responsive to individual children's needs. Designing authentic, intrinsically motivating learning tasks that can be assessed through performance is a high, although hopefully achievable, goal. Portfolios and grade-level benchmarks seem to be promising assessment avenues, as are the ecobehavioral observations systems and implementation aides described by Greenwood. If ecobehavioral methods become easy to use in both small and large schools and systems, such that their use is reasonably affordable and consistent with a broad array of curricula, they can help us design learning environments that have the inherent benefits of the transactional model, while being maximally beneficial to the broadest possible spectrum of children.

REFERENCES

Calkins, L. M. (1986). *The art of teaching writing*. Portsmouth, NH: Heinemann.
Stone, C. A., & Reid, D. K. (1994). Social and individual forces in learning: Implications for instruction of children with learning difficulties. *Learning Disability Quarterly, 17*, 72–86.

5

Models of Classroom Instruction: Implications for Students With Learning Disabilities

Lynn S. Fuchs
Peabody College of Vanderbilt University

The chapters by Kathryn Au and Jacquelin Carroll and by Charles Greenwood characterize two theoretical and operational perspectives on the form and function of classroom instruction. These models, although distinct, are both clearly articulated and highly developed, and versions of both models are employed widely throughout the country today. Consequently, the implications of these models are broadly generalizable to the current educational climate. I begin my discussion of these chapters by summarizing the broad differences and similarities across these views on classroom instruction. I then focus my discussion on the evidence these authors have presented on the effectiveness of the two models for the variety of learners we can expect to find in general education classrooms today—including students with learning disabilities (LD). I argue for the need to consider differential effects deliberately and, in support of that argument, I briefly describe a study illustrating how classroom instruction may in fact affect different types of learners differently. I conclude by offering one important direction for future research activities.

DISTINCTIONS BETWEEN AND SIMILARITIES ACROSS THE MODELS

Au and Carroll and Greenwood have relied on different theoretical perspectives to construct contrasting visions of what classroom instruction should look like. Au and Carroll relied on an increasingly popular, social-constructivist,

81

transaction model. Within such a perspective, teachers and students exchange ideas to generate new knowledge; teachers and students share the role of learner; and the focus is on the social, intersubjective nature of knowledge.

Such a perspective leads to a vision of classroom instruction where goals are stated in terms of holistic, global outcomes that emphasize student ownership and enjoyment of learning, as well as high levels of achievement for all learners. The starting point for accomplishing these goals is motivation, where teachers arrange learning activities so that they foster high levels of interest in "authentic" activities. Instruction is designed on the basis of collaborative decisions between teachers and students, where the teacher is a member of the learning community who is sometimes called on to conduct "mini" lessons. Additionally, performance assessment creates portfolios to track students' learning accomplishments, with regular teacher/student conferences, lots of feedback to students, and teacher use of the information for planning subsequent activities. Within such a vision, key dimensions posited to influence student learning are students' active responsibility for learning; reliance on learning activities that are intrinsically motivating to children and that are anchored to authentic situations to which students bring strong background knowledge; and a strong social context for learning, where the classroom resembles a workshop.

In sharp contrast to this social constructivist perspective, Greenwood approached classroom instruction from a behavioral, interactional framework that views classroom instruction as a dynamic, reciprocal, interdependent process: Changes in alterable classroom features influence student learning, and student behavior just as surely influences instruction. Greenwood relied on three major constructs to conceptualize this process: teacher behavior, the classroom ecology, and student behavior. Clearly, however, student engagement is the key variable. Classroom instruction controls student engagement (which is an indicator of effective instruction), but it is student engagement itself that accounts for student learning.

Using such a framework, Greenwood structured the learning environment to increase student engagement with Classwide Peer Tutoring. Classwide Peer Tutoring requires students to work in pairs in highly structured activities that ensure high levels of academic responding on activities of appropriate difficulty. In addition, Greenwood relied heavily on ecobehavioral assessment to provide high-quality feedback to teachers about the effectiveness of the learning process for individual students, and on curriculum-based measures of student learning to evaluate individual growth.

Interestingly enough, despite these major distinctions, the two models do share some important features. First, each model has been derived from an unusually long-standing and impressive research and development program, conducted in naturally constituted classrooms, with teachers actually mediating treatments. Second and relatedly, both models emphasize the importance of observational feedback to teachers (a) to help teachers formatively evaluate the effectiveness of their classroom instruction in terms of student learning, and (b) to help practitioners, within and across schools, develop a common language and set of assumptions for working collaboratively to create a unified vision and to enhance the learning environment. Third, both models explicitly recognize the importance of peer-to-peer interactions for achieving learning goals.

EVIDENCE OF EFFECTIVENESS AND ESTIMATED BENEFITS FOR STUDENTS WITH LD

Both sets of authors provided impressive evidence for the effectiveness of their models, and demonstrated that we can expect most children to profit from both forms of restructured general education learning environments. For our purposes, however, it is important to scrutinize the effects more specifically for students with LD. After all, within conventional general education classrooms, these children previously have failed to achieve important literacy and numeracy goals, with 6 of 10 students with LD having been retained in at least one grade prior to their placement in special education (Vaughn & Lyon, 1994).

Au and Carroll's implicit argument was for the relevance and efficacy of a social constructivist model of classroom instruction for all children. No mention of differential efficacy was included, and there was no explicit discussion of how the KEEP instructional model addresses the serious problems presented by students with LD, such as the phonological processing difficulties that impede word learning and word recognition (e.g., Ball, 1993; Blachman, 1989; Bruck, 1992). Although reading instruction within KEEP classrooms, for example, does incorporate word recognition strategies and spelling as an explicit goal of literacy instruction, the instructional method relies on contextual cuing and a problem-solving approach. Such a strategy may be effective for assisting the typically developing child to decipher the occasionally unknown word. Two problems, however, may restrict the utility of such an approach for students with LD. First, a contextual cuing and problem-solving approach to identifying unknown words is at odds with the strongly automatic processes on which fluent readers routinely rely (e.g., Humphreys, 1985; Stanovich, 1990). Moreover, as revealed in the empirical literature on reading disability (e.g., Cunningham, 1990; Liberman & Liberman, 1990; Mather, 1992), a more explicit approach to decoding instruction typically is required for the development of literacy in this group of learners.

In a similar way, Greenwood argued that student engagement is the mediator of learning across student types. Greenwood did, however, take a different approach in his discussion of efficacy. First, he clearly acknowledged the importance of the individual student's learning history in determining engagement. He argued that although a classroom structure, such as Classwide Peer Tutoring, may create high levels of engagement for the group, individual students may still respond idiosyncratically. He further emphasized the related need to conduct ecobehavioral assessments at the individual student level and to plan and alter instruction at the individual level to increase the probability of high levels of engagement for all children. In addition, he addressed the efficacy of Classwide Peer Tutoring specifically for students with LD.

For example, Greenwood documented that Classwide Peer Tutoring's recurring opportunity for students to engage in meaningful fluency and comprehension practice activities has been shown to enhance the reading achievement of students of low socioeconomic status, who clearly are at risk for poor learning outcomes, and for at least some segments of the school population with LD. Such an outcome is impressive and important: It provides a strategy for addressing the needs of important segments of the school population— needs that frequently remain unmet within conventional classrooms.

Nevertheless, it also seems important to question whether the practice activities incorporated within Classwide Peer Tutoring will be adequate for the group of students with LD who have severely limited strategies for word decoding. After all, as documented in the reading disability literature, to achieve literacy, students with severe reading problems can be expected to require structured phonics instruction delivered by skilled instructional clinicians (e.g., Hatcher, Hulme, & Ellis, 1994; Liberman & Liberman, 1990; Mather, 1992; Stanovich, 1994).

Given the diversity of learners we can expect to find in general education classrooms today (Hodgkinson, 1992; Jenkins, Jewell, Leceister, Jenkins, & Troutner, 1990), it may be necessary for developers of classroom instructional models to scrutinize effects by learner types within the context of single studies. With such designs, the field may be able to identify strategies for extending the instructional procedures that address the greatest range of learners, while specifying precisely for whom the model can be expected to produce acceptable growth. As illustrated in the school-based experiment described next, we have begun to incorporate such designs within our research program.

ASKING QUESTIONS ABOUT DIFFERENTIAL EFFICACY FOR DIFFERENT TYPES OF LEARNERS

During the 1993–94 school year, Fuchs, Fuchs, Hamlett et al. (in press) combined the use of classwide curriculum-based measurement and peer-assisted learning strategies to provide general educators with (a) an assessment-rich environment for planning instruction and (b) a restructured instructional routine with which they could feasibly differentiate instruction on the basis of the assessment. Earlier research (Fuchs, Fuchs, Phillips, Hamlett, & Karns, in press) had demonstrated impressive overall effects within heterogeneous general education classrooms during mathematics instruction. Nevertheless, given persistent and well-documented problems in encouraging students to work constructively together (e.g., Cooper & Cooper, 1984; Fuchs, Fuchs, Bentz, Phillips, & Hamlett, 1994; Michaels & Bruce, 1991; O'Connor & Jenkins, 1994), we experimented with methods for enhancing students' instructional interactions during the peer-assisted learning sessions, and we explored effects for four types of learners.

One group of 10 classrooms was taught during peer-assisted learning sessions to seek and provide elaborated help (where explanations lead children to apply and practice methods for solving problems themselves, rather than telling each other answers or saying that answers are wrong; see Webb & Farivar, 1994). A second group of 10 classrooms was taught these elaborated helping methods as well as five specific strategies for providing conceptual mathematical explanations. Another 20 classrooms served as a contrast group, which used the same mathematics basal program to structure teacher-directed instruction lessons. Treatments lasted 18 school weeks.

Within each classroom, we sampled outcomes for students with LD, other nondisabled but low-achieving students, average-achieving students, and high-achieving students. On the basis of videotaped interactions during peer-assisted learning sessions, we found that students in the conceptual explanations treatment did in fact provide more constructive help to their partners and incorporated more conceptual explanations. In addition, across types of learners, students in the conceptual explanations treatment achieved more than did the elaborated help treatment, which in turn achieved more than the contrast group.

Despite these overall positive outcomes, exploratory follow-up tests suggested that the conceptual explanations treatment may have been more effective for nondisabled low-achieving and for high-achieving students than for LD students or for average-achieving students. We speculated that the conceptual explanations treatment may have operated with differential efficacy due to the decision rules incorporated into the computer-managed assessment program that formulated dyads for peer-mediated instruction. These rules paired the highest-achieving student with the lowest-achieving student, then paired the next highest- with the next lowest-achieving student, and so on. This formula created challenging opportunities for high-achieving students to construct rich explanations for their low-achieving partners. These decision rules, however, tended to pair average achievers together, and such dyads may have offered fewer opportunities for students to elaborate on their own understanding in a manner that facilitated new learning and retention of previously learned material. This pairing strategy may account for the larger effects of the conceptual treatment for high achievers who formulated explanations (effect size of .63) and for low achievers who received those explanations (1.14), than for average achievers who had fewer opportunities to formulate or receive explanations (.45).

This line of reasoning does not, however, explain the smaller effect size associated with the LD students: Although LD and low-achieving students had similar opportunities to benefit from the explanations created by their high-achieving peers, the effect size of low-achieving students (1.15) was considerably larger than for LD students (.26). The reason for this relative lack of responsiveness is open to question. It may, however, reside with the nature of the learning problems this population experiences: A large body of literature clearly documents important differences between LD and low-achieving populations on multiple dimensions (e.g., Cleaver, Bear, & Juvonen, 1992; Tur-Kaspa & Bryan, 1994). The more serious nature of the learning problems of LD students may require explanations formulated by professional adult clinicians, even though we corroborated Greenwood's findings that these children do profit (effect size of .26) from those provided by peers.

As illustrated in this study, the efficacy of classroom innovations may be mediated by the seriousness of students' learning problems. This finding, in combination with the increasing diversification of the student population within general education (Hodgkinson, 1992), highlights the need for researchers to examine effects separately by learner type. By investigating differential effects within the context of a single study, we were able to identify methods for revising our instructional procedures with the hope of addressing the needs of a greater range of learners. We were also able to begin to specify potential limits on efficacy for certain types of learners.

With respect to the efficacy research presented by Au and Carroll and by Greenwood, it seems fair to ask similarly hard questions about exactly how well students with LD actually fare in these restructured general education classrooms. By investigating differential effects, these and other developers of innovative classroom structures may extend their methods to address the serious learning problems experienced by students with LD. In addition, the field may gain important insights into the learning characteristics of students who are likely to profit from restructured general education classrooms, and identify those children who are likely to require more intensive services.

ACKNOWLEDGMENTS

Some research discussed in this chapter was funded by Grant #H180E20004 from the U.S. Department of Education, Office of Special Education Programs to Vanderbilt University. Statements do not, however, represent official positions or policies of the agencies.

REFERENCES

Ball, E. (1993). Phonological awareness: What's important and to whom? *Reading and Writing: An Interdisciplinary Journal, 5*, 141–159.

Blachman, B. A. (1989). Phonological awareness and word recognition: Assessment and intervention. In A. G. Kamhi & H. W. Catts (Eds.), *Reading disabilities* (pp. 133–158). Boston: College-Hill Press.

Bruck, M. (1992). Persistence of dyslexics' phonological awareness deficits. *Developmental Psychology, 28*, 874–886.

Cleaver, A., Bear, G., & Juvonen, J. (1992). Discrepancies between competence and importance in self-perceptions of children in integrated classrooms. *The Journal of Special Education, 26*, 125–138.

Cooper, C. R., & Cooper, R. G. (1984). Skill in peer learning discourse. In S. A. Kuczaf (Ed.), *Discourse development* (pp. 89–102). New York: Springer-Verlag.

Cunningham, A. E. (1990). Explicit versus implicit instruction in phonemic awareness. *Journal of Experimental Child Psychology, 50*, 429–444.

Fuchs, L. S., Fuchs, D., Bentz, J., Phillips, N. B., & Hamlett, C. L. (1994). The nature of student interactions during peer tutoring with and without prior training and experience. *American Educational Research Journal, 31*, 75–103.

Fuchs, L. S., Fuchs, D., Hamlett, C. L., Phillips, N. B., Karns, K., & Dutka, S. (in press). Increasing students' use of conceptual mathematical explanations during peer-mediated instruction. *Elementary School Journal.*

Fuchs, L. S., Fuchs, D., Phillips, N., Hamlett, C. L., & Karns, K. (in press). Acquisition and transfer effects of classwide peer-assisted learning strategies on students with varying learning histories. *School Psychology Review.*

Hatcher, P., Hulme, C., & Ellis, A. W. (1994). Ameliorating early reading failure by integrating the teaching of reading and phonological skills: The phonological linkage hypothesis. *Child Development, 65*, 41–57.

Hodgkinson, H. L. (1992). *A demographic look at tomorrow.* Washington, DC: Center for Demographic Policy, Institute for Educational Leadership.

Humphreys, G. W. (1985). Attention, automaticity, and autonomy in visual word processing. In D. Besner, T. Waller, & G. MacKinnon (Eds.), *Reading research: Advances in theory and practice* (Vol. 5, pp. 253–309). New York: Academic Press.

Jenkins, J. R., Jewell, M., Leceister, N., Jenkins, L., & Troutner, N. (1990, April). *Development of a school building model for educating handicapped and at risk students in general education classrooms.* Paper presented at the annual meeting of the American Educational Research Association, Boston.

Liberman, I. Y., & Liberman, A. M. (1990). Whole language vs. code emphasis: Underlying assumptions and their implications for reading instruction. *Annals of Dyslexia, 40*, 51–77.

Mather, N. (1992). Whole language reading instruction for students with learning disabilities: Caught in the cross fire. *Learning Disabilities Research and Practice, 7*, 87–95.

Michaels, S., & Bruce, C. (1991). *Discourses on the seasons* (Technical Report). Champaign: University of Illinois, Reading Research and Education Center.

O'Connor, R. E., & Jenkins, J. R. (1994). *Cooperative learning as an inclusion strategy: The experience of special education students.* Manuscript submitted for publication.

Stanovich, K. E. (1990). Concepts in developmental theories of reading skill: Cognitive resources, automaticity, and modularity. *Developmental Review, 10*, 72–100.

Stanovich, K. E. (1994). Constructivism in reading education. *The Journal of Special Education, 28*, 259–274.

Tur-Kaspa, H., & Bryan, T. (1994). Social information-processing skills of students with learning disabilities. *Learning Disabilities Research and Practice, 9*, 12–23.

Vaughn, S., & Lyon, R. (1994). *Inclusion: Can it work for students with learning disabilities.* Manuscript submitted for publication.

Webb, N. M., & Farivar, S. (1994). Promoting helping behavior in cooperative small groups in middle school mathematics. *American Educational Research Journal, 31,* 369–395.

PART II

Classroom Interaction

6

Inclusion Into What?: Thoughts on the Construction of Learning, Identity, and Affiliation in the General Education Classroom

Frederick Erickson
University of Pennsylvania

The aim of this chapter is to provide an overview of the social and cognitive organization of classroom life and, more specifically, of academic learning tasks. Its focus is on the general education classroom in the elementary school. The chapter considers how engagement of teachers and students in everyday routines and tasks constructs differing students as more or less "with it" or "out of it." My assumption is that *with it* and *out of it* are social constructions, not simply individual traits of students. The question I want to address is, "What's the *it* in relation to which a given student is constructed as *out* or *with?*" That question is the central focus of the chapter.

There are two current movements in educational policy and reform that raise basic questions about the nature of classrooms as learning environments. One is the movement toward inclusion of special education students in the general education classroom. The other is the movement toward raising the standards of what is to be learned in the classroom. These standards press for curriculum and pedagogy that will foster reasoning and higher-order thinking rather than the teaching and learning of low-order skills and facts.

Both movements place tremendous pressure on general education classrooms to change in fundamental ways. But such change is difficult. It reminds us of the joke about how many psychiatrists it takes to change a light bulb: Only one, but it takes a long time and the light bulb really has to want to change. Special educators and general educators are in for a long haul. Not only are they being asked to develop new relationships with one another as colleagues but to do so within a classroom environment that, one way or another, is likely to be changing in response to the standards movement.

I begin the chapter by reviewing some thoughts on the nature of learning, and then consider the nature of the school classroom as a social form, emphasizing surveillance, sorting, and the nature of everyday classroom participation structures as learning environments. Then I consider the classroom as a site for the production of student social identities in relation to learning. I discuss student affiliation and disaffiliation with classroom life, with the teacher, and with learning, treating issues of inclusion and student identity within the classroom social and cultural ecosystem.

THOUGHTS ON LEARNING
AS POLITICAL ASSENT

Learning has many definitions. Here I want to consider learning as a matter of politics; of assent that can be withheld, not necessarily with conscious awareness or intent. The notion of learning as a political act of assent directs our attention to the social conditions in which such assent is granted or withheld.

Think of what is one of the most basic aspects of human learning—acquiring the capacity to speak a language fluently. Virtually everyone except those who are severely impaired physically or neurologically learns to speak a mother tongue. Yet which language (and dialect or register) in which we develop fluency varies nonrandomly across the demographic map. In south Texas, for example, there are many native speakers of Spanish as well as native speakers of English. Yet a far smaller proportion of Anglos become reasonably fluent in Spanish than the proportion of Latinos who develop fluency in English. This has to do with the politics of language learning situations and with the politics of assent.

I think as well of the apparent difficulty of teaching a middle-class English oral register to working class students in school. Year after year teachers enjoin students not to say "ain't" or "he be goin'." Yet working-class adolescents who discover themselves to be gay learn a middle-class gay register very quickly. Is this likely to be a matter of neurology or of politics?

Schools are places for the acquisition of written literacy. In the United States some children learn to read with little difficulty and others with great difficulty. To what extent is this a matter of differential "readiness" or "dyslexia" and to what extent is it a matter of the politics of learning situations? We know from ethnography and cross-cultural psychology that there are places where almost everyone succeeds in nonschool literacies. Scribner and Cole's work (1981) on the Vai of Liberia is one example. Conklin's research on the Hanunoo in the Philippines provides another example (Conklin, 1959). Teenage boys learn a syllabary script and a special vocabulary analogous to our "pig Latin," by which the normal order of syllables is transformed in various ways. This special language is used for courtship songs. The script is carved on sticks of bamboo as a memory aid. By dressing in special ways, playing musical instruments whose use is restricted to courtship, and by singing the courtship songs the young men attract young women to small elevated sleeping houses for assignations.

I am told by my colleague Ray McDermott that the Hanunoo love song illiteracy rate is close to zero. Pre-adolescent boys and girls learn the songs, adolescents use them in courtship, and older people continue to sing them. Apparently there is no dyslexia in that literacy system. My point here is that under conditions of high motivation most youth will assent to learn. The circumstances of politics of learning in general education classrooms in schools, however, appear to be ones in which significant proportions of students withhold that assent.

THOUGHTS ON THE NATURE OF
CLASSROOMS AS A SOCIAL FORM

The Ubiquity of Surveillance

As Jackson (1968) and others observed, classrooms are both crowded (20+ juveniles to one senior) and students are members of a crowd. As such, their behavior is constantly available for surveillance. And as Foucault showed in his monograph *Discipline and Punish* (1979), the exercise of attention by the dominant senior member (and by fellow students as members of the crowd) is a medium for the exercise of power. All student behavior is potentially available to be *audienced*—by the teachers and by other students.

The traditional school classroom's physical arrangement, with students in rows facing front and with the teacher on a raised platform at the front of the room, enables surveillance of students by the teacher. Foucault observed that this kind of classroom arrangement developed in the same time period— roughly 1820–1840—as did prisons whose architecture enabled surveillance of all inmates from a central observation tower.

It should be noted that attention by the teacher to students isn't simply negative. Many students in the United States seek such attention—although this is not universally the case cross-culturally, either within the United States or internationally. That some students seek the teacher's attention may be due in part to the workings of hegemony, but I think it is more complicated than that. There can and should be genuine connections of mutual concern that arise between teachers and their students (see Noddings, 1992). In order for the teacher's attention to be regarded as positive by students, however, a basic kind of bonding between the student and the teacher needs to have been established. This is a matter of what we can call the *social construction of affiliation.* It is considered in a later section of the chapter.

Surveillance by a teacher is close or more distant, not only in a spatial sense (this is technically called *proxemics,* the study of interpersonal space in social interaction) but in a temporal sense as well. Through temporally proximal surveillance, as the "spotlight" of teacher attention moves around the room, the teacher observes and in so doing exercises control over student compliance. Proximal surveillance globally monitors the social and academic performance of students in the immediate moments of classroom life. By temporally distal surveillance, through testing at the end of an instructional unit or in standardized testing at the end of a school year, the teacher observes evidence of learning.

A basic problem in the general education classroom is that distal surveillance of student learning (as formal assessment) produces evidence of learning that comes too late to inform ongoing instruction. Surveillance of student compliance, although temporally proximal and thus available to inform midcourse corrections in instruction, doesn't provide direct evidence of student learning. Thus, it doesn't inform instruction in a fundamental way. Indeed, because immediately visible and audible evidence of student compliance is used as a proxy for evidence of student learning, this can be very misleading for a teacher. It substitutes a focus on what Dewey called the student's *outer attention*—the appearance of engagement in learning—for what he called *inner attention*—the genuine, interior quality of student interest and engagement that is not directly observable (Dewey, 1904).

Surveillance of compliance thus substitutes for temporally proximal attention to evidence of student learning. Students and teachers get confused by their mutual relations of "faking it." The experienced teacher learns to seem to monitor learning, and the experienced student who wants to appear as if he or she is learning develops behavioral displays as a way of appearing to learn. But all too often this is pretense and shadow boxing. One of the challenges for the reconstruction of classroom learning environments is for teachers to develop usable and valid ways of assessing student learning as it is happening, in temporally proximal time frames. This is noted in the discussion by Au and Carroll (chap. 2, this volume). Also relevant is Greenwood's (chap. 3, this volume) discussion of curriculum-based measures.

Ranking and Sorting Students

Social and academic sorting and ranking of students, a social gatekeeping responsibility of the teacher, is accomplished by spatially and temporally proximal and distal surveillance. Students are ranked according to their relative positions in mastery of subject matter and of deportment.

There is a cultural assumption in U.S. schools of a sequential "ladder of skills" from simple to complex—the usual assumption is that one proceeds from mastery of lower-order skills to higher-order ones (see Erickson, 1987a). This normatively elitist frame underlies both curriculum and assessment, constructing students as rank ordered within the crowd.

There is also a notion of a "ladder of deportment" that appears to operate in classrooms. Teachers distinguish between those students who are highly trustable and those less trustable, between those who try and those who do not. These ratings are often intercorrelated with the level of overall kinesic activity (i.e., body motion); those students who are more kinesically active and those who are not. The classroom system privileges certain kinds of language use (oral and written). The system also privileges those students who keep their kinesic activity within certain bounds. A good student is one who learns to use his or her mouth in certain ways and yet to sit still or stand quietly in line. The normative frame of a *ladder of deportment* underlies the assessment of students as motivationally worthy and it interacts with the assessment of their rank on the *ladder of skills*.

Depending on how rigidly and literally a teacher holds to the framing of the ladders of skill and deportment, some students appear to the teacher as "slower," or "behind," or "lower" than others academically, and some look "hyper" or "squirrely" in their deportment. When the frames are held rigidly, these assessments are seen by teachers as unproblematic—the kid who wiggles in his seat really *is* hyperactive. Hyperactivity is thus not considered to be a judgment, located as it were in the eye of the teacher as beholder, but is seen as a trait that actually exists within the student.

There is considerable variability among teachers in how rigidly they hold the frames and in how narrowly or widely they set the tolerances—the threshold levels—for what is neither too much nor too little activity. Consider, for example, the threshold level held by a teacher that defines how much kinesic activity it takes for a student to be judged "hyper." What is "too much"—what is "hyper" or "squirrely"—is defined differently by different teachers, perhaps for cultural reasons or for reasons of the individual teacher's temperament. Currently we know little systematically about how or why these threshold levels vary among teachers.

Students rank one another on ladders of skills and deportment just as teachers do. "What page are you on?" (in a math or reading skills workbook) is a question that appears ubiquitously in those early grades classrooms in which the ladder of skills assumption drives curriculum and instruction.

The formal and the informal pecking orders in the classroom (the former defined by the teacher and the latter by the students) are dimensions that interact to form the local classroom "underlife," in Goffman's terms (Goffman, 1961). This is a local ecology that is distinctive from room to room. The particular combinations of dimensions of differentiation and the locations in social space (statuses and roles) that are generated by the multiple dimensions considered together are unique to each local classroom. Although there may be general similarities in construction of statuses across classrooms (e.g., the class clown, the bottom reading group, the math whiz, those students who get *asked* to take the attendance roll slip to the school office for the teacher), the locality of the production of student status, role, and rank makes the lived experience of each classroom unique in subtle ways. This is true from one room to the next in a given grade level and from year to year across a given teacher's career.

Thus, in different classrooms students are differentially constructed as deviant or nondeviant, according to local standards of teacher and student judgment that are largely implicit. I assume that no amount of attempting to make such standards universal and explicit across classrooms can by itself have much influence on the local production and use of standards within each classroom as a local sociocultural entity unless the teacher comes to fundamentally change his or her pedagogical commitments. Such commitments can be thought of as aspects of an implicit philosophy of practice that is embedded in that practice. Two teachers, for example, may have very different implicit assumptions of what "classroom order," "trying hard," or "writing clearly" look like as behavioral displays. Those differing assumptions may be related to differences between the teachers in their conceptions of classroom discipline and the nature of the teacher's authority, of effort attributions and expectations, and of the nature of written discourse and of standards for and purposes of writing. Often many aspects or facets of these assumptions, what we can call pedagogical commitments, which taken together can be thought of as a teacher's overall philosophy of education, are not held in reflective awareness by teachers, especially as they are immersed in the midst of their daily practice. They are implicit aspects of the teachers' pedagogical knowledge in use.

A Model for the Organization of Classroom Tasks as Learning Environments

Let us turn now to consider everyday classroom participation structures. Overall academic task structures (ATS) can be thought of as consisting of both a social participation structure (SPTS) and a subject matter task structure (SMTS). The social participation structure influences the ways in which students and the teacher relate in such functional ways as seeking help, giving help, taking turns at talk in a classroom conversation, doing work individually, doing work collectively, joking, and taking a break. The subject matter task structure involves such matters as logical relationships of sequence in completing the task, levels of difficulty at various points along the way, closed-ended ("right answer") or open-ended framing of the knowledge, and skill that is to be encountered in the task.

Often within a subject area (e.g., math, reading) certain SPTS arrangements predominate (e.g., usually if students "go to the board" they do so in math rather than in reading). It is curious that in many classrooms a fairly narrow range of variation in SPTS occurs, and that within subject matters an even narrower range of SPTS's occurs. For example, in elementary grades reading instruction teachers often employ a small group format, the "reading group," in which students read together and discuss a written text. Very often the social participation structure for the reading group is what is called "round-robin reading," that is, individual students successively read aloud a page or paragraph from a textbook they all have opened in front of them, as the teacher either corrects their errors in oral reading or models correct reading by reading aloud him- or herself. At issue in the subject matter task structure is the fluency and coherence with which the various students make sense of the written text, and the provision of feedback and assistance by the teacher. Round-robin reading is a very frequent interactional means for accomplishing those pedagogical ends. Yet other interactional means could be employed; for example, repeated choral reading of a passage by all group members and the teacher together, or silent reading by the children followed by discussion of the passage with the teacher with reading aloud by individual children occurring only very infrequently or not at all. Au and Mason (1983) reported a change in social participation structure in reading group discussion that appears to have had a profound influence on motivation and understanding by native Hawaiian students in the Kamehameha school. Instead of the round-robin arrangement of turn-taking, students were asked to read a passage silently and then discuss it with the teacher in conversations in which more than one student spoke at the same time. This resembled the turn-taking organization of informal conversation in the children's homes in a native Hawaiian speech event called "talk story." The children's participation and reading achievement were clearly superior when the talk story turn-taking structure was used, and clearly inferior when the reading passage was discussed in a conversational arrangement in which only one child could talk at a time. The academic content (SMTS) was the same—what differed was the social participation structure (SPTS). The round-robin conversational format was apparently much more uncomfortable and confusing for the children than was the talk story format.

In my own research (Erickson & Mohatt, 1982) I found that a Native American teacher whom I videotaped in a village school in northern Ontario consistently avoided round-robinlike reading discussion. She taught reading either by having whole class discussions in which she allowed choral answers to her content questions, or by walking around her room among the students' desks in a figure-8 pattern and waiting for individual students (who were reading silently at their seats) to summon her with a glance or some other subtle nonverbal sign. She would then lean over the child's desk, engage in quiet conversation with the individual child, and by that means evaluate the child's performance and provide feedback and support. In so doing she was finding an alternative SPTS means to a standard SPTS end. Unfortunately, most teachers do not arrange the interactional engagement of academic tasks so that there are alternative interactional roads to Rome, as did the teachers in Hawaii and in northern Ontario, Canada, who were teaching differing minority populations in differing cultural ways, each of which was culturally appropriate for the students who were being taught. Teachers can accommodate other sources of diversity in classrooms besides cultural differences (e.g., differences in temperament between students, and particular learning handicaps or strengths) by alternating the social participation arrangements by which academic tasks are to be accomplished.

SPTS and SMTS always covary in the enactment of academic task engagement. As change occurs on either dimension the nature of the classroom learning task changes and the possibilities for being "with it" or "out of it" change—because the ecological "it" of the conduct of interaction as a learning environment has changed. This can be illustrated by a common example from a conventional early grades classroom (see Figure 6.1).

Classroom tasks as experienced in real time are always sequential and are usually recursive as well. Think of the moment-by-moment enactment of the simple arithmetic worksheet shown in Fig. 6.1. Students usually begin by writing their names in the upper righthand corner. Then they turn to the top numeral in the leftmost problem in the first row of problems. In order to complete this problem, they must have a conception of twoness, understand addition and its operation sign, and have a conception of threeness. Moving sequentially from 2 to + to 3 and then summing, the students arrive at the answer of 5. Then they turn to the top numeral in the problem that is located immediately to the right of the first problem. After completing that problem, they turn to the next rightmost problem. They consider the 3, the operation sign for addition, and then the 9. When they reach the 9, they need to possess a qualitatively differing kind of knowledge from that which was necessary to complete the previous two sums correctly. At the sequential moment in which they encounter the 9, some conception of "place value" is required. Perhaps in that moment they are not sure what to do next. Here is where the

Name _____

2	4	3	x
+3	+5	+9	x	etc.

x	x	x
x	x	x	etc.

FIG. 6.1.   An arithmetic worksheet.

SPTS bears on the SMTS. At the moment of experiencing a "bump" in difficulty in the SMTS can students get help? If so, from whom? Only the teacher? Or another student? Can it be a student's best friend or must it be the person sitting next to him or her? Can students ask the teacher for help at any time or only immediately after the teacher has dismissed the reading group he or she was working with while the other students were working on this problem sheet?

To underscore the mutually constitutive relation between social participation task structure and subject matter task structure in an overall academic task structure (ATS), consider the following. The SMTS may be identical in usual practice seatwork and in a test. What makes the overall ATS a "test" is a matter of social participation rather than of subject matter. In a test, the SPTS principle is that under no circumstance at any time can the student get help from any one else, whether teacher or student. Intuitively we are aware that "test" and "not test" conditions make an academic task a very different experience subjectively.

The point here is that in the moment-by-moment enactment of classroom tasks, some SPTS arrangements and some SMTS arrangements are always encountered simultaneously. Change in the structure of either dimension of task structure reframes the overall academic task as a differing entity subjectively for the student—the form of social relations constitutes the "task" just as much as does the form of subject matter knowledge or skill entailed in the task. Some students work better on some things alone, whereas others work better in constant interaction with others. Some students actively seek out the teacher's attention, whereas others do not. By paying attention to the specific content of SPTS in relation to SMTS, general education teachers can widen the range of ways in which differing students can engage the same subject matter.

Learning, Risk, and Face Work

Why is provision of a variety of ways to learn so important? Because not only do students have differing preferences, they also have differing aversions and perceptions of risk in engaging academic tasks. Because of the crowded conditions of classroom life and because of the surveillance of the teacher and of other students, trying to learn something while others are watching raises issues of maintaining "face." It is risky business. Let us consider academic task structures as sites for risk, respect, and trust.

In engaging students at the "zone of proximal development," we take the student to the leading edge of that person's competence to perform without assistance and then ask the student to move just beyond that edge, cooperating with a more expert partner in some kind of scaffolding interaction. That involves risk. The student needs confidence that he or she will be respected and not shamed before the ubiquitously present audience of teacher and class-mates. This asks of the learner a "leap of trust" in order to learn. That is, the so-called "domains" of the social and cognitive, although analytically separa-ble, are in the engagement of actual academic tasks inseparable; indeed they are mutually constitutive (see Erickson & Shultz, 1991, for elaboration on this point).

Thus, everyday classroom life constantly presents students with issues of safety, not to mention justice. Given the face-threatening potential of trying to learn, one reasonable adaptation for a student who is anxious about doing well is to become what can be called a "phantom woodworker." This is the be-haviorally compliant student who becomes adept at disappearing into the woodwork as the spotlight of teacher attention sweeps across the room. Be-cause of crowding in the classroom, teacher surveillance can never be com-plete. The inherently fragmentary character of teacher attention to student learning is compounded by an institutional press toward "batch processing" of students instructionally (e.g., basal readers and reading groups, math workbooks at different levels) and by the tendency of teachers to use behav-ioral evidence of surface compliance by students as a proxy for evidence of student learning, as discussed earlier. This leaves the phantom woodworker plenty of room to stay out of the teacher's attention. If the woodworker is hav-ing difficulty in learning, the specifics of such difficulty can stay invisible— sometimes for years across such a student's career. Woodworking students are easily lost in the shuffle of classroom life.

CLASSROOMS AS SITES FOR THE PRODUCTION OF STUDENT IDENTITIES AND LEARNING: THE ENDOGENOUS ROOTS OF RESISTANCE

Identity and Affiliation as Socially Constructed

Student identities and learning are fluid. They are constructed. Their content and character shifts across classroom situations (i.e., across various acade-mic task structure configurations). When students are forced into alienating ATS circumstances they disaffiliate with the teacher, the classroom, and school learning as a life project. This is not to say the students don't learn— they are always learning, but not always what the teacher and school may want. Students are always "on task." The question is, which task, and for whose purposes (Erickson, 1986)?

When students find affirming and meaningful ATS circumstances, they af-filiate with the teacher, the classroom, and school learning as a life project. Affiliation with school can happen in spite of external circumstances, such as class or racial position, or community attitudes toward school learning

(Erickson, 1987b). It is reasonable to assume that community attitudes toward schooling will always be at least ambivalent. That is, there is some genuine positive regard for school learning among parents, no matter how mixed with conflicted feelings about their own school experience as children. Also, because all parents have had some schooling and everyone has had at least some negative experiences with school (as with any other formal institution), all parents, no matter how socially advantaged, are likely to have some fears that the school will not serve their child properly.

Students have tremendous power to withhold the learning that is desired by school, and to construct personal identity in resistance to rather than in affiliation with school. This is to say that you can lead a horse (student) to water (learning environment) but you can't make it drink (learn).

We cannot overemphasize the point that, just as is the case for trust and affiliation, resistance is not the exclusive province of a particular category of students. "Resistance" is not totally predetermined in populations of low SES or "included" students, nor is it absent among students who are socially privileged or who appear to be compliant and achieving.

The biographical and autobiographical literature on English boarding schools, for example, shows how elite students who do fairly well academically can resent and resist what they see as the unjust exercise of authority. This theme is repeated in American popular culture in movies about high school life, such as *Ferris Buehler's Day Off*. Resistance is not necessarily a manifestation of an emotional disorder; it can be a reasonable response to forced labor in an irrational, alienating work situation. Recall the stories in African American communities of the slave who spits in the soup in the kitchen before bringing it into the dining room to serve to the master and mistress. Resistance by students in school can be devious, subtle, and principled.

CONCLUSION: STRETCHING THE ENVELOPE OF THE CLASSROOM LEARNING ENVIRONMENT

Inclusion as Adaptation

By making classroom frames more elastic—curricular frames and deportment/social participation frames—one makes possible a wider range of non-alienated labor in the classroom for all students, not only for the special education students who are now "included." Loosening the frames (which is not to create chaos but to make flexibility) can be seen as achieving inclusion in its most fundamental sense, providing a variety of academic task structures so as to make room for all learners.

This is to say that although "being out of it" may never be fully eliminated in classrooms, teachers can reduce the incidence and the prominence on the classroom landscape of those who appear "out of it" by changing the "it" of routine classroom life. The issue is to adapt the "it" in the direction of the learner in addition to asking the learner to adapt to the "it." Too little of this was done by teachers (and administrators) in schools in the past. Now that mainstreaming is happening there is an opportunity to open up general education classrooms to a wider variety of learning modes and styles than has characterized practice there in the past. But such an attempt will be resisted, because the pressures are still intense in the direction of pedagogical batch processing and teaching toward a steering group of students just above the middle level in achievement. With the press toward national standards that call for much more higher-order thinking on the part of students and for instruction for reasoning rather than memorization of facts, the batch processing approach of teachers may not necessarily change. It is possible that instead of attempting to differentiate instruction for a variety of learning needs and strengths, teachers will use the same old batch processing approach but simply adapt their pacing of instruction to a set of students closer to the top of the achievement range in their classroom. In consequence, a higher proportion of students will be regarded as falling further and further behind. Perhaps special education teachers can help general education teachers attempt to differentiate instruction for a variety of learning styles and rates, providing alternative instructional roads to Rome.

Three Approaches to Adaptation

Three main avenues along which learning environments might be adapted in general education classrooms are (a) in the direction of variation in types of learning styles as psychologists have been identifying them, (b) in the direction of cultural differences in preferred interaction frameworks, and (c) in the direction of differences in learning rates and physical functioning. The first direction in adapting for greater ATS/student congruence recapitulates Cronbach and Snow's "Aptitude-Treatment Interaction" work in somewhat different terms (see, e.g., Gardner, 1983). The second direction can be seen in the work of Kathryn Au and others at the Kamehameha School (e.g., Au & Mason, 1983; and as discussed in Tharp & Gallimore, 1988), which has been called *culturally responsive pedagogy* (see also Ladson-Billings, 1994, on the related notion of culturally relevant pedagogy).

The third direction involves adapting for greater "special needs" congruence. One aspect of this is changing the pacing of instruction to accommodate differing learning rates. This is done now, invidiously, by such practices as assigning students to differing "ability groups" in reading. One must be careful that adaptation to learning rate is not unintendedly invidious (but discussion of how to do that raises complex and subtle issues that go beyond the scope of this paper). Another aspect of adaptation to the inclusion of students with special needs involves the kinesic and temporal demands of classroom tasks. By literally slowing down the kinesic pace, especially at certain transition moments, a teacher can minimize the salience of moderate cerebral palsied or paraplegic students on the classroom landscape. Through decreasing the tempo of classroom participation activity one makes the physically handicapped student less visibly "out of it." For example, insisting for reasons of student control that all students leave the room in lockstep fashion makes the child with a brace or wheelchair more visible in the scene than arranging a more casual pattern of classroom departure. Students with learning disabilities might be accommodated by a teacher's generally increasing "wait time" in classroom discussions (i.e., giving all students more time to answer questions orally). Another adaptation might be to allow learning disabled students more time to complete written assignments. Ways of doing this that do not call invidious attention to such students can be devised. Time–space arrangements in classrooms can be changed if teachers set their minds to do it.

Another way to change the timing of classroom activity is in terms of the distinction made by Edward T. Hall between timing as one-dimensional or multidimensional—what he called the *monochronic* or *polychronic organization of activity* (Hall, 1976). Polychronic time is "more than one thing at a time"—for example, combining what we usually think of as work with what we usually think of as play by allowing small groups of students whose desks are placed together to chat quietly while they do academic tasks, or having periods of time in which some students are working on mathematics while others are working on science and still others are working on social studies. Having all students in the classroom working on mathematics in the same time block every day may not be the best way to organize instructional time. Another way in which instructional time becomes more polychronic is when students work on projects that integrate subject areas—in the completion of a project that interests them, students may be working on language arts, social studies, science, and mathematics simultaneously and also may be putting effort into social relationships—helping one another academically and providing emotional support for one another. Cooperative learning arrangements can be thought of as allowing qualitatively differing kinds of activity to be going on at the same time, which is to make classroom temporal organization more polychronic than monochronic. Through judicious use of polychronic temporal organization—which might seem to allow students to "goof off" but which actually increases opportunity to learn—a skillful teacher can increase the amounts of high-quality learning time for a wide variety of students. Through presenting intellectually and emotionally better tasks (and often polychronically organized tasks are better in just those ways), teachers can make for more "time on task" that is not just busywork.

A final adaptation is to focus teacher attention on learning rather than on compliance. There is a need for temporally midrange assessment of student learning by their instructors. The temporally distal assessment of standardized tests provides information too late for midcourse correction in instruction. Temporally proximal assessment of student deportment, as we have seen, also can miss the subtleties of students' immediate learning difficulties and achievements. Through the extremely temporally distal or proximal means of surveillance, the phantom woodworker is left lots of room to fall between the cracks in classroom learning environments. Some focal attention is needed, of a sort that is temporally closer to the action, but not so immediate as the teachers' momentary scanning of the room for overall compliance.

A Special Role for the Special Educator

A potential role for the special education teacher in the general education classroom is that of keeper of attention to the ongoing course of student learning. The special education teacher could have the responsibility of shepherding the sheep who are somehow straying academically, whether they are general education students or special needs students. By monitoring student work products for evidence of learning and by attending closely to students working in the classroom to see when they are conceptually or procedurally in a muddle, the special education teacher could be a consultant on learning and instruction for the general education teacher. In such a partnership, the special education teacher would be continually on special assignment to watch out for learning and to engage in continual dialogue with the general education teacher about the particulars of students' learning in the room. Through such dialogue the general and special education teachers would be engaged in temporally midrange assessment of the ongoing course of the learning of all students. The special education teacher would provide intervention not only for special needs students but for others who find themselves momentarily in trouble in their learning.

In such a partnership between the general and special education teacher there would no doubt be tensions and role conflicts, just as there are bound to be tensions and contradictions in adapting classroom learning environments and routine practices so as to accommodate student diversity more adequately. But loosening the frames of classroom ATSs and focusing teachers' attention more centrally and immediately on learning are both necessary if classrooms are to become places in which reasoning and understanding are taught and learned, and in which fewer students are alienated in their learning than is presently the case. Perhaps in the future the special education teacher might play a special role in helping to accomplish both kinds of change in the general education classroom.

REFERENCES

Au, K. H., & Mason, J. M. (1983). Cultural congruence in classroom participation structures: Achieving a balance of rights. *Discourse Processes, 6*(2), 145–167.

Conklin, H. (1959). Linguistic play in its cultural context. *Language, 35*(4): 631–636.

Dewey, J. (1965/1904). The relation of theory to practice in education. In M. L. Borrowman (Ed.), *Teacher education in America: A documentary history* (pp. 140–171). New York: Teachers College Press.

Erickson, F. (1986). Tasks in times: Objects of study in a natural history of teaching. In. In K. K. Zumwalt (Ed.), *Improving teaching: 1986 yearbook of the Association for Supervision and Curriculum Development* (pp. 131–147). Washington, DC: ASCD.

Erickson, F. (1987a). Conceptions of school culture: An overview. *Educational Administration Quarterly, 23*(4), 11–24.

Erickson, F. (1987b). Transformation and school success: The politics and culture of school achievement. *Anthropology and Education Quarterly, 18*(4), 335–356.

Erickson, F., & Mohatt, G. (1982). Cultural organization of participation structures in two classrooms of Indian students. In G. Spindler (Ed.), *Doing the ethnography of schooling* (pp. 133–174). New York: Holt, Rinehart & Winston.

Erickson, F., & Shultz, J. (1991). Students' experience of the curriculum. In P. W. Jackson (Ed.), *The handbook of research on curriculum.* New York: Macmillan.

Foucault, M. (1979). *Discipline and punish: The birth of the prison.* New York: Random House/Vintage.

Gardner, H. (1983). *Frames of mind: The theory of multiple intelligences.* New York: Basic Books.

Goffman, E. (1961). *Asylums: Essays on the social situation of mental patients and other inmates.* New York: Doubleday Anchor Books.

Hall, E. T. (1976). *Beyond culture.* New York: Doubleday.

Jackson, P. W. (1968). *Life in classrooms.* New York: Holt, Rinehart & Winston.

Ladson-Billings, G. (1994). *The dreamkeepers: Successful teachers for African American students.* San Francisco, CA: Jossey-Bass.

Noddings, N. (1992). *The challenge to care in schools.* New York: Teachers College Press.

Scribner, S., & Cole, M. (1981). *The psychology of literacy.* Cambridge, MA: Harvard University Press.

Tharp, R., & Gallimore, R. (1988). *Rousing minds to life: Teaching, learning and schooling in social context.* New York: Cambridge University Press.

7

Classroom Ecologies: Classroom Interactions and Implications for Inclusion of Students With Learning Disabilities

Sharon Vaughn
Jeanne Shay Schumm
School-Based Research
University of Miami

The general education classroom is the location of choice for educating students with learning disabilities (LD). In fact, it is likely that over the next few years considerable effort will be expended to reconsider general education so that it is better suited to meet the needs of all students with disabilities. This reconsideration will no doubt include an examination of professional development (at the preservice and inservice levels), curricula and standards, teacher planning, monitoring and adapting, and the classroom climate that supports individuals with disabilities. This chapter addresses teacher and student interactions with consideration of the classroom climate and the adjustments that will need to occur to ensure successful inclusion for students with LD.

From our perspective, there are two critical questions: What accommodations are feasible and sustainable for general education teachers to make to meet the individual academic and social needs of students with LD? What are the consequences of these accommodations for students with LD as well as students who represent other achievement groups? Over the past 5 years, we have conducted a series of studies designed to address those questions. Furthermore, we are presently engaged in a 4-year study of the effects of inclusion programs on the academic and social progress of students with LD in the general education classroom. This chapter summarizes the findings from these studies from the perspective of teachers and students. Furthermore, the chapter provides a description of general education classroom climate and the extent to which this climate is likely to ensure academic and social progress for all students. Our focus has been on those academic and social factors that contribute to an effective classroom climate that are feasible and sustainable by general education teachers given the resources that they can expect to have available to them.

TEACHERS' PERSPECTIVES

Perhaps the most central issue for general education teachers is the extent to which students with LD can be accommodated in general education classrooms without extensive preplanning on their part, specialized materials, or adaptations that call attention to the student or require extensive time from the teacher. Our studies have focused on two samples of teachers: randomly selected teachers and teachers identified as effective with students with LD. Within both samples we have examined teachers' perspectives across grade levels: elementary, middle, and high school. The studies conducted have included surveys, case studies of teachers, and extensive classroom observations. Findings from the surveys, conducted with large numbers of teachers, further refined the knowledge base about teacher planning and accommodations for students with disabilities, and influenced our subsequent in-depth studies. The case studies, conducted with general education teachers identified as effective with students with LD, provided an in-depth and expanded examination of what accommodations were made by willing teachers. The classroom observations yielded data about the type and quality of interactions between student and teacher and between student and student.

Surveys

Our first study was conducted with 775 elementary, middle, and high school general education teachers (Schumm & Vaughn, 1992). Our findings indicated that information sources used by teachers for planning for students with disabilities included other teachers, the mainstreamed student, and parents.

Information sources that are rarely used included other agencies, the IEP, and psychological reports. Overall, teachers were more likely to make adaptations during instruction than to consider adaptations as part of their pre- or post-planning.

As a follow-up to this study, we were interested in determining which adaptations general education teachers would find desirable and feasible for use in the classroom (Schumm & Vaughn, 1991). A total of 93 teachers participated: 25 elementary, 23 middle school, and 45 high school. Adaptations teachers identified as most desirable and feasible were those that required no instructional or curricular alterations and could be done relatively easily by the teachers. The most desirable and feasible adaptations identified by teachers included: provide reinforcement and encouragement, establish a personal relationship with the student, involve the student in whole class activities, respect the mainstreamed student as an individual, establish appropriate routines, adapt classroom management strategies. Adaptations that were the least desirable and feasible were those that required extensive changes in their planning, curriculum, or instructional practices and included: adapt long-range plans, adjust physical arrangement of room, adapt regular materials, use alternative materials, adapt scoring/grading criteria, communicate with mainstreamed students, and provide individualized instruction. Our conclusion was that teachers are willing to make accommodations that demonstrate "acceptance" of the student with LD, but less willing to make adaptations that require planning, instructional, or environmental adaptations.

We were also interested in teachers' beliefs about planning and making adaptations for students with LD in the general education classroom (Schumm, Vaughn, Gordon, & Rothlein, 1994). Sixty general education teachers identified as effective with students with LD, all of whom had had students with LD mainstreamed into their classroom, completed the survey and interview. Not surprisingly, teachers identified as effective reported high ratings of beliefs, skills, and practices in working with students with LD. The two items in the low range were long range planning and modifying tests. As in the previous surveys, teachers believed that interactive planning (monitoring and altering instruction on the spot, responding to the needs of the student) was the best way for them to make modifications for students with LD. Teachers were also reluctant to alter the content for students with LD and for the most part felt that students should be expected to cover the same content as other students in the class. The importance of all students covering the same content is a finding that appears again in our case studies.

These studies revealed that general education teachers find many more accommodations desirable than feasible, and are unlikely to make extensive, time consuming adaptations to meet the individual needs of students. While this does not mean that teachers are not willing to make changes that fit their

beliefs about effective instructional practice, but instead that the accommodations and adaptations requested of general education teachers need to be
considered within teachers' framework of beliefs about effective practice.

The information provided by these teachers and observations of their classrooms have informed our thinking, such that the fundamental question for us
is no longer "What are the most effective practices for students with LD in the
general education classroom?" but "What are the most effective practices for
students with LD in the general education classroom that (a) are feasible to
implement, (b) are likely to be sustained by teachers over time, and (c) will
positively influence the performance of all learners in the classroom, including average- and high-achieving students?" We have reframed the question because we have learned that teachers' beliefs about instruction focus on meeting the needs of the class as a whole and not on implementing specific instructional practices that will meet the needs of target students (e.g., students
with LD).

Case Studies

Twelve teachers who were principal-, teacher-, and self-identified as effective
with students with LD participated in this year-long case study (Schumm et
al., 1995). These teachers represented elementary (n = 4), middle school (n =
4), and high school (n = 4) grade groupings. All 12 teachers had at least one
student with LD mainstreamed into their classroom. Multiple data sources
were collected over the course of an entire school year and included interviews, surveys, open-ended questionnaires, written lesson plans, videotapes
of their lessons, stimulated recalls, and classroom observations.

Results indicated that students with LD cannot expect that general education teachers will individually plan to meet their specific academic needs.
Some teachers (mostly at the elementary level) will consider their needs as
they plan for the class as a whole. Teacher planning and thinking addressed
content and classroom activities, and not the individual needs of learners.
Content coverage drives instructional decision making, and students with LD
were expected to cover the same content and at the same pace as other students (middle and high school), although modifications are more likely to be
made at the elementary school level. Monitoring of students with LD occurred
largely by checking on what they were doing; little systematic monitoring of
understanding that included feedback was observed. Teachers monitored by
moving quickly around the room and checking to ensure that students were
working on an appropriate activity. We saw few mini-instructional lessons
where the teacher would "teach" for 1–3 minutes to move the student along.

The data from three of the middle school teachers who were included in
this study were further examined to determine the planning and adaptations
middle school teachers make for students with LD (Vaughn & Schumm,

1994). Teachers considered planning for the class as a whole and rarely considered planning for individual students or subgroups of students. They determined both the success of the lesson and when it was time to introduce new content based on the performance of the class as a whole and the amount of content they needed to cover. Teachers allocated a specific amount of time to segments of content and, although there was some flexibility, when the time was up the class moved on, whether the students understood the material or not. Reference to students' knowledge acquisition was surprisingly missing from extensive dialogues with these teachers. Teachers did not comment on whether students learned the lesson or which students might have experienced difficulty and needed further explanation or assistance. Rather, teachers were more interested in whether the students demonstrated interest in the lesson, were creating discipline problems, and seemed to "like the show."

Further examination of the case studies of the high school teachers revealed that they were similar to middle school teachers in their emphasis on content coverage and concern with the lesson "entertaining" the students and reducing discipline problems (Saumell, McIntosh, Schumm, & Vaughn, in press). However, high school teachers were even more concerned with treating all students the same, not identifying students with special needs or making accommodations to meet their special needs for fear that they would "stand out" and this would not prepare them for the real world. In marked contrast were the views and behavior of elementary teachers who described the students in their classrooms as a "family," all of whom had special needs that they felt had to be acknowledged and accommodated as well as possible. Concern with the self-concept and social acceptance of students with LD was a theme from the elementary case studies (Schumm et al., 1995).

Summary: Teachers' Perspectives

The central theme from our surveys and case studies was that these teachers were accepting of students with LD and treated them much as they would other students in the classroom. There is a positive and a negative outcome from this acceptance. On the positive side, students were not singled out and certainly did not feel as though they were "different" from others in the class. On the negative side, students with LD could expect few accommodations and adjustments in assignments, teaching routines, expectations, homework, or testing. Because most students with LD require these accommodations to ensure academic success in the general education classroom, we felt that learning was hindered. Our confidence in this conclusion is enhanced by the fact that these results have been confirmed through both qualitative and quantitative methodologies across several studies and with a range of teachers.

STUDENTS' PERSPECTIVES

We have been interested in students' views of the instructional practices of teachers for several reasons (for review, see Schumm & Vaughn, 1994). First, students' preferences for instructional practices are likely to be communicated directly to teachers and are likely to influence teachers' practices. If, for example, adaptations to meet the special needs of students with LD are viewed as highly undesirable by other students, it is likely that this will influence teachers' use of adaptations. Second, students' perceptions of instructional modifications could offer guidelines for procedures that students find helpful and thus increase student motivation to learn. Third, students' responsibility for their own learning, although traditionally overlooked (Goodlad, 1984; Gutmann, 1987), is receiving increased attention (Ericson & Ellett, 1990). If success and failure to learn is partly attributed to the learner, then students' perceptions of teaching practices need to be discerned.

Surprisingly little work has examined students' views despite the call for consideration of students' perceptions in research on teaching (e.g., Babad, Bernieri, & Rosenthal, 1991; Nicholls & Thorkildsen, 1989). Weinstein and colleagues established that students are highly aware of differential teacher behavior and can describe it sensitively and consistently (Brattesani, Weinstein, & Marshall, 1984; Marshall & Weinstein, 1986; Weinstein, 1983, 1985, 1989). Students are surprisingly good judges of teachers' behavior and are particularly sensitive to differential treatment of other students, even when teachers believe that they are able to conceal how they really feel (Babad et al., 1991; Tal & Babad, 1989, 1990).

With this in mind, we hypothesized that students would be highly sensitive to the accommodations and adaptations made for target students and that their perspective on these issues could influence the guidelines provided to teachers about best practices for including students with LD. We also felt that students' perceptions influence teacher behavior and also affect their motivation to learn. Our research has addressed students' perceptions of teachers who make adaptations to meet the special learning needs of students versus teachers who make few or no adaptations. Our research has included over 3,000 students who represent all achievement groups: low achieving, average achieving, high achieving, and LD. Furthermore, we included the perspectives of students who represented all grade groupings: elementary, middle, and high school.

Instruction

Our first study was conducted with over 800 middle and high school students who were asked to examine the instructional practices of two hypothetical teachers: one who made adaptations in instruction, pacing, homework, and tests to meet the special needs of students; and the second teacher who made few or no adaptations (Vaughn, Schumm, Niarhos, & Daugherty, 1993). In two related studies, one with elementary students that used a similar measure plus an individual interview (Vaughn, Schumm, Niarhos, & Gordon, 1993) and one that addressed the preferences of students with LD (Vaughn, Schumm, & Kouzekanani, 1993), we obtained similar findings.

First, students prefer teachers who adapt the pacing of instruction to promote learning for all students. Thus, although teachers feel pressure to cover content to meet district and state guidelines, students appreciate the teacher who is aware that some students are not "getting it" and slows down to ensure that all students have a chance to learn. In a study that included interviews from middle and high school students, 91% felt that the teacher should slow down or make instructional adaptations when some students do not understand the lesson content. How do high-achieving students feel about this issue, because they have the most to lose? Seventy-five percent agreed that the teacher should slow down. One student put it this way: "This will help struggling students and show that the teacher cares about them. Teachers are here to help students learn, not to make it more difficult for them." Several students stated that "Everyone has the same right to learn."

Second, because homework is an obvious marker of class membership, students generally prefer that homework remain the same for all students. The most frequently cited reason was that it was fair. They felt that all students who were in the same class should have the same work. A second reason was that it allowed students in the same class to communicate with each other, thus promoting their social acceptance. Because homework is the primary reason given to parents for making telephone calls to friends in the evening, different homework could potentially remove certain students from the social telephone call loop. Although the overwhelming majority of students preferred the same homework and assignments, there were a few exceptions: a subgroup of elementary students (Vaughn, Schumm, Niarhos, & Gordon, 1993), middle school students with LD, and the students with LD and low achieving students at the high school level (Vaughn, Schumm, Klingner, & Saumell, 1995).

Third, students find learning from textbooks difficult and boring. Although many realize the need for instruction based on textbooks, they request strategy instruction and direct learning experiences that facilitate their instruction. Students at the middle and high school level were particularly concerned about the difficulty of textbooks and teachers' lack of instructional support to facilitate learning from text. One student reflected, "It seems in grade school or elementary school, my teachers were much more helpful with my textbooks. Also, my textbooks were a little more interesting. But as I got into my higher grades, teachers got a little more lazier and my books got harder." Students at the secondary level consistently reported that there was a huge gulf between their need for hands-on learning experiences, strategy instruction, and textbook adaptations and their reports of the extent to which teachers implemented those practices in their classrooms (Schumm, Vaughn, & Saumell, 1992; Vaughn et al., in press).

Fourth, students prefer flexible grouping practices that provide them an opportunity to work and learn with their peers. Interestingly, middle and high school students realize that there is the potential that these groups will turn into social "chat" sessions, and many students suggest that the teacher identify which students should work together. The issue of grouping seems particularly important in light of the move toward more inclusive education for students with disabilities. In fact, one of the most frequently stated suggestions for increasing the mainstreaming of students with disabilities is to use cooperative groups. This suggestion is not viewed positively by all stakeholders. Many parents and teachers of children who are high achieving and gifted (Vaughn, Schumm, Jallad, Slusher, & Saumell, in press) feel that the education of these children is compromised as teachers provide instruction and support for poorer-achieving students.

Students' preferences differ for mixed versus homogeneous learning groups in their classrooms. Some students see advantages to mixed groups in that higher-achieving students can help lower-achieving students and that "cliques" can be avoided; others were concerned that their grades might be affected or that they would make slower progress if they worked with lower-achieving students. One thing is clear: Students have strong feelings about grouping and are able to clearly identify situations in which they feel they learn best. Some students feel that they learn best when they work with just one other student, whereas some other students work and learn best alone.

Fifth, students feel that all students should have the same tests, although modifications in test procedures are acceptable. Teachers at the elementary level are more willing to make test adaptations for students with LD; however, middle and high school teachers are much less likely to do so.

Students have strong and clear preferences for the types of instructional practices and adaptations they view as helpful and fair for themselves and for students with disabilities in the general education classroom. For the most part, students across grade and achievement groupings prefer that teachers make more adaptations to meet the individual learning needs of all students and to meet the special needs of some students. Students were particularly emphatic about teachers slowing the pace and ensuring that students "get" the information before moving on to a new topic. Particularly at the middle and high school level (Vaughn & Schumm, 1994), students pleaded for strategy instruction that would provide them with the tools to be more independent, successful learners. In general, adaptations that were not viewed positively were those that called special attention to students with LD. These included adaptations in homework, tests, and using different textbooks.

Social

Most of the data that examine the social functioning of students with LD have addressed the extent to which they are accepted, liked, and/or have friends in the general education classroom. To better understand these findings, research has also addressed their self-perceptions, social skills, and behavior problems. In summary, students with LD, when compared with their classmates, are more poorly accepted and more frequently rejected, have lower self-perceptions and social skills, and more frequent behavior problems (for review, see Hazel & Schumaker, 1988). However, when compared with other low-achieving students who are not LD, the data reveal that low-achieving students and students with LD frequently do not differ from each other on most measures of social functioning (e.g., Haager & Vaughn, 1995; Vaughn & Haager, 1994; Vaughn & Hogan, 1994). This raises questions about how to account for the low peer acceptance and high rejection of students with LD. For example, to what extent is the problem a function of how significant others (e.g., teachers and students) treat low achievers rather than behaviors related to students' learning disabilities?

We have a limited understanding of the social climate in the classroom and how this affects the social acceptance of students with LD. Of particular interest is the extent to which teachers' acceptance of students with LD might influence the acceptance of their classmates. Teachers' perceptions of students influence peers' perceptions (Tal & Babad, 1990), and students are aware of what teachers think of students (Babad et al., 1991; Tal & Babad, 1989, 1990). Because many teachers view students with LD as undesirable to have in the classroom (Garrett & Crump, 1980), and teachers' interactions with students with LD are often negative (Dorval, McKinney, & Feagans, 1982), teachers' perceptions of students with LD would likely be communicated to other students and affect the peer acceptance of students with LD.

In an attempt to examine this issue, we assessed the social status, peer acceptance, and reciprocal friendships of students who were in classrooms with teachers who were principal-, teacher-, and self-identified as accepting of students with LD (Vaughn, McIntosh, Schumm, Haager, & Callwood, 1993). Overall, the findings indicate that students with LD in classes where they are accepted by their teachers are not less well liked or less well known by their classmates than are students from other achievement groups. Most encouraging was that 90% of the students with LD had a mutual best friend (reciprocal friendship). Reciprocal friendships hold promise for buffering the negative effects associated with low peer acceptance and rejection (Howes, 1988) and are an important indicator of social functioning.

The social climate in the classroom is orchestrated by the classroom teacher who provides the model for acceptance, understanding, and social support. Our observations (McIntosh, Vaughn, Schumm, Haager, & Lee, 1993; Schumm et al., 1995; Vaughn, McIntosh, et al., 1993) indicate that teachers have an enormous influence on whether students with LD will be accepted and even liked by their peers. Accepting teachers set a tone in the classroom that all students are prized, and cooperating with and teaching each other are valued behaviors in the classroom. Furthermore, accepting teachers do not tolerate "put-downs" by other students (Schumm et al., 1995; Vaughn & Schumm, 1994).

We also examined the social perceptions of students (LD and NLD) in general education classrooms to determine the extent to which their perceptions might influence the success of inclusion (Saumell et al., 1994). Students' perceptions of classmates and teachers related to inclusion issues were assessed in a rating scale/individual interview conducted with 267 students representing grades three through five in two elementary schools. Each school provided pull-out resource room services as well as teacher consultation for students with LD who were mainstreamed into general education classrooms more than 50% of the day. The NLD students who participated in this study were from general education classrooms that included students with LD. The findings revealed that 63% of students with LD and only 33% of NLD students had negative feelings about their classmates (e.g., "They are mean;" "They make noise and get you in trouble"). When asked what they liked about their classmates, 28% of NLD students indicated that "They are my friends," whereas 0% of the students with LD gave that response.

In the same study, we were interested in students' judgments related to leaving the classroom for help and having a special teacher come to their room. Students' responses to the question, "What do you think about leaving your classroom to get extra help?" were overwhelmingly negative on the part of students with LD (75%) and NLD students (64%). In response to how the student would feel about having another teacher come into his or her class to help, only 13% of the students with LD had a negative response whereas 52% of the NLD students felt negatively about it. We were most alarmed by students' responses to the question, "How do you feel about the way your teacher helps children who do not learn as quickly as others?" One hundred percent of the students with LD and 84% of the NLD students provided a negative response to this question (e.g., "She only works with the children who are above LD. She doesn't give the others time.").

We felt that these responses provided insights into alternative service delivery models that might hold promise for students with LD. Many students with LD do not like to be "singled" out or to leave the classroom to receive support services from another teacher. Educational models that provide direct, intensive instruction within general education classrooms are likely to result in positive outcomes for many of these students. There are, however, some students who benefit from pull-out resource room help. Alternatively, some students, teachers, and parents feel that selected students need the break from the general education classroom and benefit from intensive one-on-one instruction provided in a special setting for part of the day.

Summary: Students' Perspectives

Students' perspectives on academic accommodations yield several significant findings. Students want the pacing adjusted so that they learn material rather than simply cover it. They want to be taught learning strategies to acquire information from text, and prefer instructional adaptations from teachers who consider the learning of all students. Homework and tests should be the same for all students, although modifications in test administration procedures are generally accepted. Students have preferences for how they learn in groups, including opportunities to work with their peers and friends that do not turn into "chat" sessions.

Overall, students' perspectives on the social functioning and acceptance of students with LD who are pulled out of the general education classroom for part of the day indicate that they are higher on behavior problems and lower on social acceptance than their peers. Findings from students with LD from classrooms where teachers are highly accepting of them reveal that they are not less well liked or less well known by their classmates than are students from other achievement groups. Students' perspectives of issues related to inclusion reveal that students do not like leaving the classroom for extra help and feel that the teacher does not spend adequate time with students who need help. A summary of teacher and student perspectives is provided in Table 7.1.

TEACHER–STUDENT INTERACTIONS: CLASSROOM CLIMATE

In an attempt to better understand the general education classroom ecology for students with LD, we developed the Classroom Climate Scale (CCS) (McIntosh et al., 1993) as a tool to measure teacher and student academic and social behavior. The scale was designed to examine the behavior of the target student (a student with LD) as compared with the behavior of other NLD students in the general education class. We were particularly interested in capturing the classroom interactions between teacher and student and student and student. How students responded to teachers and to each other in general education classrooms was also assessed.

Although other previously developed measures addressed teachers' behavior (e.g., Bailey, 1984), instructional practice (e.g., Callaway, 1988), student's social behavior (e.g., Schumaker, Hazel, Sherman, & Sheldon, 1982), and student's social interactions (e.g., Bryan & Bryan, 1978), we were unable

TABLE 7.1
Teacher and Student Perspectives about Academic and Social Implications
of Including Students with Learning Disabilities in the
General Education Classrooms

Perspective	Teacher	Student with LD
Academic		
Content instruction	Students with LD should learn same content as others.	Teachers should provide instructional strategies and adapt pacing of instruction.
Adaptations	Many are more desirable than feasible to implement. Few instructional adaptations made to meet the individual learning needs of students.	Desires individual adaptations without calling attention to student with LD. More adaptations to meet the individual needs requested.
Grouping	Education of higher-level students is compromised by lower-level students.	Prefers to work and learn from peers. Strong preference about grouping procedures and how they influence learning.
Comprehension	Little systematic monitoring and feedback is provided.	Infrequently asks teacher for help or engages in class discussion.
Social		
Acceptance	Treat students with LD like others; few accommodations.	Depends on the acceptance of the student by the teacher.
Involvement	Students with LD are often ignored and receive infrequent praise or feedback.	Uninvolved in instructional or social interactions in the classroom.

to locate an instrument that assessed teacher and student interactions. Thus, the CCS was developed to provide a reliable and valid measure of teacher and student behavior in general education classrooms that included students with LD. The CCS contains 21 items that address four major areas:

- *Teacher-initiated behavior* (nine items)—Instructional grouping, monitoring students, instructional modifications, praise, and teacher fairness and impartiality.
- *Student-initiated behavior* (five items)—Student's level of involvement in class, asking for help, volunteering to answer, and observed level of frustration/confusion.
- *Student participation and interaction* (three items)—Student–student interaction, participation in class activities, and interactions between the student and teacher.
- *Classroom climate* (four items)—The extent to which the classroom climate is consistent or discrepant for the target student with LD and other NLD students in the class.

Sixty general education teachers (grades three through twelve) were observed during three full lessons over a period of five months. Teachers were selected based on principal-, special-education teacher-, and self-identification as effective teachers of students with LD. All participating teachers had at least one student with LD in their classroom. The students with LD (21 females, 39 males) were randomly selected from the target class (if more than one LD student was present). Each of the 60 teachers' classrooms were observed on three occasions for a total of 180 observations.

Perhaps the best way to review the findings is to use the four components from the CCS as an organizational format. When interpreting findings, consider that all observations were conducted during social studies and science (when students with LD in this school district are most frequently mainstreamed).

Teacher-initiated behavior can be first examined by reporting teachers' grouping preferences. Teachers were consistent across grade levels (elementary, middle, and high school). Teachers provided the majority of instruction to the whole class with limited opportunities for small group instruction and even fewer opportunities for students to work in pairs. Few instructional modifications were observed for any student, including students with LD. Elementary teachers made more instructional modifications for students with LD than NLD students; however, this was not true at the middle and high school levels. Although teachers checked in with students at a relatively high rate, systematic monitoring of their academic progress was rarely observed. Middle and high school teachers monitored the work/activity of NLD students at a higher rate than they did that of students with LD. These teachers also made more negative comments to NLD students. We interpret the higher rate of monitoring and negative comments of NLD students at the middle and high school levels as an indication of higher interest and involvement with these students. We view this as one source of evidence, along with the teacher case studies previously discussed, that the classroom climate for students with LD, particularly at the middle and high school levels, is one in which they are most likely to be ignored. Teachers made few negative comments that would include sarcasm or personal ridicule to any student. Although the rate of praise for elementary teachers was significantly higher than for middle and high school teachers (lowest rate), overall, teachers used praise and positive feedback at what we interpreted as a low level.

For *student-initiated behavior* there were significant differences between students with LD and NLD students. Students with LD were engaged in academic behaviors at a significantly lower rate when compared with their NLD classmates. Students with LD infrequently asked the teacher for help, volunteered to answer questions, or engaged in class discussions. With respect to more social-related items such as interfering with others and making negative comments to peers, students with LD were rated significantly lower (displayed these behaviors less frequently) than their classmates. In summary, students with LD were less involved both academically and socially in the classroom environment.

The *student–teacher participation and interaction* items were similar to the student-initiated items for students with LD. The NLD students interacted with the teacher, other students, and classroom activities at a significantly higher rate than did students with LD. The *overall classroom climate* for students with LD was similar to that for NLD students. With few exceptions, it was not possible to distinguish the NLD students from the students with LD by the materials the students were using, the seating arrangement or seat location of students, or the activities in which they participated. Students with LD distinguished themselves significantly from NLD students by the low level of engagement and involvement they exhibited toward other students, the teacher, and the academic task.

Across settings, grade levels, and teachers the most consistent finding is that students with LD are uninvolved both socially and academically in the classroom environment. This lack of engagement is observed in the few questions and answers they attempt, the lack of social interaction with peers, and the low levels of engagement in academic tasks. Students with LD are unengaged in the learning process by both their own and the teacher's initiation. Because the primary method of instruction across all grade groupings was whole class instruction, students with LD must acquire participation and self-monitoring skills to have a chance at keeping up with the high concept and content load presented.

We feel that the low interaction rate of students with LD in the general education classroom is related to the large cognitive gap between their knowledge and the material presented in class. The vocabulary and concept load of the content these students were supposed to be learning was sufficiently dense that the students with LD turned off and tuned out. Because so little of the classwork was adapted to meet their learning needs and the primary mode of instruction was whole class (large group), the students with LD were not engaged in the learning process. Although the amount of class discussion was not recorded with the CCS, the consensus among the observers was that there was little opportunity for students with LD to discuss what they already knew about the topic and then to relate it to the new information presented.

This lack of "with-it-ness" as learners on the part of students with LD has also been previously characterized as inactive learning (Torgeson, 1982; Torgeson & Licht, 1983). Inactive learners have a response style that is passive and disengaged, with little self-monitoring of what they are learning or what they are missing. We feel that this study provides additional confirmation for the passive learning style of students with LD. Despite their low rates for requesting assistance and volunteering to answer, the students scored low on frustration and confusion. Thus, they did not seem to "mind" not knowing what was happening.

We cannot help but wonder to what extent the passive, low interaction learning style of the student with LD and the lack of teacher adaptations are part of a mutual pact between student and teacher—"You don't bother me and I won't bother you." This agreement was better represented at the middle and high school levels than at the elementary level.

Summary: Teacher–Student Interactions and Classroom Climate

Observations of the general education classroom climate, elementary through secondary, provided little evidence that students with LD would have their individual learning needs met. The majority of instruction was whole class, and few instructional modifications or systematic monitoring of learning were observed for any student. Praise and feedback were infrequently observed. Students with LD were less involved both academically and socially in the classroom. Overall, teachers expected little of students, and the behavior of students with LD could be described as passive although not uncooperative.

IMPLICATIONS AND FUTURE DIRECTIONS

So, back to the questions we initially posed: What accommodations are feasible and sustainable for general education teachers to make to meet the individual academic and social needs of students with LD? What are the consequences of these accommodations for students with LD as well as students who represent other achievement groups?

Over time, the teachers and students with whom we have worked have taught us that the critical components of this question are *feasibility, sustainability,* and *effectiveness for all learners.* Interventions that are effective in laboratory settings, under controlled conditions, implemented by either highly trained teachers or research groups, with resources or class sizes that do not represent the realities of the classroom situation may hold promise for providing guidelines for the further development of interventions, but will do little to directly inform teacher practice. In fact, teachers are highly suspicious of these intervention models and consider them the work of "ivory tower" researchers.

Unfortunately, even though "lab setting interventions" may provide much needed information about what components of an intervention are powerful, with whom, and under what conditions, unless they are adapted to meet the realities of the classroom they will not be implemented by teachers (Malouf & Schiller, 1995). Most classroom teachers do not have the time or expertise to consume the research literature and consider what components of it make sense in their setting and then take it the next step—developing an effective intervention practice that works in their classrooms. They find much more trustworthy those instructional practices that their teaching peers have developed, implemented, and evaluated—ones that have passed what they consider to be the true tests of feasibility and sustainability. Moreover, teachers in the general education setting are more likely to espouse instructional practices that promote learning for all students. Practices that require an inordinate amount of teacher effort for an individual child or subgroup of children are not likely to be adopted.

What are the implications for researchers? How do we move knowledge about instructional practice into knowledge use? If our findings about the classroom climates and practices in general education classrooms reflect most classrooms, what hope is there for successful inclusion of students with LD in general education classrooms? First, in the research and development of instructional interventions, attention must be given to feasibility. Teachers' perceptions of ease of implementation must be taken into consideration. Second, research needs to document instructional practices that teachers will sustain over a period of time. Of particular interest is how teachers adapt instructional practices to meet the particular needs of their students and classroom settings. If teachers elect not to sustain a particular practice, documentation should be made of the reasons why. Moreover, students' perceptions of the classroom practice must be taken into account. Teachers are acutely aware of student responses to methods and strategies and are not likely to continue their use if students (i.e., the consumer) find them to be boring, repetitive, or unnecessary. Third, continued research needs to be conducted on multilevel instructional practices that can be implemented in heterogeneous classrooms. Focus should be given to the impact of such practices on the learning of students with disabilities as well as their general education peers. Such a research agenda necessitates intensive classroom-based research as well as research on professional development programs. It also necessitates a partnership among researchers, teachers, administrators, parents, and students.

ACKNOWLEDGMENTS

Special thanks to Ellen Schiller, Chief, Directed Research, Division of Innovation and Development, U.S. Office of Special Education Programs, whose comments regarding translating research into knowledge use influenced this chapter.

REFERENCES

Babad, E., Bernieri, F., & Rosenthal, R. (1991). Students as judges of teachers' verbal and nonverbal behavior. *American Educational Research Journal, 28,* 237–242.

Bailey, G. D. (1984). An evaluator's guide to diagnosing and analyzing teaching styles. *NAASP Bulletin, 68,* 19–25.

Brattesani, K. A., Weinstein, R. S., & Marshall, H. H. (1984). Student perceptions of differential teacher treatment as moderators of teacher expectation effects. *Journal of Educational Psychology, 76,* 236–247.

Bryan, T. S., & Bryan, J. H. (1978). Social interactions of learning disabled children. *Learning Disability Quarterly, 1,* 33–37.

Callaway, R. (1988, April). *A study of teacher's planning.* Presented at the annual meeting of the American Research Association, New Orleans, LA.

Dorval, B., McKinney, J. D., & Feagans, L. (1982). Teacher interaction with learning disabled children and average achievers. *Journal of Pediatric Psychology, 7,* 317–330.

Ericson, D. P., & Ellett, F. J. (1990). Taking student responsibility seriously. *Educational Researcher, 19,* 3–10.

Garrett, M. K., & Crump, W. D. (1980). Peer acceptance, teacher preference, and self appraisal of social status among learning disabled students. *Learning Disability Quarterly, 3,* 42–48.

Goodlad, J. I. (1984). *A place called school: Prospects for the future.* New York: McGraw-Hill.

Gutmann, A. (1987). *Democratic education.* Princeton, NJ: Princeton University Press.

Haager, D., & Vaughn, S. (1995). Parent, teacher, peer, and self-reports of social competence of students with learning disabilities. *Journal of Learning Disabilities, 28*(4), 205–215.

Hazel, J. S., & Schumaker, J. B. (1988). Social skills and learning disabilities: Current issues and recommendations for future research. In J. F. Kavanagh & T. J. Truss, Jr. (Eds.), *Learning disabilities: Proceedings of the National Conference* (pp. 293–344). Parkton, MD: York.

Howes, C. (1988). Peer interaction of young children. *Monographs of the Society for Research in Child Development, 53,* (1, Serial No. 143).

Malouf, D. B., & Schiller, E. P. (1995). Research and practice in special education. *Exceptional Children, 61*(5), 414–424.

Marshall, H. H., & Weinstein, R. S. (1986). Classroom context of student-perceived differential teacher treatment. *Journal of Educational Psychology, 78,* 441–453.

McIntosh, R., Vaughn, S., Schumm, J. S., Haager, D., & Lee, O. (1993). Observations of students with learning disabilities in general education classrooms. *Exceptional Children, 60*(3), 249–261.

Nicholls, J. G., & Thorkildsen, T. A. (1989). Intellectual conventions versus matters of substance: Elementary school students as curriculum theorists. *American Educational Research Journal, 26,* 533–544.

Saumell, L., McIntosh, R., Schumm, J. S., & Vaughn, S. (in press). General education high school teachers: What can students with learning disabilities expect? *Learning Disabilities Research & Practice.*

Saumell, L., Rothlein, L., Wilson, C., Hughes, M., Sinagub, J. M., Vaughn, S., & Schumm, J. S. (1994). *Students' views of inclusion.* Manuscript submitted for publication.

Schumaker, B., Hazel, J. S., Sherman, J. A., & Sheldon, J. (1982). Social skill performances of learning disabled, non-learning disabled, and delinquent adolescents. *Learning Disability Quarterly, 5,* 388–397.

Schumm, J. S., & Vaughn, S. (1991). Making adaptations for mainstreamed students: Regular classroom teachers' perspectives. *Remedial and Special Education, 12*(4), 18–27.

Schumm, J. S., & Vaughn, S. (1992). Planning for mainstreamed special education students. *Exceptionality, 3,* 81–90.

Schumm, J. S., & Vaughn, S. (1994). Students' thinking about teachers' practices. *Advances in Learning and Behavioral Disabilities, 8,* 105–129.

Schumm, J. S., Vaughn, S., Gordon, J., & Rothlein, L. (1994). General education teachers' beliefs, skills, and practices in planning for mainstreamed students with learning disabilities. *Teacher Education and Special Education, 17*(1), 22–37.

Schumm, J. S., Vaughn, S., Haager, D., McDowell, J., Rothlein, L., & Saumell, L. (1995). Teacher planning for individual student needs: What can mainstreamed special education students expect? *Exceptional Children, 61*(4),

Schumm, J. S., Vaughn, S., & Saumell, L. (1992). What teachers do when the textbook is tough: Students speak out. *Journal of Reading Behavior, 24,* 481–503.

Tal, Z., & Babad, E. (1989). The "teacher's pet" phenomenon as viewed by Israeli teachers and students. *Elementary School Journal, 90,* 99–110.

Tal, Z., & Babad, E. (1990). The teacher's pet phenomenon: Rate of occurrence, correlates, and psychology costs. *Journal of Educational Psychology, 82,* 637–645.

Torgeson, J. K. (1982, April). The learning disabled child as an inactive learner: Education implications. *Topics in Learning and Learning Disabilities, 5,* 45–52.

Torgeson, J. K., & Licht, B. G. (1983). The learning disabled child as an inactive learner: Retrospect and prospects. In J. D. McKinney & L. Feagans (Eds.), *Current Topics in Learning Disabilities* (pp. 3–32). Norwood, NJ: Ablex.

Vaughn, S., & Haager, D. (1994). Social competence as a multifaceted construct: How do students with learning disabilities fare? *Learning Disability Quarterly, 17,* 253–256.

Vaughn, S., & Hogan, A. (1994). The social competence of students with learning disabilities over time: A within-individual examination. *Journal of Learning Disabilities, 27*(5), 292–303.

Vaughn, S., McIntosh, R., Schumm, J. S., Haager, D., & Callwood, D. (1993). Social status, peer acceptance, and reciprocal friendships revisited. *Learning Disabilities Research & Practice, 8*(2), 82–88.

Vaughn, S., & Schumm, J. S. (1994). Middle school teachers' planning for mainstreamed special education students. *Remedial and Special Education, 15,* 152–161.

Vaughn, S., Schumm, J. S., Jallad, B., Slusher, J., & Saumell, L. (in press). Teachers' views of inclusion. *Learning Disabilities Research and Practice.*

Vaughn, S., Schumm, J. S., Klingner, J., & Saumell, L. (1995). Students' views of instructional practices: Implications for inclusion. *Learning Disability Quarterly, 18*(3), 236–248.

Vaughn, S., Schumm, J. S., & Kouzekanani, K. (1993). What do students with learning disabilities think when their general education teachers make adaptations? *Journal of Learning Disabilities, 26*(8), 545–555.

Vaughn, S., Schumm, J. S., Niarhos, F., & Daugherty, T. (1993). What do students think when their teachers make adaptations? *Teaching and Teacher Education, 9,* 107–118.

Vaughn, S., Schumm, J. S., Niarhos, F., & Gordon, J. (1993). Students' perceptions of two hypothetical teachers' instructional adaptations for low achievers. *Elementary School Journal, 94,* 97–102.

Weinstein, R. S. (1983). Student perceptions of schooling. *Elementary School Journal, 83,* 287–312.

Weinstein, R. S. (1985). Student mediation of classroom expectancy effects. In J. B. Dusek (Ed.), *Teacher expectancies* (pp. 329–350). Hillsdale, NJ: Lawrence Erlbaum Associates.

Weinstein, R. S. (1989). Perceptions of classroom processes and student motivation: Children's views of self-fulfilling prophecies. In R. Ames & C. Ames (Eds.), *Research on motivation in education: Vol. 3. Goals and cognitions* (pp. 187–221). New York: Academic Press.

8

Constructing Knowledge in Inclusive Classrooms: What Students Know and Teachers Need to Know

Elba I. Reyes
University of Arizona
Department of Special Education and Rehabilitation

As our nation's schools move full speed toward the inclusion of students with learning disabilities (LD) into the general education classrooms, one cannot help but reflect on the question raised by Frederick Erickson (chap. 6, this volume): "Inclusion into what?" A previous chapter by Vaughn and Schumm (chap. 7) and the chapter by Erickson address that question by examining the interactions within classroom environments from the teachers' perspective (Vaughn & Schumm) and from the students' perspective (Erickson; Vaughn & Schumm). In this chapter I first synthesize and then compare those perspectives for the purpose of identifying components of classroom interactions that could assist students with LD to be successful and learn along with their peers in general education classrooms.

The notion of classroom interaction has diverse definitions, and it appears that the definition is influenced by the perspective of the person or persons doing the defining: researcher, teacher, or student. Vaughn and Schumm defined classroom interaction by looking at the academic and social climate of the classroom. Academic climate was identified by the teachers' perceptions of what could feasibly be done during instruction in classes that included students with LD, by the students' perception of what teachers do and should do during instruction in classes that included students with LD, and by the teacher–student interactions during instruction. Teachers reported on their classroom interactions based on what worked for them in achieving their academic goals. Social climate was identified by teachers' and peers' social acceptance of students with LD, by the perceptions of students with and without learning disabilities regarding issues related to inclusion, and by the observed teacher–student and student–student interactions. For the students in that same study, classroom interactions were defined by what worked for them, academically and socially, within the classroom's social environment.

Teachers chosen for the study were those teachers who were principal-, peer teacher-, and self-identified as effective in working with students who had learning disabilities. Unfortunately, the term *effective* was not defined. Teacher effectiveness can be gauged by various measures: for example, teacher's popularity with administrators and peers, classroom behavior control skills resulting in the least number of referrals of students with LD to the principal, student academic progress, and so on. This notion of effective teachers becomes important when we analyze teachers' and students' perceptions of desired classroom environments and when we compare the instructional preferences of teachers and students.

In his thesis on the construction of learning in classrooms, Erickson presented some clues regarding the differences between students' and teachers' understanding of classroom environments when he suggested that educators need to examine their perceptions on teaching and learning. Erickson also proposed that teachers need to consider how present classroom environments might be changed to correspond to the social nature of classroom life.

His definition of classroom interaction stems from the construct of sociocultural organization and is based on the classroom's ecosystem. How the students "look" socially and academically and whether they are "with it" or not becomes a function of the relationships within the classroom and the interaction that is designed by the teacher and acted on by the students, either consciously or unconsciously. The result of the interaction, according to Erickson, is that the students assent to learn or withhold that assent, again either consciously or unconsciously. That is a powerful tenet: Students choose to learn or not to learn depending on how they feel about themselves within the classroom environment. Furthermore, that choice to learn or not to learn is targeted toward the academic nature of the classroom interaction.

The notion of students assenting to learn when motivated to do so was illustrated through Erickson's example of the Hanunoo boys' love notes. Those examples brought to mind instances of students' underground literacy that I encountered while teaching in public schools. Many of the students with LD were identified as having a written language disability and were reluctant writers in their general education classrooms. Yet, those same students wrote letters and notes to peers on a variety of topics: who was seeing whom, inquiries regarding dates and times of school sports events, predictions of the day's lunch menu, sharing of news (e.g., the death of a grandfather), and so on. It became evident that those students had acquired knowledge regarding writing but they were not participating in the academic learning of writing while in the general education classroom. Analogous to those examples were students who often withheld assent to participate in "school" math, yet could be observed calculating team members' sport scores and predicting points needed to top competitive teams' composite scores. One of Erickson's clues as to why learning may not be occurring in classrooms lies in his suggestion that the social climate and interaction within the classroom environment is not only shaped by academic activity, but also influences students' motivation to participate or to learn.

If researchers, teachers, and students can recognize that learning success will or will not occur depending on the learning environment and the interactions within that environment, where is the problem for students with LD? One method to address that question may be to look at the incongruencies between the perceptions of teachers and the perceptions of students. Then we would then identify those components of classroom interactions that may result in success for students with LD. Finally, we can examine how those components may be incorporated into inclusive classrooms.

EXAMINING PERCEPTIONS
OF TEACHERS AND STUDENTS

As we examine the perceptions of teachers and students presented by Vaughn and Schumm and by Erickson, we can detect several incongruencies that appear to center around behaviors, attitudes, and the integral structure of the classroom environment. In this section these areas are addressed and some ideas regarding the source of such incongruencies are proposed.

Incongruencies regarding teacher behaviors and attitudes are evident in both chapters 6 and 7. Furthermore, teacher and student responses reveal that teachers view classrooms primarily as academic environments, whereas students view classrooms as social environments. This is not new information. However, such information becomes vital when we consider how classroom ecologies affect students' motivation to learn, and that students' viewpoints may possibly be more useful than teachers' (see Table 8.1).

Behaviors

While teachers do not want to accommodate for individual students' needs and find feasible only those adaptations that do not require additional instructional training or curricular modifications, students report these behaviors as undesirable. Certainly, teaching to 25 or 30 individuals can dissuade teachers from planning and implementing instruction for individualized needs. Increasing research, however, is demonstrating that students with LD can and do benefit from the same type of instruction and curriculum as do non-LD students when teachers' behaviors change from transmitters of in-

TABLE 8.1
Teachers' and Students' Perceptions of Desired Classroom Environments

Teachers	Students
Behaviors	
Teach to the whole class	Teach to the needs of each student
Content drives instruction, activities, and time	Lessons and instruction should be designed to ensure learning
Teachers survey and assess learning	Students often can "fake" learning
Prefer little to no adaptation of instruction	Adapt instruction without singling out students
Attitudes	
Teachers treat all students fairly	Teachers have differentiated behaviors toward students and are more negative with students who have learning disabilities
Pull-out or pull-in is preferable for students needing special assistance	Pull-out or pull-in is highly undesirable
Environment: academic versus social	
Completion of an academic task is influenced by the student's mastery of the subject matter	Completion of an academic task is influenced by conditions of the social structure of the classroom
Classrooms are academic environments	Classrooms are social environments where academics are learned

formation to facilitators of learning (Bos & Reyes, 1989; Reyes, 1990, 1994). Some students with LD can learn grade-level curriculum using grade-level materials and instructional practices that have proven effective in general education classes *once the teacher facilitates the process through a change in the teacher's instructional behavior.*

Affiliated to teachers' classroom behaviors are students' behaviors. Teachers assert that they can assess learning by monitoring students' behaviors. Yet, as Erickson suggested, the observed or measured behavior may be an indicator of the ecology of the classroom rather than an indicator of students' learning or potential to learn. Students with LD are often deft at contriving ways to appear "with it" when in fact they are not. They attempt to mask their disabilities from an unknowing teacher, peers are ready allies in the teacher deception, and oftentimes teachers' behaviors may transmit a mismessage that the student with LD is not "really" expected to "get it." Hence, students with LD are often pulled out of classrooms or specialized teachers are brought into the general classroom to assist the students. The result in either case, within such classroom ecologies, is that students with LD are singled out as deficient.

Attitudes

Teacher behaviors are consistent with their attitudes, and those attitudes are frequently garnered by students. For example, findings reported by Marshall and Weinstein (1986) as they observed classroom interactions and recorded students' perceptions of those interactions indicated that the attitudes teachers thought they were conveying to the students during interactions were not what the students were perceiving. Similar findings were evidenced with the teachers and students in the Vaughn and Schumm study. Although teachers said that they accepted students with LD in their classrooms, students perceived differential teacher treatment toward the students with LD, and that treatment was negative. Erickson provided additional clues regarding teacher attitudes when he discussed the importance of how teachers orient the environment: the instructional and interactional tempo, the classroom layout, who interacts with whom, and how such orientation ultimately sets the classroom environment and the resulting educational ecology.

Vaughn and Schumm aptly suggested that teachers operate from their "orienting premise." Yet when teachers throughout the country have been asked to identify the major difficulties they perceive with the inclusion of students with special needs into general education settings, teachers have identified reasons external to their orienting premise; that is, the lack of effective teacher training and the scarcity of opportunities for collaboration. Certainly, these are essential ingredients. However, the teachers surveyed perceived these as the foundation for successful inclusion of students with special needs into general education classrooms. Teachers who are not provided with needed training and ongoing opportunity for collaboration adopt a business-as-usual attitude and continue teaching to content and remaining within the comfort of what is known (CASE, 1994; California Research Institute, 1989; NASBE, 1992). However, even when they *are* provided with additional quality training by accomplished researchers, teachers often return to their previous methods of teaching (Zigmond, chap. 11, this volume). A clue to the source of this teacher attitude was suggested by Vaughn and Schumm as teachers reported that they were more comfortable in accepting, or at least considering, those teaching techniques and practices that stemmed from their ranks, and of teacher suspicion regarding the strategies suggested by researchers in "ivory towers."

Environment: Academic versus Social

If we understand that learning takes place as an interactive process within a context of community and society, and that the classroom environment sets the foundation for classroom interaction, then the last two perceptions noted in Table 8.1 may be the most important. As Erickson reported, the social structures and the subject matter structures are interdependent: As the social climate changes, the academic task changes. Students attach meaning to their classroom accomplishments or lack of accomplishments and determine what is important in the environment based on that meaning. Consistent with behaviors in other social milieus, risk levels increase or decrease, roles are released or assumed, and students will or will not participate.

A behavior that teachers perceive as an inability to perform an academic task may be a social posture that students have chosen and that can be counter to academic achievement. An excellent illustration of the incongruency between perceptions of academic versus social environment is evident in the experience of one of my previous students whom I shall call Luisa.

Luisa was a third-grade student with LD who, according to standardized testing, had a reading level below first grade. Once a week Luisa and several other of my students participated in a story circle program. That program was a collaboration between general education teachers (usually of kindergarten and first grades) and my students, during which my students were scheduled to go into the classroom and read to the younger students in a relaxed, circle-time environment. On the Friday of each week my students chose their selection for the next week's story circle. Readings included, for example, poetry, fables, and children's classics (e.g., "The Emperor's New Clothes"). Although the students practiced their readings in my room, I never attended the story circle times. Instead, after their return to my class I conferenced with my students regarding their performance, and I also conferenced with the teachers receiving my students as story circle readers regarding the progress of my students' reading.

On one occasion, after several weeks of participating in the story circle program, Luisa requested to schedule her story time with a third-grade class—her peers. On this particular, eventful day, Luisa returned to my resource room class elated. With still-trembling hands and a shaky voice, she shared, "They clapped for me and asked me to read the story again." Her teacher noted, "I didn't know Luisa could read!" We were in the second semester of the school year. Based on my students' comments, the story circles were perceived as social events and were consistent with their sociocultural experiences. However, they perceived reading in their general education classrooms as academic tasks.

Earlier in this chapter I identified the need for a definition of the effective teacher. This issue is critical because of the disparities between teacher perception and student perception of classroom climate. To arrive at a definition of effective teachers, some questions we need to investigate are: What is a successful classroom environment for students with LD? How do the sociocultural experiences of students with LD affect the social climate of the classroom environment? What does the teacher know and do to facilitate learning in that environment?

For the last several years I have been addressing these questions in both the special education and the general education classrooms. I have looked at and compared several learning environments in which students with LD were consistently being unsuccessful in content learning. What I initially found was that these students often were not participating in constructing knowledge, they were not engaged in making meaning of information to which they were exposed, and they were not consistently (if at all) expected to engage in these activities. Some of those students withheld assent to learn, whereas others appeared not know how to learn even when they wanted to. The teachers I observed were caring, dedicated, and "effective" teachers by school standards; yet, they mirrored the perceptions, the learning environments, and the classroom ecologies presented by Erickson and by Vaughn and Schumm.

WHAT STUDENTS KNOW AND TEACHERS NEED TO KNOW

In spite of the present turmoil being experienced in the field of education, I remain an optimist. I am convinced that we are able to glean features of classroom environments that may facilitate the success of students with LD in general education classrooms when that is the setting of choice for the effective learning of the student. The students with LD in the Vaughn and Schumm study demonstrated in their responses that they knew some of those features. For example, they will often choose a special education setting because there they get the assistance that general education does not provide. But what if their "regular" teacher knew how to integrate, for example, the development of reading skills and critical thinking skills for students with LD into their social studies instruction in such a way that the entire class was involved in the same activities and all students were encouraged to construct knowledge based on their abilities and experiences?

Teachers need to acknowledge that classrooms are social communities where the social environment affects academic achievement and where students will seek opportunities to interact, talk, challenge, and share with other students. Teachers can channel that social activity into academic learning by designing opportunities for authentic problem-solving where students with LD can participate along with peers. Clearly, the classroom environment needs to be designed to encourage such participation as teachers plan and implement instruction.

My most resent research focused on incorporating students' sociocultural experiences as they constructed knowledge during their social studies in-

struction. Concepts taught were those covered in the regular fourth-grade curriculum and included such abstract ideas as democracy, freedom, rights, privileges, responsibilities to community, and the function of government. The
students discussed how industries developed, where and why, as well as the
concepts of the need for goods and services. These students, all with LD and
at reading levels from primer to second grade, used their fourth-grade-level
social studies texts. They learned not only to take responsibility for their learning, but also learned how to assist each other construct meaning as they challenged each other's concepts and engaged in research to confirm or modify
their understanding. Results of the study indicated that the students were
learning content as they engaged in classroom activities. Students' test scores
demonstrated significant gains over baseline grades. In the classroom setting
we designed, the students experienced an ecology in which the social and cultural patterns of the classroom resulted in learning resources for everyone.
Another interesting finding was that there was substantially less off-task
activity.

In an inclusive classroom, all students need to be taught how to negotiate
learning. This can be done by adapting grade-level curriculum to meet the
needs of all students in the classroom. Videos, guest lecturers from the students' communities, problem posing and solving, role playing, research, debates, and experiments are not new types of curriculum supplementation and
enrichment. What may be new is how students with LD are taught to and expected to participate. Instruction becomes the result of conscious and pragmatic teacher planning where learning styles and rates of learning are considered and where learners can collaborate with each other. The roles of expert and novice learners are not fixed, and become more fluid or elastic. Students' needs are met and teachers can observe how students are learning as
the students' construction of knowledge is facilitated.

CONCLUSION

Erickson and Vaughn and Schumm offered valuable information regarding
the current dilemma confronting students with LD in many inclusive classrooms. Learning environments are not providing these students with the kind
of interaction conducive to learning and success, and teachers appear reluctant to change those environments. We now need to analyze what students,
teachers, and researchers are saying, and then operationalize that knowledge
into practices that can be field tested by the practitioners: the classroom
teachers.

Teaching as a profession needs to be redefined as we listen to and consider
teachers' responses to the Vaughn and Schumm survey. Action-oriented research could provide the venue for teachers to be researchers as they imple-

ment familiar practices in systematic ways. In such an environment, "The art of teaching is also the art of research" (Wansart, 1995), and teachers have opportunities to evaluate their own behaviors and the impact of those behaviors on students' ability to learn.

It is essential for us to remember that today's teachers were part of a classroom ecology in teacher preparation programs that often did not model the social, interactive environments I am suggesting. If we expect teachers to design the type of classrooms that foster successful inclusion of students, then we must ensure that in higher education we are training them how to do it as we develop reciprocal partnerships of learning and research. Finally, it is my conviction that teacher preparation programs need to model inclusive practices and collaboration between general education and special education faculty as we move toward a new and exciting orientation of teaching and learning.

REFERENCES

Bos, C. S., & Reyes, E. I. (1989, December). *Knowledge, use, and control of an interactive cognitive strategy for learning from content area texts.* Paper presented at the annual meeting of the National Reading Conference, Austin, TX.

California Research Institute (1989). What makes integration work? *Strategies 1*(1), 1–4.

Council of Administrators of Special Education, Inc. (1994). *CASE future agenda for special education: Creating a unified education system.* (Report of the CASE Research Committee.) Bloomington, VA: Author.

Marshall, H. H., & Weinstein, R. S. (1986). Classroom context of student-perceived differential teacher treatment. *Journal of Educational Psychology, 78,* 441–453.

National Association of State Boards of Education (1992). *Winners all: A call for inclusive schools.* (The Report of the NASB Study Group on Special Education). Alexandria, VA: Author.

Reyes, E. I. (1990, April). *The thinking, reading, writing connection: Facilitating the process with learning disabled, bilingual students.* Paper presented at the meeting of the Council for Exceptional Children, Toronto, Canada.

Reyes, E. I. (1994). *Classroom discourse communicative competency of bilingual students with learning disabilities during content learning in three learning environments.* Unpublished doctoral dissertation, University of Arizona, Tucson, AZ.

Wansart, W. L. (1995). Teaching as a way of knowing: Observing and responding to students' abilities. *Remedial and Special Education, 16,* 166–177.

9

Reconfiguring Professional Communities on Behalf of Students With Special Needs

Annemarie Sullivan Palincsar
University of Michigan

> *Believing, with Max Weber, that man is an animal suspended in webs of significance he himself has spun, I take culture to be those webs, and the analysis of it to be therefore not an experimental science in search of law but an interpretive one in search of meaning.*
>
> —Geertz (1973, p. 5)

The interesting metaphor and course of action that Geertz proposed in this brief quote provide an appropriate springboard for the call I wish to issue in responding to the chapters authored by Erickson and by Vaughn and Schumm. My call is for a partnership between special education researchers and teachers, the purpose of which would be to jointly engage in an exploration of the webs in which teachers, students, researchers, and other members of the educational community find themselves as well as create. In the first part of this response I identify some of the observations that inform this call. In the second part, I describe some efforts underway that exemplify how we might go about the process of engaging in these partnerships.

The first observation is prompted by Vaughn and Schumm, who began their chapter with the declaration that the general education classroom is the location of choice for educating students with learning disabilities. This declaration has been echoed by many and has appeared in many guises (mainstreaming, the regular education initiative, the inclusion movement). Although the *Zeitgeist* may favor this declaration, it is clearly an assumption that needs to be, and in fact, has been problematized (Baker & Zigmond, 1990; Fuchs, Fuchs, & Fernstrom, 1993; McIntosh, Vaughn, Schumm, Haager, & Lee, 1993). My intention here is not to try to characterize the debate surrounding this declaration (for a recent entry, see Roberts & Mather, 1995) but rather to suggest that regardless of one's position on this issue, the onus on each and every one of us who profess to care about promoting success in school for students identified as learning disabled is to first understand the contexts (both special education as well as general education) in which students with diverse learning needs are educated.

This leads to my second observation: Schools are cultures, and cultural change is far more complex than is suggested by the simple notion that new curricula or pedagogical techniques—no matter how much more efficacious they may prove to be—can simply be delivered and assimilated into teachers' practices. Sarason (1971) eloquently described the powerful norms that tie a school together. He referred to these norms as "behavioral and procedural regularities." They are the patterned ways of being to which Erickson referred in his chapter. We need to understand these norms, and I would argue that we need to understand them from the participants' perspective.

Hence the third observation, which is clearly demonstrated in the thoughtful program of research that has been conducted by Vaughn and Schumm and their colleagues, in which they characterize teachers' "orienting premises": Change requires an understanding not only of the culture of the classroom and school but also an understanding of what the participants value and understand, and to what they aspire and are committed. In our research, conducted with special educators, we have been struck by the power of these orienting premises. Much of our recent work has been devoted to redesigning the contexts in which young children who are experiencing significant developmental delays learn about reading and writing and about themselves as readers and writers (Klenk & Palincsar, in press; Palincsar & Klenk, 1992). The objective of our work has been to bring developmental and sociocultural perspectives to the literacy curriculum and instruction of primary-grade students in self-contained special education settings for children identified as learning disabled. From these perspectives, children are given multiple occasions to bring to bear whatever forms of writing are currently in their repertoires (e.g., pictures, rebuses, invented spellings, sight words) for the purpose of using writing to communicate. Furthermore, the role of the teacher in this instruction is to assist performance (Tharp & Gallimore, 1989), supporting the children's efforts and guiding them to more refined uses of writing.

We began this program of research by simply observing the nature of literacy instruction in special education settings, and were struck by how seldom the students were given opportunities to use written language in purposeful ways; instead, the emphasis was on manipulating written language as a code (e.g., copying and tracing). Conversations with the teachers were very helpful to understanding this practice: The teachers articulated their beliefs that children must first master the tools of writing and understand its conventions before they can use writing in more meaningful ways. Multiple and sustained conversations with the participating teachers were necessary before we were able to introduce changes that were anything more than simple and ineffective add-ons to their programs of instruction.

My fourth observation reflects the social constructivist perspective eloquently characterized in the chapter by Au and Carroll. Just as we must attend to children's construction of knowledge in socially supported ways, so also must we attend to teachers' construction of knowledge in socially supported ways. Bolstering this observation is the fact that the kinds of interventions that represent the unique contributions that the special education research community might offer to educators are not superficial in nature. For example, drawing on a 10-year program of research on the use of reciprocal teaching as a means of enhancing children's ability to learn from text, we found that, despite the fact that reciprocal teaching is, in essence, a metascript, providing very specific guidance to the teacher vis à vis the teaching of four specific strategies in the context of discussions about shared text, there was significant variability with regard to the amount of support that teachers required to become proficient in the use of this metascript (Palincsar, Stevens, & Gavelek, 1989). For example, teachers for whom this dialogic form of instruction represented a dramatic departure from their traditional instructional practice were initially inclined to subordinate the activity of making sense of text to the activity of teaching the strategies as an end in itself.

The challenge of reciprocal teaching rests not in the teaching or modeling of strategies but in the scaffolding of students' efforts to make sense of text, using the instructed strategies as tools to attain this goal. There are enormous complexities involved in scaffolding children's understandings; some of the most successful means that we determined for enhancing the ability to scaffold included sharing transcripts of teachers engaged in reciprocal teaching using identical text, coteaching in the context of reciprocal teaching dialogues, viewing and analyzing videotape of reciprocal teaching lessons; in other words, using socially supportive means.

My fifth observation is that teachers possess a wealth of knowledge to bring to the partnership proposed, but too few occasions to call it forth. Borrowing from the scheme proposed by Grossman and Shulman (Grossman, 1990), teachers have *subject-matter knowledge;* that is, substantive as well as syntactic disciplinary knowledge. Teachers also demonstrate *general pedagogical knowledge;* that is, knowledge of pedagogical principles and techniques that exceeds the bounds of specific subject matter. Finally, teachers demonstrate *craft knowledge,* or intelligent and sensible know-how in the activity of teaching. The knowledge of teachers and knowledge about teaching are not issues that have received much inquiry on the part of special education researchers (Malouf & Schiller, 1995). Yet, an awareness and appreciation for these various types of teacher knowledge may provide successful points of entrée in conducting research with teachers on accommodating the needs of diverse learners.

Based on these observations, my proposal is that we join other educational researchers in constituting reconfigured professional communities that involve teachers in the processes of systematically inquiring and reflecting on their own practice. What purposes might guide the interactions of such communities? First, to provide forums in which teachers (general education and special education) and researchers can make public their conceptual frameworks or orienting premises. Second, to provide a context in which the conditions that are necessary to productive school change can germinate. For example, Elmore (1991), among others, cautioned that without consensus among the members of the school community regarding school goals, change efforts will be frustrated. Furthermore, these communities would provide a means of identifying and building on the resources and talents of all the members of school communities. There is yet another critical role that such communities might play—actively resisting prescriptive shortcuts, refusing to be engulfed by new trends and fads before critically evaluating evidence that these changes ought to be pursued.

In the next portion of this response, I identify several efforts to establish the kinds of communities to which I refer. The first project was undertaken by the Institute for Education in Transformation at the Claremont Graduate School and was codirected by Mary Poplin and Joseph Weeres. The description that follows was taken from a report on this project entitled Voices from the Inside.[1] The purpose of their work was to identify "the perceptions, complaints, satisfactions, fears and hopes of students, teachers, parents, administrators, and staff inside four schools" (p. 6). All of the participants in this endeavor were regarded as both researchers and subjects of their own research. Using research methodologies that included participatory research, teacher research, action research, phenomenological research, and narrative analysis, the team set about to identify the problems in these four schools.

Perhaps one of the most interesting of their outcomes was the suggestion that what have historically been identified as problems in these educational settings (e.g., lowered achievement, high dropout rates, and problems within the teaching profession) were, in fact, the consequences of deeper, more fundamental problems. These fundamental problems included poor interrelationships in school settings, experiences of racism and cultural alienation,

---

[1]A copy of this report can be obtained at a cost of $5 each from: The Institute for Education in Transformation at the Claremont Graduate School, 121 East Tenth Street, Claremont, CA 91711–6160.

curricula and teaching methods that were unengaging, failure to find physical and psychological safety in the contexts of schools, and a sense of despair regarding the possibility for change.

In addition to the consensus that emerged during the course of this research, there were two other outcomes that the authors reported. The first is that, springing from these conversations, there was a sense of hope that was nurtured by the awareness that there were many common values on which to build more ideal schools. In addition, although change was not the purpose of this phase of the research, changes did indeed begin to emerge out of the conversations.

A second, quite different model is the teacher–researcher study group constituted by C. S. Englert and her colleagues (Englert & Tarrant, in press). In their work, special education teachers shared a primary role with educational researchers in the development of innovative literacy practices. In the context of study groups, where attention was paid to teachers' conceptual understandings, beliefs, concerns, attitudes, and self-efficacy, university and school participants coconstructed innovations. The group shared readings and viewings of videotape of exemplary literacy instruction, discussed which features of the instruction might be introduced in their respective classrooms (given their instructional goals), tried these ideas out, and returned to the group to collaboratively address the problems they experienced in implementation. Through this process, teachers gradually introduced significant curricular and instructional changes in their classes with concomitant gains reflected in the students' literacy learning.

Clearly the time is ripe for the formation of new, inclusive educational communities. Since PL 94-142, the translation of special education research into practice has historically been the art of implementing new ideas and technologies into the "second system" of education already in place in the school, without having to disturb the general culture of the school.[2] There was relative unanimity of beliefs regarding the "separate to varying degrees" service delivery model for special needs children in the mid-1970s. In addition, until recently this model was supported by legislation and strong parent advocacy groups; hence change efforts in special education were accepted into the schools with relative ease.

Because these change efforts could be characterized as mostly affecting the instructional technologies of the teaching–learning situation in special education classes, they required changes in ideas and materials but not basic beliefs concerning special needs learners. Even within this relatively hospitable climate, the successful implementation of special education research into practice was uncommon. As Batemen (1992) remarked, "The real world

---

[2]The author gratefully acknowledges her colleague, Jean McPhail, for conversations regarding the role of special education in contemporary education that influenced the writing of this section.

of public school I.E.P.'s, teachers, students, and their parents seem frankly untouched by the academic world of educational interventions" (p. 35). However, the radical shift from special education as a second system of education to its inclusion in the cultural world of general education has created a new milieu in which special education efforts must be conducted. Changes in special education service delivery models have disrupted the everyday cultural life of the school, and will continue to do so. Special educators interested in implementing effective change in schools, interested in contributing to the call for "political assent to learning" (in the words of Erickson), must come to understand, appreciate, and effectively interact in the cultural life of the school.

REFERENCES

Baker, J., & Zigmond, N. (1990). Are regular education classes equipped to accommodate students with learning disabilities? *Exceptional Children, 54,* 515–526.

Bateman, B. (1992). Learning disabilities: The changing landscape. *Journal of Learning Disabilities, 25,* 29–36.

Elmore, R. F. (1991, April). *Teaching, learning, and organization: School restructuring and the recurring dilemmas of reform.* Paper presented at the annual meeting of the American Educational Research Association, Chicago, IL.

Englert, C. S., & Tarrant, K. (in press). Creating collaborative cultures for educational change. *Remedial and Special Education.*

Fuchs, D., Fuchs, L., & Fernstrom, P. (1993). A conservative approach to special education reform: Mainstreaming through transenvironmental programming and curriculum-based measurement. *American Educational Research Journal, 30,* 149–177.

Geertz, C. (1973). *The interpretation of cultures: Selected essays.* New York: Basic Books.

Grossman, P. (1990). *The making of a teacher.* New York: Teachers College Press.

Klenk, L., & Palincsar, A. S. (in press). Enacting responsible pedagogy with students in special education. In M. Pugach & C. Warger (Eds.), *What's worth knowing: How curriculum trends will affect special education.* New York: Teachers College Press.

Malouf, D. B., & Schiller, E. P. (1995). Practice and research in special education. *Exceptional Children, 61*(5), 414–424.

McIntosh, R., Vaughn, S., Schumm, J. S., Haager, D., & Lee, O. (1993). Observations of students with learning disabilities in general education classrooms. *Exceptional Children, 60*(3), 249–261.

Palincsar, A. S., & Klenk, L. (1992). Fostering literacy learning in supportive contexts. *Journal of Learning Disabilities, 25*(4) 211–225, 229.

Palincsar, A. S., Stevens, D. D., & Gavelek, J. (1989). Collaborating with teachers in the interest of student collaboration. *International Journal of Educational Research, 13,* 41–53.

Poplin, M., & Weeres, J. (1992). *Voices from the inside.* Claremont, CA: The Institute for Education in Transformation.

Roberts, R., & Mather, N. (1995). The return of students with learning disabilities to regular classrooms: A sellout? *Learning Disabilities Research and Practice, 10*(1), 46–58.

Sarason, S. (1971). *The culture of the school and the problem of change* (2nd ed.). Boston: Allyn & Bacon.

Tharp, R., & Gallimore, R. (1989). *Rousing minds to life: Teaching, learning, and schooling in social context.* Cambridge, England: Cambridge University Press.

PART III

Classroom Management

10

Designing Classrooms for Inclusion: Beyond Management

David H. Cooper
Linda R. Valli
University of Maryland at College Park

Management, a fancy educational term for what often feels like glorified group baby-sitting.
— *The Washington Post* (December 10, 1994, p. A1)

This chapter's purpose is to revisit and build upon Doyle's (1986) comprehensive review of research on classroom management. We begin with an acknowledgment that defining the term *management* is likely to reveal the writer's theoretical perspective rather than explicating any consensus in the field. As the *Washington Post* story (quoted at the start of the chapter) indicates, management of classrooms has gained a negative connotation among both professional educators and the public. We would argue that negativity is to be expected given the prevailing behaviorist approaches to management, which were and continue to be essentially corrective approaches. These corrective approaches reflect an assumption that the disengaged learners' intrinsic motivation is inadequate. The management strategy that follows from this assumption is a teacher-directed system of contingencies installed in the classroom environment. In this chapter we describe a change in the field that is marked by a constructive rather than a corrective approach. Our view of classroom design focuses on the interaction of learners and the learning environment, and, specifically, the active involvement of learners in the construction and interpretation of the cognitive and social aspects of that environment; in other words, a social constructivist approach. From this perspective, we argue that order can be a consequence rather than a condition of an engaging learning environment.

Our intent is not simply to update Doyle's work, but rather to elaborate on it in terms of: (a) recent trends in theoretical perspectives, specifically the shift from behaviorist to social constructivist views of teaching; (b) current national efforts in the area of school reform, specifically as these relate to adoption of high standards in content areas for a diverse student population; and (c) the design of classrooms that are welcoming and supportive of inclusion of children with learning disabilities.

RECAPPING THE HISTORY OF RESEARCH ON MANAGEMENT OF INSTRUCTIONAL ENVIRONMENTS

Before Constructivism: Order Versus Learning

Brophy and Putnam (1979) astutely decried the absence of a strong theory of classroom management. The prevailing behaviorist theory had indeed made significant contributions to the understanding of the conditions of learning. However, the nature of the learning accounted for by behaviorist theory is limited to discrete, declarative knowledge, learned by rote methods, and packaged in measurable fragments. Although the behaviorist approach had demonstrated its usefulness in the control of student behavior, Brophy and Putnam nevertheless expressed a dissatisfaction with teachers taking a reactive stance, using behaviorist techniques to manage merely for the sake of order. The theory they sought, but did not find, was one that would explain the interplay among teachers, students, and learning in classrooms. The goal was to proactively achieve prevention of disarray, and several studies were cited in support of careful planning, preparation, and routine as preventive factors. Of particular interest for this history of management research is the preview Brophy and Putnam provided of the coming of the cognitive era. If preventive classroom management was to be successful, they argued, then students would need to internalize the values and skills necessary for independent learning; thus there was a need for "cognitive structures" to be built. (The advantages and challenges in this approach for inclusion of students with learning disabilities is addressed in a later section.)

The situation seems to have changed little by the time Doyle set about reviewing the literature in 1986. Classroom rules were still very much the dominant theme in management. One could argue that this period of rule promulgation was a necessary yet reactive stage in the evolution of classroom discipline from behaviorism to cognitive (self) control of student behavior. Rule-governed classes were still not focused on the nature of learning, but at least included some attention to the importance of explicit teaching of rules. The teacher continued to be viewed as the transmitter of social knowledge. One additional problem with rules seems to lie more in their targeted behaviors than in the notion of rules per se. In Doyle's (1986) view:

> Classroom rules are usually intended to regulate forms of individual conduct that are likely to disrupt activities, cause injury, or damage school property. Thus, there are rules concerning tardiness, gum chewing, fighting, bringing materials to class, and the like. (p. 410)

> Some student actions, for example, tardiness or wearing hats to class, fall fairly clearly into the category of misbehavior and require teacher intervention. (p. 419)

Gum chewing and hat wearing hardly seem to be the targets that Brophy and Putnam had in mind when they advocated prevention over behaviorist reactivity. Even the admonition to "teach the rule-governed routine explicitly" (Emmer, Evertson, & Anderson, 1980) leaves the teacher reliant on an authoritarian (i.e., rule maker/enforcer) as opposed to an authoritative (i.e., knowledgeable facilitator) style of management, which is not the most effective approach to building cognitive structure. The role of the rule maker would always be to try to anticipate numerous and varied instances of misbehavior and to devise enough rules to cover all possibilities. This implies a behaviorist analysis or fragmentation of behavior. The knowledgeable facilitator role, in contrast, plans a more open-ended approach that permits social participation structures to be built ("socially constructed") by the participants themselves.

Doyle once again deserves credit for having recognized the inadequacy of classroom control in the absence of content and social learning. He called attention to the devil's bargain that teachers and students strike: Students agree to "behave" as long as there is no expectation that they do serious cognitive work. In these cases, behaviorist approaches to management may actually impede rather than foster learning.

In contrast to teaching rules designed to prevent disruption, some work in the area of early acquisition of literacy was pointing in the direction of learning itself as a management strategy. Snow (1993), in her studies of adults reading to children, and Au (1980), in her studies of alternative formats for reading instruction, showed the effect that learning in a culturally authentic "ritualized context" could have, namely that attention could be redeployed in the service of learning of complex academic content instead of rules.

Doyle (1986) pointed out one important source of variability in the management of classrooms that may be relevant to the inclusion of students with learning disabilities. He noted that *learning* is a psychological process whose unit of study is the individual, a perspective more likely in special then in general education. On the other hand, *order* is a process that looks to the group as its unit of study. The holy Grail of classroom management, *engagement,* is a result of interest in group as opposed to individual behavior management. But the limitations of engagement as a construct are nevertheless the same: Engagement is not learning, only a prerequisite. The fact that teachers in general education classrooms define activities rather than learning as central to their instructional planning (Vaughn & Schumm, chap. 7, this volume; Zigmond, chap. 11, this volume) may well be a reflection of this perspective, which may be inexplicable to teachers who focus on the individual learning outcomes of students with learning disabilities. The irony is that although they need not be as concerned with order, special educators have nevertheless still adopted a very behaviorist approach.

Doyle's review ended on a social constructivist chord. He stressed that the teacher's understanding of the dynamic nature of classroom order and its dependence on planned organization is the "key to success" (1986, p. 423). He referred to the classroom's "program of action," and concluded that it is "jointly constructed" by teachers and students. This view is markedly different from the behaviorist view of management by contingent response, which starts from an assumption that the natural contingencies in the learning environment are generally adequate, needing to be supplemented only for the disengaged learner. By identifying the differences in approaches, Doyle's review marked the advance of theory in the years since Brophy and Putnam (1979) and clearly pointed to the need for closer examination of the active role of the learner in the learner–environment interaction.

Behavior in the Postbehaviorist Years

What follows is an illustrative summary of two studies that have examined student behavior within the new paradigm, the constructivist view of classrooms. In this paradigm, instruction, teachers, and students are organized around learning objectives and a social context rather than activities designed primarily to maintain order (i.e., "busywork").

Day and Libertini (1992) examined the cognitive effects of child-directed reading and mathematics lessons on primary-grade children. Three lesson structures were used. The first was traditional, behaviorally oriented, teacher-directed, and didactic. Time for learning and type of learning was strictly controlled. The second was child-directed and constructivist. Children freely elected when, where, how, and for how long they would engage in the reading and mathematics lessons. A third group received a mixed type of lesson structure, including teacher demonstrations followed by small-group independent learning.

Child responses coded by Day and Libertini were arrayed on a scale ranging from intellectually complex to simple, on-task behavior. Cognitive, linguistic, and social domains were tapped. Higher-order cognitive and language responses were observed more in the child-directed group than in the other groups. The child-directed group also produced more lesson-related speech. The children in the didactic group were coded as exhibiting more on-task behaviors than did the groups that were less didactically managed. Unfortunately, there was no statistical treatment of the data, and all results were given as overall percentages, without mention of individual differences within groups and lesson types. We can conclude little that is certain from this one study, but the results indicate that further analyses of cognitive performance beyond behaviorist engagement are likely to produce distinctively different outcomes, and may provide further evidence of the advantages of a constructivist approach in facilitating learning.

But did not Doyle (1986) warn that higher-order thinking can throw a class into management disorder? This underscores the importance of a study by Hiebert and Wearne (1993) in which the trade-off for order at the expense of cognitive understanding was evaluated. Hiebert and Wearne observed second-grade classes, equivalent as determined by a pretest of math facts and skills. Classes were divided into those characterized as "high/average" versus "low/average." One class at each level received alternative math instruction; the others followed the textbook. Alternative methods included materials use, problem-solving activity focus, group discussion, and use of story contexts for math algorithms. Alternatively managed classes did fewer problems, spent more time on each problem, used more manipulative or figural representations of tasks, used more stories, and spoke more words relative to the teacher (both overall and per response). They were asked relatively fewer recall questions. Although it is not immediately clear from the data whether order was actually traded for understanding, it is very clear that student talk was dramatically increased in the low/average classes taught using the alternative methods.

The instructional differences appeared to be associated with outcome scores on the specially designed posttest. Specifically, the low/average ability group that was instructed in a alternative design made gains relative to other low/average groups and made achievement gains that resulted in their looking more like a high/average group. Likewise, the high/average ability group that received the alternative treatment surpassed the traditionally managed control group. Unfortunately, subjects were not randomly assigned, the Hawthorne effect cannot be ruled out, statistical treatment of the data was missing, and no validity evidence for the test was reported.

On posttesting, the thinking processes in low/average students in the control (traditional) groups were described in ways suggesting success in behaviorist terms as "procedural and, perhaps, rather mechanical" (Hiebert & Wearne, 1993, p. 421). Emphasis was on execution. On the other hand, the groups whose instruction was more discursive yet less busy, regardless of their initial level of ability, was "reflective and analytic" (Hiebert & Wearne, 1993,

p. 421). Understanding was "deep" (see later discussion) as demonstrated by these students' success in modifying previously learned strategies for attacking novel computational problems. This is why, the authors speculated, that doing more seatwork problems may not have been the most efficient route to learning, despite its semblance of order. Together, tasks and *discourse* influence students' perception and construction of knowledge. How school climate can promote such discourse is the subject of the next section.

MANAGEMENT IN THE CONTEXT
OF SCHOOL REFORM

The conceptual bases of several school reform initiatives implicitly support this paradigm shift from a behaviorist to a social constructivist approach to classroom management. Reforms such as developing national standards, teaching for understanding, designing authentic assessments, attending to student diversity, and multi-age grouping challenge dominant instructional practices. The sections that follow indicate how each of these reforms support the paradigm shift from behavior to constructivist management approaches.

These reforms are designed to create classroom conditions in which students are motivated to learn how to learn and help each other learn to learn. The intent is to create learning environments that tap into student needs and interests, help students analyze their life situations and experiences, support the development of independent and self-regulatory cognitive structures, and provide for differences in style and pace of learning (Bredekamp, 1987; National Council of Teachers of Mathematics, 1991). Initial research suggests that such learning environments enhance teachers' sense of efficacy and increase student achievement (Rosenholtz, 1989).

Teaching for Understanding

School reform efforts aimed toward teaching for understanding come from a number of disparate sources. They find their roots in: theories of developmentally appropriate practice, general dissatisfaction with the process and products of the American educational system (especially in international comparisons), the ascendancy of constructivist over behaviorist theories of learning, concern about America's declining role in a global economy, and the belief that the shift from the industrial age to the information age requires drastic changes in what and how students learn.

The name most often connected with teaching for understanding is Howard Gardner, director of Project Zero at Harvard University. Gardner (1991) has often contrasted "what passes for understanding" with that which is deep and genuine. By this he meant that understanding requires "a sufficient grasp of concepts, principles, or skills so that one can bring them to bear on new problems and situations, deciding in which ways one's present competencies can suffice and in which ways one may require new skills or knowledge" (1991, p. 18).

In Jerome Bruner's words, understanding goes "beyond the information given" (cited in Perkins, 1992, p. 75). It implies generative rather than static knowledge, enablement rather than possession. Rather than giving "a central place to the transmission of factual and procedural knowledge from one person to another, through an essentially *imitative* process" (Jackson, 1986, p. 117), teaching for understanding involves students in "looking for patterns in ideas, finding personal examples, and relating new ideas to prior knowledge" (Perkins, 1992, p. 5).

The problem is that teaching for understanding seldom occurs in American schools, and classrooms are not organized to promote deep understanding. What, then, are the implications of this reform movement for classroom organization and management? Teachers must first start with the premise that "what students learn has to do fundamentally with how they learn it" (McLaughlin & Talbert, 1993, p. 1). This requires a radical transformation in the culture and social organization of most classrooms, which are presently designed for a knowledge transmission mode of instruction in which teachers are authoritative repositories of knowledge who pass on their wisdom to passive and compliant students. As seen in a series of classroom studies, when teaching for understanding is the goal, classroom activities, routines, roles, and relationships all change (Cohen, McLaughlin, & Talbert, 1993). For example, in traditional classrooms, students work alone about 60% of the time, often spend two thirds of their time listening to the teacher talk, and reproduce textbook information in response to 90% of teacher questions directed to them (Tisher, 1987). In classrooms designed for understanding, *activities* no longer follow this rote-learning model where teachers initiate, students respond, and teachers evaluate (IRE). Participation and discourse structures shift dramatically. Students initiate and evaluate as well as respond. They are seldom engaged in individual and silent seatwork (Cohen, McLaughlin, & Talbert, 1993).

This implies a significant role change for both teachers and students. Roles become blurred. Authority is no longer vested solely in the adult. Instead, it is "diffused from teachers and texts to anyone who makes persuasive arguments" as students learn to both "respect others' views" and to "subject those views to the intellectual discipline of historical or mathematical thought" (Cohen & Barnes, 1993, pp. 234–44). *Routines* must then accommodate this less predictable classroom life. Rules and routines that promote deep understanding deemphasize silence, order, and turn taking. Purposeful noise, movement, and groupwork take their place.

One teacher who consciously changed her approach to teaching described her new role this way:

> I have learned that children already come with a lot of knowledge, and that they can teach one another. I didn't feel that way before. I felt that I had to be the teacher, whatever that meant. But anyway, I am thinking more about what it means to teach. A lot of the teaching in the classroom goes on between children, and the teacher acts kind of like a facilitator, picking up on the comments that children make that are purposeful for discussion. . . . (quoted in Ball & Rundquist, 1993, p. 28)

Others talk about involving students in classroom decisions, watching students and listening to backtalk, asking questions like "What do you think?" and wondering when to be more directive if discussions become muddled. They struggle with their own passive images of learning, adjust levels of structure and control in their teaching, and begin to trust that students can progress on their own (Russell & Munby, 1991). These teachers spend less time formally planning lessons, and more time providing materials, identifying student interests, and "searching for ways to 'get at the content that is within the kids'" (Ball & Rundquist, 1993, p. 32).

Classrooms organized for the purpose of maintaining order, maximizing ontask behavior, and transmitting knowledge are not well designed to facilitate individual learning and deep understanding. Radical transformations in classroom management occur when teaching shifts from a behaviorist to a cognitive orientation. These changes involve all aspects of the social system: activities, routines, roles, and relationships. Studies cited earlier in this chapter drew parallel conclusions. Didactic groups produced more ontask behavior, whereas child-directed groups produced more higher-order cognition (Day & Libertini, 1992). Similarly, traditional whole-group, textbook-based mathematics instruction resulted in more problems answered, whereas small-group, inquiry-based instruction produced higher achievement (Hiebert & Wearne, 1993).

But teaching for understanding is often accompanied by high levels of ambiguity and complexity. Tasks are not broken down into small, structured components. Students are encouraged to discover multiple ways of solving problems or answering questions. When trusting relations, sound pedagogy, and support systems are not in place, students lose interest or patience, become confused and frustrated, and negotiate with teachers to reduce standards and to make product specifications more explicit. Classroom order and learning can easily become threatened (Doyle, 1992). It is possible that the press for higher levels of achievement by setting high academic content standards will increase this threat even more. For students with learning disabilities, the benefits of inclusion in such classrooms will not be worth the cost. Substantial efforts to study the differentiated effects of such reformed classrooms will be needed before the inclusion and reform movements can proceed in harmony.

Designing Classrooms to Meet National Standards

The drive to develop national standards is based on the premise that "American education is in trouble because standards in our schools are too low—children aren't challenged to work hard and fulfill their potential . . . " (U.S. Department of Education, 1994). Like the teaching-for-understanding movement, reform efforts to create national standards in core school subject areas can have radical implications for the design of traditional classrooms. The reason is that many of these standards require students to develop skills and habits of sustained and rigorous inquiry. Standards in the areas of science and mathematics, for example, emphasize learning from experience, risk taking, exploring challenging concepts, developing sound problem-solving strategies, evaluating arguments, experimenting with alternative approaches, thinking critically and logically about the relationships between evidence and explanation, and using appropriate tools and technologies to analyze data (National Council of Teachers of Mathematics, 1989, 1991; National Research Council's National Committee on Science Education Standards and Assessments, 1994). Standards currently being developed in the areas of English language arts and the various social sciences follow this same pattern of inquiry.

These constructivist learning processes stand in stark contrast to those associated with the traditional behavioral objectives: recalling, completing, knowing, listing, memorizing, summarizing, and reciting. While behavioral objectives promote classrooms designed for teachers to transmit information, monitor ontask behavior, and evaluate student work products, constructivist objectives encourage classrooms designed for teachers to facilitate learning and evaluate student thought processes. To accomplish these constructivist objectives, those who promote national standards recommend breaking out of the time and space constraints of traditionally organized classrooms. They recommend assigning group problems that would require a long block of time, perhaps several days, to complete, and having students design learning activities for other classes.

As with teaching for understanding, the national standards place pressure on classroom teachers to change role expectations, classroom routines, and support structures. Lost time and classroom chaos can result unless students are prepared for and supported in high-risk-taking activities. To avoid such disasters, the science standards from the National Research Council's National Committee on Science Education Standards and Assessments (1994) emphasize the importance of teachers developing learning communities. They call for giving students a voice in content and context discussions, nurturing collaboration, requiring students to take responsibility for their learning (singly and collectively), and promoting a respect for others' ideas.

Although the creation of inquiry-oriented learning communities is not easy, anecdotal evidence by those engaged in teaching for understanding suggests it is possible. Teachers and researchers involved in such efforts write, for example, that "[students] learned to listen politely and attentively to other students, and it was rare to hear anyone snicker at anyone else's idea. Only eight years old, they participated effectively in a half-hour (or more) discussion every day" (Ball & Rundquist, 1993, p. 30).

Unfortunately, we do not yet know a great deal about how these learning communities are developed and sustained. Nor do we know how students with learning disabilities will fare in such environments. The teachers and researchers involved in the classroom studies reported in Cohen, McLaughlin, and Talbert (1993) did indeed give students voice, foster collaborative learning, and promote respect. But specifically how they did these and under what conditions they were successful remain murky. Some general factors do, however, surface across this body of literature that can guide future research efforts. Those factors are: teacher training and mentoring, time and practice, institutional support, and structuring for student success.

As Tharp and Gallimore (1989) reminded us, "Teachers have not been trained to do anything but the traditional recitation script" (p. 5). Even when aspects of their professional preparation focus on promoting inquiry and higher-order thinking, that intervention is often too weak to disrupt more traditional and more ingrained notions of teaching (Zeichner & Gore, 1990). Creating inquiry-oriented learning communities will require long-term staff development and mentoring programs that include examination of personal theories, beliefs, and practices; intensive coaching and constructive feedback; and regular opportunities to learn from and with colleagues. This, of course, implies a change in school culture and a commitment to transform the regularities of schooling on an institutional scale. Anything less threatens the likelihood of success. As Fullan (1995) concluded from his review of the educational change research, when staff development and school cultures collide, school culture inevitably wins. Prospects of bringing about change in student behavior are also diminished without institutional commitment. Without a consistent transformation of their schooling experience, students have difficulty developing inquiry-oriented skills and habits of mind. They are often unwilling to put forth the effort necessary to be the active learners such communities demand (Haberman, 1991).

To help students acquire these skills and habits of mind, the literature further suggests the necessity of methodically teaching students how to successfully participate in these redesigned classroom environments. An analysis of Brown's (1994) Community of Learners (COL) project, for instance, reveals highly structured activities such as reciprocal teaching and cooperative "jigsaw" whose participation structures students must learn in order to successfully engage in the project. Both teachers and students need explicit and intensive training to participate in these types of communities of learning. Otherwise we can surmise that little learning and much disorder could result. Achieving high national standards through the creation of such classroom environments would be then an unobtainable goal, and students at risk for failure due to learning disabilities would not be well served by inclusion.

Using Authentic Learning and Assessment

Another aspect of school reform that moves the concept of classroom management away from behavior control is the use of authentic learning and assessment. The call for authentic—or performance—assessment runs throughout the national standards as well as state and school system standards that are based on them. Under this umbrella term are a variety of approaches that engage students in tasks and activities that closely resemble life out of school. Included in this approach may be field-based experiences in disciplinary projects, such as environmental studies, or involvement in civic activity and advocacy. Just as the activities and tasks themselves are authentic, so must be the assessment strategies that are used to determine students' understanding of the concepts and principles embedded in the experiences. One recalls the history of literacy education in postrevolutionary Cuba. Universal literacy was the national goal, and the assessment of each Cuban's attainment was writing a "Letter to Fidel" (Kozol, 1978).

A recent study by Weade (1992) illustrates the power that is possible when authentic learning, authentic assessment, and subject matter integration are combined. Weade asked, "What counts as learning?" In the process of answering this question, she sought to debunk the myth of the "teachable moment" by adopting a constructivist rather than a behaviorist view of the elongated processes of learning, from teachers' planning through authentic assessment of students' deep understanding. Weade stressed the need to examine layers of context, as well as the events before and after the lesson, in order to fully apprehend the learning event. The teachers in Weade's exemplary case study began by announcing nontraditional quarterly math and science themes (e.g., "Acacadabra . . . the magic of math and science, problem solving, and scientific process"), which broke away from the traditional subject matter boundaries. Step two in planning was motivation, which translated into devising tasks and activities that were authentic and salient (i.e., hands-on, exciting, involving props and costumes). It is essential for this discussion to note that lesson plans and specific objectives were near the bottom of the list of the planning sequence. One math and one science teacher working in a combined fourth- and fifth-grade program were engaged in "the prospective creation of occasions for learning" (p. 111).

This approach may appear too loosely structured, particularly for special educators who carefully control learning objectives and data-based documentation of progress. However, assessment of outcomes was designed into the units, although it differed in format from the usual paper-and-pencil tests. Students demonstrated their knowledge of the math and science content by means of authentic exhibitions. For example, after designing and constructing a space colony, students led guided tours of the structure for peers and adults. Their docent-like presentations were used as indicators of their grasp of the concepts and principles that entered into the design of the colony. Validation of this approach to measurement should be the subject of future studies.

Research on developmentally appropriate practice as well as teaching for understanding suggests the importance of authentic, situated learning. In real contexts, learning is supported by apprenticelike relations, social networks, and progress made on real tasks with real consequences (Perkins, 1992). Learning in classrooms is facilitated by mirroring these real contexts as much as possible (Brown, 1994).

Authentic assessment practices are classroom based, involve evaluation standards that are individual as well as criterion or norm-referenced, inform teaching practice formatively, and sample a variety of intellectual operations and knowledge forms associated with student use of information. Assessments emphasize risk taking, question posing, problem solving, and reasoned judgment. As in teaching for understanding, the use of authentic assessment has significant implications for classroom management including significant student movement, construction, purposeful noise, and extended, purposeful interactions among students of diverse abilities.

We see great potential benefits for students with learning disabilities from inclusion in classrooms where learning and assessment are authentic. When learning proceeds from student interest without the interference of decontextualized written work, the LD student's linguistic deficits will not pose such impermeable barriers. There is more flexibility in how knowledge is exhibited; content competency is not confounded by literacy and numeracy. The emphasis on primary sources of knowledge, rather than textbooks once-removed from the "data," should assist LD students whose linguistic processing skills function best when information is contextualized, concrete, familiar, salient, and interesting.

Attending to Student Diversity

One reform movement that promotes a social constructivist approach to classroom organization focuses on the academic success of a group of at-risk students: poor children of color. These reformers argue that students who are most at risk of school failure often have schooling experiences that put them further at risk. This reform position is supported by research indicating that both the instructional and social aspects of schooling play important roles in student learning (Shulman, 1986) and that both aspects create problems for at-risk learners. Although reasons for academic problems are numerous and differ by types of students, this research suggests the importance of negotiating meaning and establishing classroom norms in keeping with students' knowledge and backgrounds (Erickson, 1987; Irvine, 1990; Zeichner, 1993). Ethnographic studies of classroom life offer concrete images of what social and learning expectations based on student culture and cognition looks like.

Dillon (1989) provided such a study of a lower-level reading classroom based on constructivist principles. The teacher, Mr. Appleby, used students' language and cultural background as a basis for instruction and jointly constructed the social organization of the classroom with them. He allowed his students "to use their natural language during lesson interactions" and sometimes transformed his own language "to that of his students" (p. 244). He encouraged them to freely call out answers and to "interact with each other and with him, in the way they spoke to peers and adults in their family/community," whom he had visited. Appleby accepted sarcasm, interruptions, and overlapping speech, which he interpreted as engagement in learning rather than disrespect for each other or traditional classroom norms. Although no academic achievement data was given, Dillon (1989) claimed that "this practice promoted active participation and allowed students to focus on learning the content" (p. 245).

Heath (1982) arrived at a similar conclusion in her ethnographic study of children from a poor African American community she calls Trackton. Wondering why these seemingly bright and articulate children failed to respond to simple instructional questions, Heath compared classroom questioning patterns to those in the children's family and neighborhood environment. Seeing important differences, the teachers Heath worked with incorporated materials from the children's community and Trackton kinds of questions in their instruction. The teachers "openly discussed different types of questions with students, and the class talked about the kinds of answers called for by certain questions" (p. 125). This helped the Trackton children understand that even though classroom questions were strange, they did not threaten their own culture. Responding to them was necessary for school success.

These practices are in keeping with Irvine's (1990) synthesis of research on effective strategies with African American children and with Au's (1980) now-classic study of participation structures in a reading lesson with Hawaiian children. Both encouraged less formality in the social organization of the classroom to maximize oral participation. Irvine recommended greater congruence or scaffolding between the classroom culture and the culture of the home. Au promoted the creation of a hybrid setting that blends elements of both home and school culture, is comfortable for students and teacher, and produces academic achievement.

This theme of culturally congruent or responsive teaching resonates across numerous classroom studies (Erickson, 1987; Ladson-Billings, 1994). Cultural responsiveness often seems to open up necessary space for students to feel invited into and be able to participate in the social and academic life of classrooms. As can be seen from these examples, culturally responsive pedagogy takes into account the socially mediated nature of learning. It provides for integrative, meaningful learning—the "creative process of restructuring current understandings"—and the social factors that facilitate new understandings (Stone & Reid, 1994, p. 73).

For children with learning difficulties, Stone and Reid (1994) reminded us, these social factors are particularly important. Although interactive settings can stimulate new ways of thinking, past interactions and understandings influence further discoveries and linkages. Because children reconstruct their views through conversational inferences, classroom discourse must be carefully structured to be relevant, clear, and limited to the information needed. It must provide conversational tension to move students beyond current understandings and into new forms of meaning making.

Teachers, however, must resolve the tension through careful scaffolding for students who cannot assimilate normal classroom instruction. This includes careful and deliberate word choice, question forms, nonverbal gestures, sequenced inferential directives, multiple channels of information, and the use of familiar social and instructional patterns. Traditional recitational forms of instructional practice such as teacher initiation, student response, and teacher evaluation (IRE) violate the notion that learning is dependent on social and cultural factors. Its overly formulaic nature stifles "self-regulated efforts at meaning making" (Stone & Reid, 1994, p. 77).

Classroom organization for poor children of color and for children with learning difficulties must account for individual and cultural differences in knowledge construction by providing well-scaffolded, culturally responsive, and socially mediated instructional activities (Irvine, 1990; Stone & Reid, 1994; Zeichner, 1993). This body of research suggests that the imposition of behavior and learning expectations apart from student culture and cognition is a self-defeating educational approach. The social organization of classroom life as well as specific instructional activities can result in students being either unable or unwilling to successfully participate in learning.

Regrouping Classrooms By Age

One feature of schools that is not unique to recent reform efforts but does represent a form of restructuring is multi-age grouping. Montessorians have long practiced this form of instructional design. It is also an essential element of Brown's (1994) Community of Learners. Because the desired number of adult experts in each classroom is unrealistic, the project is structured to rely on student experts. Cross-age teaching occurs through face-to-face interactions and through electronic mail. Older students are used as discussion leaders who guide reciprocal teaching and jigsaw activities for younger students.

A number of empirical efforts have demonstrated its usefulness. In the earlier-cited study by Weade (1992), the grouping of grades four and five was a key element in the thematically organized, authentic learning and assessment program. In contrast to combination grade classrooms, in which students of more than one grade level are housed together in classes but instructed separately according to grade-level curricula, the teachers in Weade's study fully integrated the students regardless of age, and thereby capitalized on this aspect of diversity. One important advantage was the maintenance of institutional memory, that is, a system in which returning students can be expected to retain concepts and routines from the previous year, and provide the teachers with a basis for beginning instruction. Further, the "veterans" can assist in the induction and mentoring of the "rookies."

A study of leadership among children in mixed-age groups (French, Waas, Stright, & Baker, 1986) provides careful documentation of the potential advantages of this arrangement. Given a problem to solve as a group, children's behaviors were coded as facilitative, domineering, organizing, and so on. In contrast to children in same-age groups, children in multi-age groups were more likely to be organizers and leaders. The style of leadership was not merely dominance; rather, it was characterized as facilitating participation by younger children. The study's findings have implications for all children, but especially for children who for reasons of disability could benefit from being on both the giving and receiving ends of facilitative social interaction, and thus developing prosocial skills that may be critical for their success in inclusive settings.

Several studies have documented differences between multi-age and single-age classroom arrangements in terms of ontask behavior (Veenman, Lem, & Roelofs, 1989), achievement and language development (Psacharopoulos, Rojas, & Velez, 1993), and work-related skill development (Epstein & Cooper, 1994). Together, these studies suggest that the advantages of multi-age grouping may also be available to classes that integrate children with disabilities, potentially capitalizing on this dimension of diversity.

MANAGEMENT RISKS AND DESIGN
OPPORTUNITIES FOR INCLUSIVE EDUCATION

Management is the number one problem identified by beginning teachers

(Evertson & Harris, 1992), and because of high rates of teacher turnover, there is a constant and large supply of beginning teachers. This fact poses significant risk to the academic and social success of students with learning disabilities when they are included in regular classes. As if learning itself were not hard enough, a disorderly environment is likely when there has been inadequate planning and failure to establish routines (Doyle, 1986) and, therefore, not a setting in which disabilities of language or attending behavior can be easily accommodated. The good news is that the design of instruction for proactive management *and* for deep understanding are virtually identical. The bad news is that translating this theoretical linkage into everyday classroom reality is difficult. Fortunately, Evertson, who conducted much of the research, gave appropriately equal attention to the problem of this theory-to-practice translation (Evertson, 1987). For Evertson, the key is a staff development process that (a) treats teachers as equal partners in the planning and delivery of the knowledge, (b) emphasizes reflective practices based on principles rather than specific techniques, and (c) has institutional commitment to follow through. As for the content of this staff development curriculum, Evertson and Murphy (1992) proposed a process of "backward mapping," that is, starting the consideration of management from the point of the individual student's learning, and then working backward to classroom and instructional design strategies that aim precisely at the kind of learning desired. Currently, that means teaching for understanding rather than teaching for engagement.

In science, for example, starting at the point of scientific learning through logical reasoning, hypothesis testing, controlled observation, and experimentation, teachers should learn to view students not as "assembly-line workers" but rather as "teams of scientists" (Brown, 1994; Evertson & Murphy, 1992). The first and obvious point is that scientists engage in a sophisticated from of cooperative learning, learning as much (if not more) from the community of scientists working in their content area as from their own direct observations. Thus, students of science would have frequent occasions for sharing observations with "colleagues": moving from audience to speaker and back again such as a scientist might do at a symposium. The community of learners concept suggests a second point: Scientific learning is an iterative process of reading and discoursing, alternating with experimentation. Accordingly, management of the science classroom would involve opportunities and resources for students to move easily back and forth between the literature and the lab bench. A third point is that scientific knowledge is seldom (if ever) settled. Even after one has reached a valid conclusion, replications and extensions of the inquiry are pursued until the community as a whole is ready to move on, or until such time as a technological breakthrough reopens the question for analysis at another level. Following this model, students of science of whatever age would be encouraged to and supported in their efforts to revisit seemingly mastered knowledge. In the classroom of diverse learners, this spiral route through the curriculum would allow groups of students at varying levels of mastery to engage and reengage the same task, but to take from it new knowledge based on experience and cognitive development. Finally, in science, knowledge is demonstrated by means of the publication of empirically based reports. In the classroom, students' knowledge would be exhibited, rather than tested. The concept of "content coverage" would be replaced by individualized assessments of authentic knowledge.

Orienting prospective and (reorienting) experienced teachers in the direction of constructivist management will not be easy. Most teachers have experienced school as assembly-line workers. Powerful traditions, institutional structures, and habits of mind prevent an easy shift from a control to a learning perspective. Nonetheless, research indicates that such shifts can occur in both new and experienced teachers if new ideas are supported by theory, teachers are given the support and resources needed to change their practice and classroom environment, and teachers see evidence that new modes of practice are successful (Hollingsworth, 1989; Mallory & New, 1995; Richardson, Anders, Tidwell, & Lloyd, 1991; Valli, 1992).

Preservice preparation in classroom management would need to expand its horizons well beyond direct instruction (teaching as transmission) and reactive, behavioral control. Such instruction is often given in a separate course and is implicitly grounded in behaviorist rather than constructivist theories of learning. In its place would be an emphasis on classroom organization for deep understanding and cultural responsiveness, preferably integrated in methods classes and internship experiences. Prospective teachers would have to learn how to help their students build cognitive structures for independent, constructivist learning. Instead of concentrating on behavioral rules (do not chew gum, do not wear hats, etc.), emphasis would be placed on rules and procedures for authentic, cognitive engagement and self-regulated learning. Prospective teachers would, for example, need to be taught how to create culturally authentic, ritualized contexts (Au, 1980); judge the difference between learning and engagement; facilitate self-directed and collaborative learning; challenge misconceptions; create activities, routines, roles, and relationships for active, authentic learning and its assessment; and scaffold for success for *all* students.

This is not to say that teachers, teacher educators, and classroom researchers should ignore the problem of order. This will always be an issue because teachers work with groups of children who are required by law to attend school. What we are proposing is the idea that order can be a consequence rather than a condition of an engaging learning environment. From our review of the literature, it is obvious that more research needs to be done in classrooms that are socially constructed, inquiry oriented, and inclusive. We need a more detailed and theoretical understanding of this approach to classroom management and the kinds of professional preparation that will

enable classroom teachers to maintain order through a social constructivist
approach to student learning.

REFERENCES

Au, K. H. (1980). Participation structures in a reading lesson with Hawaiian children: Analysis of a culturally appropriate instructional event. *Anthropology & Education Quarterly, 11*(2), 91–115.

Ball, D., & Rundquist, S. (1993). Collaboration as a context for joining teacher learning with learning about teaching. In D. Cohen, M. McLaughlin, and J. Talbert (Eds.), *Teaching for understanding: Challenges for policy and practice* (pp. 13–42). San Francisco, CA: Jossey-Bass.

Bredekamp, S. (Ed.). (1987). *Developmentally appropriate practice in early childhood programs servicing children from birth through age 8*. Washington, DC: NAEYC.

Brophy, J. E., & Putnam, J. G. (1979). Classroom management in the elementary grades. In D. L. Duke (Ed.), *Classroom management: The 78th Yearbook of the National Society for the Study of Education* (pp. 182–216). Chicago: University of Chicago Press.

Brown A. L. (1994). The advancement of learning. *Educational Researcher, 23*(8), 4–12.

Cohen, D., & Barnes, C. (1993). Conclusion: A new pedagogy for policy? In D. Cohen, M. McLaughlin, and J. Talbert (Eds.), *Teaching for understanding: Challenges for policy and practice* (pp. 240–275). San Francisco, CA: Jossey-Bass.

Cohen, D., McLaughlin, M. W., & Talbert, J. (Eds.). (1993). *Teaching for understanding: Challenges for policy and practice*. San Francisco, CA: Jossey-Bass.

Day, D. E., & Libertini, G. (1992). Profiles of children's learning behavior. *Journal of Research in Childhood Education, 6*(2), 100–112.

Dillon, D. (1989). Showing them that I want them to learn and that I care about who they are: A microethnography of the social organization of a secondary low-track English-reading classroom. *American Educational Research Journal, 26*(2), 227–259.

Doyle, W. (1986). Classroom organization and management. In M. Wittrock (Ed.), *Handbook of research on teaching* (3rd. ed., pp. 392–431). New York: Macmillan.

Doyle, W. (1992). Curriculum and pedagogy. In P. Jackson (Ed.), *Handbook of research on curriculum* (pp. 486–516). New York: Macmillan.

Emmer, E. T., Evertson, C., & Anderson, L. (1980). Effective classroom management at the beginning of the school year. *Elementary School Journal, 80*(5), 219–231.

Epstein, A., & Cooper, D. H. (1994). *Work-related and interpersonal skills in Montessori kindergartens*. Unpublished manuscript. Department of Special Education, University of Maryland, College Park.

Erickson, F. (1987). Transformation and school success: The politics and culture of educational achievement. *Anthropology & Education Quarterly, 18*(4), 335–356.

Evertson, C. M. (1987). Creating conditions for learning: From research to practice. *Theory Into Practice, 26*(1), 44–50.

Evertson, C. M., & Harris, A. H. (1992). What we know about managing classrooms. *Educational Leadership, 49*(7), 74–78.

Evertson, C. M., & Murphy, J. (1992). Beginning with the classroom: Implications for redesigning schools. In H. H. Marshall (Ed.), *Redefining student learning: Roots of educational change* (pp. 293–320). Norwood, NJ: Ablex.

French, D. C., Waas, G. A., Stright, A. L., & Baker, J. A. (1986). Leadership asymmetries in mixed-age children's groups. *Child Development, 57,* 1277–1283.

Fullan, M. (1995, April). *New paradigms in professional development: International perspec-

tives. Paper presented at the Annual Meeting of the American Educational Research Association, San Francisco, CA.

Gardner, H. (1991). *The unschooled mind: How children think and how schools should teach.* New York: Basic Books.

Haberman, M. (1991). The pedagogy of poverty versus good teaching. *Phi Delta Kappan, 73,* 290–94.

Heath, S. B. (1982). Questioning at home and at school: A comparative study. In G. Spindler (Ed.), *Doing the ethnography of schooling* (pp. 102–127). New York: Holt, Rinehart & Winston.

Hiebert, J., & Wearne, D. (1993). Instructional tasks, classroom discourse, and students' learning in second-grade arithmetic. *American Educational Research Journal, 30*(2), 393–425.

Hollingsworth, S. (1989). Prior beliefs and cognitive change in learning to teach. *American Educational Research Journal, 26*(2), 160–189.

Irvine, J. J. (1990). *Black students and school failure: Policies, practices, and prescriptions.* New York: Greenwood.

Kozol, J. (1978). A new look at the literacy campaign in Cuba. *Harvard Education Review, 48*(3), 341–377.

Ladson-Billings, G. (1994). *The dreamkeepers: Successful teachers of African-American children.* San Francisco, CA: Jossey-Bass.

Mallory, B. L., & New, R. S. (1995). Social constructivist theory and principles of inclusion: Challenges for early childhood special education. *Journal of Special Education, 28,* 322–337.

McLaughlin, M., & Talbert, J. (1993). Introduction: New visions of teaching. In D. Cohen, M. McLaughlin, and J. Talbert (Eds.), *Teaching for understanding: Challenges for policy and practice* (pp. 1–10). San Francisco, CA: Jossey-Bass.

National Council of Teachers of Mathematics. (1989). *Curriculum and evaluation standards for school mathematics.* Reston, VA: Author.

National Council of Teachers of Mathematics. (1991). *Professional standards for teaching mathematics.* Reston, VA: Author.

National Research Council's National Committee on Science Education Standards and Assessment. (1994). *National science education standards: Discussion summary.* Washington DC: Author.

Perkins, D. (1992). *Smart schools: From training memories to educating minds.* New York: Free Press.

Psacharopoulos, G., Rojas, C., & Velez, E. (1993). Achievement evaluation of Columbia's Escuela Nueva: Is multigrade the answer? *Comparative Education Review, 37*(3), 263–276.

Richardson, V., Anders, P., Tidwell, D., & Lloyd, C. (1991). The relationship between teachers' beliefs and practices in reading comprehension instruction. *American Educational Research Journal, 28*(3), pp. 559–586.

Rosenholtz, S. (1989). *Teachers' workplace: The social organizaton of schools.* New York: Longman.

Russell, T., & Munby, H. (1991). Reframing: The role of experience in developing teachers' professional knowledge. In D. Schon (Ed.), *The reflective turn* (pp. 164–187). New York: Teachers College Press.

Shulman, L. (1986). Paradigms and research programs in the study of teaching: A contemporary perspective. In M. Wittrock (Ed.), *Handbook of research on teaching* (pp. 3–36). New York: MacMillan.

Snow, C. E. (1993). Families as social contexts for literacy development. *New Directions for Child Development, 61,* 11–24.

Stone, C. A., & Reid, D. K. (1994). Social and individual forces in learning: Implications for instruction of children with learning difficulties. *Learning Disability Quarterly, 17,* 72–86.

Tisher, R. P. (1987). Students roles. In M. Dunkin (Ed.), *The international encyclopedia of teaching and teacher education* (pp. 432–436). Oxford: Pergamon Press.

Tharp, R., & Gallimore, R. (1989). Rousing schools to life. *American Educator* (summer), 20–52.

U.S. Department of Education. (1994). *Goals 2000.* Washington, DC: Author.

Valli, L. (Ed.). (1992). *Reflective teacher education: Cases and critiques.* New York: SUNY Press.

Veenman, S., Lem, P., & Roelofs, E. (1989). Training teachers in mixed age classrooms: Effects of a staff development programme. *Educational Studies* (Oxfordshire), *15,* 165–180.

Weade, G. (1992). Locating learning in the times and spaces of teaching. In H. H. Marshall (Ed.), *Redefining student learning: Roots of educational change* (pp. 87–118). Norwood, NJ: Ablex.

Zeichner, K. (1993). *Educating teachers for cultural diversity.* East Lansing, MI: National Center for Research on Teacher Learning.

Zeichner, K. M., & Gore, J. M. (1990). Teacher socialization. In W. R. Houston (Ed.), *Handbook of research on teacher education* (pp. 329–348). New York: Macmillan.

11

Organization and Management of General Education Classrooms

Naomi Zigmond
University of Pittsburgh

Schools are not organized with one teacher for each student. Instead, children are gathered together into classrooms and taught in groups. These classrooms are complex places. The teaching and learning that go on in them needs to be orchestrated and structured. The time that students spend in them needs to be filled productively. The diversity, inevitable in the gathering together of children into groups, needs to be accommodated. Teachers organize and manage classrooms of students so that the task of teaching the required curriculum to the required set of children is doable. When good decisions have been made and good strategies have been implemented, all the children in the classroom group achieve.

Children with learning disabilities (LD), identified, labeled, and assigned an IEP, have, by definition, not achieved adequately in the general education classroom. If they had been making academic progress, engaging in the assigned work, and behaving properly, they would not have been referred by their general education teacher for special education services. They would not have demonstrated the significant underachievement that qualified them for the label LD.

For several years, colleagues and I at the University of Pittsburgh have been studying general education classrooms: how they are organized when there are no children with LD present; whether they change when children with LD are included; and whether they change even more when teachers make conscientious efforts to accommodate, or when coteaching is installed. This chapter focuses on our efforts to understand classrooms in elementary schools, and the extent to which they are (or might be) appropriate venues for educating students with LD.

GENERAL EDUCATION CLASSROOMS
INTO WHICH NO STUDENTS WITH LD
HAVE BEEN INTEGRATED

In two separate studies, we have used qualitative and quantitative observation techniques to characterize the ecology of the general education classroom. The first was carried out in one urban elementary school (Zigmond & Baker, 1990). The target school, 1 of 53 elementary schools in the district, served 266 students in grades kindergarten through fifth during the 1987–88 school year. Located in a primarily African American neighborhood, the student body was 99.9% African American, although the racial balance of the district was approximately 54% African American at the elementary school level.

Data on classroom ecologies were collected through informal and formal observations and interviews of school personnel over a 6-month period. Qualitative information was gathered in 12 general education classes, 2 at each grade level, kindergarten through fifth grade, on types of classroom activities, students' behavior during instruction, grouping arrangements for instruction, reinforcement techniques, the variety of materials available in each classroom, and a floor plan for each room. Systematic behavioral observations (Baker, Drylie-Quinn, Gaus, & Zigmond, 1988) were collected during reading, math, and special subject classes to determine the frequency of various student and teacher behaviors. Ten homerooms were observed four times each during reading period and four times each during math period; one homeroom at each grade level was observed during art, physical education, and music classes during periods in which there were no LD students mainstreamed so as to describe the most typical general education environment. Student behaviors were coded in four areas: type of materials being used, grouping arrangement for the current activity, monitoring by adults, and student response. The student activities were measured by sampling six 10-second units during a 40-minute class period for each of six students chosen randomly at the start of each observation in each classroom. Teacher behaviors were clustered into noninstructional activities, instructional activities, and general management. Observations of teacher behaviors alternated with student observations. The teacher was observed 20 times during each 40-minute class period, with each teacher observation lasting 10 seconds. During 20% of observations, two observers coded student and teacher behaviors; overall interrater agreement for these sessions was 87%.

Results of this study were reported in considerable detail in Zigmond and Baker (1990). However, findings related to classroom organization and management of instruction are summarized here. To accomplish that, both student and teacher observation data have been aggregated across grade levels and subject matter.

Most classes operated with only one adult, the teacher. The primary mode of instruction in the entire school was the single lesson taught to the whole group, or the same seatwork activity assigned to the whole class. The time-sample, direct observation protocol showed that teachers spent only about 31% of class time teaching, and another 16% giving directions for an academic task, waiting for responses, or monitoring the class while students completed independent seatwork (a cluster of behaviors we called "instructional management"). Behavior management, generally in the form of neutral redirects, took up 17% of teacher time. Students were ontask in these classrooms for more than 85% of class time. More than half (59%) of student time was spent in whole-class instruction, and for more than half of each class period students were assigned workbook or worksheet activities.

Observers noted that instructional programs were routine. Teachers valued quiet and order. No students were ever observed working with peers in pairs or in small groups. Students raised their hands to be recognized or to get permission to move around. There was little talking among themselves.

Baker and I characterized this school as not ready for integration of students with LD into general education classrooms, because we saw no evidence of differentiated instruction and no structures in the classrooms that could support it. We observed that teachers were more committed to routine than to addressing individual differences, and that they were more responsive to district mandates than to evidence from their students that the curriculum or pacing needed to be adapted. The teachers in this school had uniform expectations for all students, and that mindset was evident in the ways they organized and managed instruction.

We wondered whether this school was unusual, noting that general education teachers are prepared to consider the group before the individual. As a recent teacher education textbook explained, "Most lesson plans [completed by elementary teachers] are designed to guide instruction for a whole class of students. Thus, the typical plan aims to motivate and involve the 'average' student. . . . No general lesson plan will be . . . a *perfect* fit for *any* individual student" (Cooper, 1994, p. 31). Another added, "[In general education classrooms] the teacher . . . provides instruction in the group to assist the individual" (Lemlech, 1994, pp. 116–117).

Thus, we analyzed a second data set of classroom observations that represented the preintervention phase of an inclusion project (see Baker, Colpo, Fulmer, & Zigmond, 1992). Again, both qualitative and quantitative data permitted us to characterize general education classroom instruction, this time in four elementary schools across Pennsylvania. The districts ranged in size from 1,400 to 5,700 students. Two districts were located in rural areas in the cental part of the state and two were located in rural/suburban areas in the eastern part of the state.

Classrooms of 32 general education teachers (8 from each school) were observed during the 1990–91 school year, the year before we implemented a full inclusion model. We used the same classroom observation protocol as in Study 1 (Baker et al., 1988) to derive estimates of the frequency of various teacher and student behaviors during reading classes. Six randomly selected nondisabled students were observed on each of four occasions. Observations of teacher behaviors alternated with student observations. During 20% of observations, two observers coded student and teacher behaviors; overall interrater reliability for these sessions was 97.6%.

Teacher behaviors were clustered into noninstructional activities, instructional activities, and activities related to management of instruction. Teachers in these sites spent 30% of reading time teaching and 47% of reading time in instructional management. Whole-class instruction was less prominent in these schools than in the urban school (only 31% of reading time), but to organize the classroom for small-group instruction, teachers assigned work to students that could be done without adult supervision; as a result, students in these four schools spent 48% of reading class working unmonitored. Students were ontask about 93% of reading time, but they spent only 40% of each reading period in reading-related activities. Almost 22% of class time was spent socializing with peers or with the teacher. Students used workbooks and worksheets for the largest percentage of time (41%) and textbooks for about 36% of the instructional time. Our conclusion: The urban school, although more strongly committed to whole-class instruction than were teachers in these rural/suburban settings, was not particularly unique in terms of the organization and management of elementary classrooms.

TEACHING TEACHERS TO TEACH DIFFERENTLY: DOES IT CHANGE ANYTHING?

In 1987, my colleague Jan Baker and I developed a full inclusion delivery model, Project MELD (Mainstream Experiences for Learning Disabled), for elementary level students with LD. Like other full-time mainstreaming models, the MELD model sought to make substantial changes in the mainstream in order to make it more accommodating to students' individual needs. MELD was a total school improvement effort in which teachers continued to use the extant curriculum, but implemented more effective delivery techniques and changed instructional strategies, grouping practices, and pacing. In the MELD model, we sought not only to accommodate students with LD in the mainstream, but also to alter the conditions (see Zigmond & Baker, 1990) that led to the referral of students to special education in the first place.

After a year of planning involving the principals and the teachers of four elementary buildings (during which the baseline data reported earlier were collected), all students labeled LD and served in pull-out programs (self-contained or resource) were returned full time to general education classrooms. The placement decisions were made thoughtfully, with a committee of special and general education teachers developing appropriate school-based decision rules for where a student with LD would "fit." The goal of the placements was to fully integrate the students with LD into the ongoing developmental instructional program of the classroom; supplemental assistance and support would be available to these reintegrated students with LD, and to any of their classmates, through the special education teacher now freed from pull-out direct teaching responsibilities and able to assume a new role of coteacher and support teacher within the mainstream.

Once students were reintegrated, however, mainstream teachers were not expected to go about business as usual. Teachers were to change grouping patterns for instruction so that students with special needs could be given special attention and full use could be made of a coteacher during those instructional periods in which the special education teacher was scheduled to work in the mainstream classroom. Teachers were to implement more effective approaches to teaching literacy skills using graphic organizers and cognitive strategies (see Calfee, 1976). Teachers were to make professional decisions about what to teach more intensively and what to skip over lightly, and about the order in which to teach various objectives (i.e., they were to break their habit of simply marching through the textbook giving each story, chapter, or workbook page the same amount of attention). And teachers and administrators were to rethink criteria for awarding grades to students to be certain that individual differences in effort and achievement were accommodated and that grades were rewarding, not punitive, to children with special needs.

The MELD model also required monitoring of students' reading achievement through administration of curriculum-based measures (CBM). Assisted by the special education teachers, mainstream reading teachers were to have each student read orally for 1 minute, twice each week, from grade-level texts, and to have students graph number of words read correctly. Special education teachers reviewed student graphs, identified any students (labeled or not) who were not meeting their goals, and met with each mainstream teacher once each week to discuss these students and to plan classroom-based instructional alternatives. CBM data as well as other achievement measures, disciplinary actions, and demographic data were maintained on a school-based microcomputer student information system designed specifically for MELD to assist the principal and teachers to identify students who were at risk and to facilitate development and documentation of action plans.

Finally, MELD promoted attitudes of accommodation rather than referral among mainstream teachers through the use of regular school-based problem-solving meetings in which teachers shared with each other problems they were experiencing and solutions they might try. This problem solving was not to be viewed as a prereferral strategy, because referral of the problem student for a special education eligibility evaluation was such an unlikely outcome of the discussions. Teachers were expected to see difficult children as challenges to be met, not as problems to be given to someone else. This attitude was encouraged by the availability of the special education teachers to work as coteachers and support personnel within the building.

MELD was implemented in the four districts for which preintervention data have previously been described. Classroom observation data collected in reading classes during the implementation year permitted us to discern what changes teachers had made in their instructional practices and in the ways they organized and managed the learning activities they gave to students. Because project staff had provided not only inservice training but also ongoing onsite technical assistance to teachers in all four schools, we hoped to find that teachers organized their reading lessons in more productive ways during the implementation year.

At each site and across sites, teachers spent significantly *less* time managing reading instruction (instructional management down from 47% to 29% of class time; $t(30) = -6.12$, $p < .001$) after the implementation of inclusion. After students with LD were added to the general education classrooms, teachers spent significantly *more* time teaching (up from 30% to 48% of class time; $t(30) = 5.54$, $p < .001$), but they did not change the amount of time they spent in noninstructional activities. Teachers also did not change how they organized reading instruction. Students still spent about 30% time in whole-class instruction and more than 40% time in independent seatwork. Students still spent less than half of each reading lesson monitored by an adult, although they now spent more time each period engaged in reading and reading-related activities (up from 41% to 47% of class time; $t(30) = 4.10$, $p < .001$). Teachers' teaching styles changed somewhat: During whole-class instruction teachers elicited more student responses (the student talk variable increased significantly from 3% to 5% of class time; $t(30) = 2.63$, $p < .02$), and teachers were more likely to introduce a graphic organizer or a writing activity than they had been before. Nevertheless, overall, the structure and organization of the 32 MELD classrooms seemed quite resistant to change.

Recently, my colleague Rita Bean and I conducted a second experiment directed at changing the ways teachers organize instruction, this time focusing not on reading but on social studies at the elementary level. Social studies is a vitally important subject in the school curriculum. It serves the function of transmitting to students the knowledge and thinking skills that will permit them to grow into open-minded adults committed to the resolution of societal problems and inequities, and prepare them to participate effectively in the democratic process. In recent years the social studies curriculum has come under sharp attack for its lack of rigor and its emphasis on lower-order thinking skills. Efforts have been made to enrich the study of social studies to include larger doses of geography and history, as well as more explicit instruction in higher-order thinking skills. Few would question the value of this enriched curriculum for all students, including those at risk for academic problems. But research on social studies achievement of students with LD reveals that even the less rigorous curriculum was often not user-friendly. Donahoe and Zigmond (1990) reported a very high failure rate of students with LD in ninth-grade social studies classes, and we also have documented problems in acquiring social studies information in elementary grades (see Zigmond, Fulmer, Volonino, Wolery, & Bean, 1993; Zigmond, Fulmer, Wolery, Meng, & Bean, 1994). Textbooks and journal articles on mainstreaming exhort general education teachers to change the ways in which they deliver social studies content to accommodate the special learning needs of students with LD (see Bos & Vaughn, 1988; Kameenui & Simmons, 1990; Schumm & Strickler, 1991; Stainback, Stainback, & Forest, 1990). Conventional wisdom holds that students with LD will require instruction that is particularly well planned and well executed if they are to derive benefit from mainstream placements; business as usual will not suffice. Students with special needs in general education classrooms will require fundamental "changes in classroom instructional practices" (NASBE, 1992, p. 4).

The research reported here was part of a larger research program on the instructional practices that would facilitate social studies achievement among students with disabilities in mainstream K–8 social studies classrooms. It focuses on the extent of implementation of new ideas by social studies teachers in elementary and middle school grades.

During 2 years of survey research, teacher interviews, and casual observation in elementary-level social studies classes in four school districts, we came to recognize several teachers as enthusiastic, competent, and cooperative. We invited 12 of these teachers to participate in a year of research on social studies instruction, if they were likely to have at least one student with LD integrated into their social studies class in the upcoming school year, and if they agreed (a) to participate in a 1-week summer workshop designed to improve their social studies instruction, (b) to be observed during a 2- to 3-week unit of social studies instruction in the fall, (c) to make themselves and selected students available for interviews, (d) to provide samples of student work and final test results, and (e) to participate in several meetings at the university over the course of the school year. Seven teachers from three different school districts volunteered for the research project. They included one first-grade, one third-grade, two fourth-grade, one fifth-grade, one sixth-grade, and one eighth-grade teacher. There were four women and three men and all but one had been teaching for more than 10 years.

Teachers were paid to participate in a 5-day inservice workshop during the latter part of August 1992. Over the course of the workshop, participants were instructed on various ways of improving social studies instruction; then, each teacher planned a unit of social studies instruction to be observed in the fall of the school year. At the start of the workshop, a set of preliminary guidelines were distributed as context, and the teachers were engaged in a discussion of factors to consider in planning, teaching, and evaluating a unit of social studies. Workshop leaders described the language and literacy problems typical of students with LD and elicited prior knowledge of teachers on ways to plan, teach, and evaluate that could make a social studies unit more accessible to these students in particular. Workshop leaders also reviewed principles of instructional delivery and introduced new instructional practices derived from research.

The 5-day inservice workshop covered various topics, including individualizing instruction, adapting materials, reward systems, and reteaching strategies, but there were four topics that received particular attention: (a) using a lesson framework, (b) mediating the use of the social studies text, (c) providing multiple exposures to new vocabulary words, and (d) arranging opportunities for peer-assisted learning. The data I present here focus only on the latter topic.

The need to address differences in capacity among diverse learners in a social studies class has led many educators to explore a variety of pedagogical techniques as alternatives to whole-class instruction. The common feature of these techniques is that they involve peer-assisted learning (see Greenwood et al., 1984; Johnson & Johnson, 1986; Slavin, 1983). Cooperative learning is especially worthwhile for heterogeneous groups of students because it encourages mutual respect and learning among students of various backgrounds and academic abilities (Sharan, 1980; Slavin et al., 1985). In the 5-day workshop, we stressed the value of small-group, cooperative learning activities and the value of partner reading in accommodating students with reading and writing difficulties. Our expectation was that, having had input on these new grouping practices, and the time and coaching to develop that input into classroom activities and materials, teachers would incorporate the ideas into the target unit of social studies instruction and we would see the fruits of this inservice effort when we observed the teachers teaching in the fall.

Four sources of data permitted an evaluation of the extent to which the workshop influenced teacher practices, and why some practices were accepted and some rejected in the actual practice of social studies instruction. First, the seven teachers were interviewed, individually, on the last day of the workshop, and the plans they had been developing were reviewed. The teachers described the proposed unit day by day and explained the materials they had developed. They described the goals of the unit, the scope and sequence of the content to be presented, and their individual plans for evaluation.

Second, a trained observer was present on every day the unit was taught, and collected qualitative, descriptive data. Further, teachers were audiotaped during each lesson; teachers wore a hip pack that housed a microcassette recorder, and a small lapel microphone was pinned on their clothing. Tape recording was done to obtain a complete record of teacher talk; student responses were recorded in the observer's qualitative notes. Observers took narrative field notes on how teachers taught their units of social studies instruction and how students of varying ability levels were engaged during the delivery of instruction. Observers made notations at least every 5 minutes indicating what the teacher was doing and what the students were doing. Student responses were noted verbatim. The observation data set consisted of 70 days of narrative notes and teacher transcripts.

Third, at the end of each lesson, the observer completed a checklist on instructional practices; the checklist had been developed to reflect the topics and suggestions covered in the workshop. The observer indicated whether any of the practices on that list had been observed in the lesson of that day. Observers completed a total of 70 checklists.

Finally, 3 months after the units had been taught, the seven teachers were released by their school districts to attend a 1-day workshop during which feedback was provided to them on the data collected for the research study. Feedback included a summary, collectively and individually, of the instructional practices during their units of social studies instruction. Teachers discussed the findings explaining why some practices seemed easier to implement than others; the discussion was tape recorded and transcribed, then analyzed to reveal the barriers to implementing specific instructional practices.

Influence on Teacher Plans

In the postworkshop interviews, six of the seven teachers believed that they would teach the target social studies unit differently than they had taught it in previous years, and all seven planned to use small-group instruction at some point in the unit. Five of the seven talked of incorporating cooperative learning group activities into the unit of social studies instruction. Two of them stated:

> I'll be grouping [students] as I said; I'll be grouping with cooperative learning groups. I will put the high achievers with the low and the middle. I am going to have them work in groups because they will be building their communities. (Teacher 1, 8/25/92)

> I use groups of 5 or 6 [students] and keep it relatively small so that you get a lot of interaction. They [the students] don't have too much background on cooperative learning so this project will be the first time that we do this in that setting. (Teacher 3, 8/25/92)

Teachers also described ways in which they would implement partner or paired activities. Two comments were:

> I do a lot of partner work and that's because of the LDs. . . . Sometimes I pair them myself, sometimes I let them choose their partners and often they know who to pick to help them. (Teacher 4b, 8/25/92)

> When you are doing mapping in pairs, lots of times they [the students] get a little competitive as to who has the better map and try to make the maps neater. They try to make them more concise. They will often divide up the work which is fine, then, swap information which is good. That seems to work out well. (Teacher 7, 8/25/92)

Influence on Teaching

Observations of the teachers teaching their units of instruction, transcriptions of teacher talk over the course of each unit, and checklists completed by the observers at the end of each lesson provided the data for analyzing whether and how teachers implemented the ideas and teaching suggestions that were the content of the workshop, and whether they followed through on the plans developed as part of the workshop. From the checklists, we derived the percentage of lessons in which an element was seen (teachers taught units varying from 6 to 13 lessons).

The data indicated that teachers spent at least part of every lesson teaching the whole class (median = 100% of lessons), and almost never (median = 0% of lessons) took a group of students or a single student aside to reteach a concept, or had students do paired oral reading. Cooperative learning groups were also rarely used by most teachers (median = 8% of lessons); the first-grade teacher used a small-group activity (but not cooperative learning) in every lesson, but three other teachers never used groups.

We conducted an alternative analysis of the use of peer-assisted activities from the narrative classroom observation notes. We counted the number of 5-second intervals during which observers recorded students as engaged in independent, whole-class, or peer-assisted learning activities, and converted the number to a percentage of total minutes of instruction by unit, by teacher. Teachers provided opportunities for peer-assisted learning from 2% to 52% of the total time devoted to the target social studies unit (median = 19%). In all but first grade, whole-class instruction prevailed as the dominant instructional mode, and time devoted to peer-assisted learning was relatively small. Our findings indicated a relatively low degree of implementation of the workshop ideas, despite the intensity and interactiveness of the week, and the time teachers were given to incorporate workshop ideas into instructional plans.

Barriers to Implementation of "New Ideas"

Several months after the units of social studies had been taught, the teachers who participated in this study convened at the university to discuss our findings and to reflect on the ways in which their practice of teaching social studies had changed. We shared with teachers the results just described (and more), and asked what the teachers thought. The teachers agreed that the data properly characterized what they had implemented in their respective classrooms. The teachers believed that what they had learned in the workshop had been valuable, and that the ideas and practices to which they had been introduced were likely to be useful for students with LD in their classes. Their explanations for the low degree of implementation, however, could be summarized in comments like, "In the real world, that's just not the way social studies is taught!" (Teacher 6). Another teacher said:

> Peer-assisted activities were a good idea, but only if you had the right mix of students. In the past I had done a lot of paired reading, although this year, I found I had more slower students. I had very few of the gifted and then of course the three boys who were basically nonreaders where I found out that [paired reading] wasn't going to work at all. (Teacher 3)

For some teachers, scheduling peer-assisted activities so that they would be useful to students with LD was often a problem. One teacher explained:

> I do a lot of partner work with the kids who work with a partner beside them and not necessarily with preset partners. I don't preset groups often. A lot of times I let them pick their own partner. And sometimes I have to say work with the person beside you and the reason I do that is because if you knew how long it takes them to pick a partner . . . there is just time efficiency here. Time is a major factor especially with the LD. They have to be in their reading classes at 1:10. And so there is my limitation, even though I am self-contained. I am still really limited with those three kids because I adjust my schedule to accommodate them. (Teacher 4b)

And some of the teachers did not use peer-assisted activities because they believed they didn't really fit. One teacher commented:

> Social studies, just the nature of the beast, is that it is a whole-class activity basically. And I think we tend to come from a whole-class angle. So if there is a way of accommodating, it is again from that whole-class angle. . . . And I think that is just a mindset that we might tend to have with social studies. That it is a whole-class activity and therefore we are not going to design something special for these two kids to do in a corner by themselves whereas the rest of the class is doing something else. I think that becomes the way we look at things, from a whole-class perspective. (Teacher 6)

The feedback discussion revealed an underlying tension in all seven teachers over the issue of accommodations for students with special needs. Some held firmly that accommodations may simply not be a good idea! One said:

> Initially, with LDs and slow learners, I needed to find where their strengths and weaknesses were first. My whole philosophy on that is try it with the rest of the

kids. Let them prove to me they can't do it, then make the adaptations. Not just jump in and say well so and so said they can't do this so I am not going to try it. I want to try it first with them because maybe with the different ways of introducing the materials they can do it. It might not be them reading it on their own or doing it a lot more independently or in groups or in projects. I can still develop concepts without doing too much with adaptations other than those types of things. Then once they prove it is just not possible, then maybe adaptations and gear it down to what they can do. The point I want to make is that I just don't want to prejudge them. (Teacher 3)

Other teachers also struggled with the idea of meeting *individual* needs, saying things like:

You know, what do you leave out? I find I don't reduce their [students' with LD] workload; I try to reduce them not understanding how to do it or not understanding what is required of them. (Teacher 8)

Several teachers were reluctant to single out students with special needs for special treatment. One commented:

I would adapt my entire class and give them all the opportunity to do the same things so that they wouldn't be isolated or pointed out as being different. (Teacher 3)

So much so, that some were blind to special needs. For example:

Your classroom population is going to determine whether or what kind of adapting you have to do. My kids this year, I have no one who is at such a low level that I have to make special accommodations. Every kid in my class had the ability to glean some information from the textbook or to understand and follow and participate in a visual organizer activity or to write a short paragraph on something. Everybody I have can do that. (Teacher 6)

Despite their plans for other than whole-class instruction, some teachers never used small-group, peer-assisted learning activities at all. In five of the seven classrooms, teachers persisted in teaching to the whole group and used only individual student work as follow-up. Teachers used as their excuse that social studies instruction does not lend itself to extensive use of small-group or peer-assisted activities. They said it so many times, and acted on that belief so regularly, perhaps it is true!

GENERAL EDUCATION CLASSROOMS WHEN THERE IS A CONSCIENTIOUS EFFORT TO FACILITATE CHANGE THROUGH COTEACHING AND COPLANNING

Many school districts have implemented full inclusion models at the elementary level, and they are very proud of these models. They describe their models at professional meetings, and invite visitors to learn how to replicate their successes. Recently, Jan Baker and I undertook a study of five such well-established full-time mainstreaming models. The five sites were selected after a review of professional conference proceedings (e.g., regional and national CEC convention programs) and federally funded programs. The sites represented a wide geographic distribution and variety in their approach to full-time integration of students with LD. The sites were located in Virginia, Pennsylvania, Minnesota, Kansas, and Washington.

Data Collection

During a 2-day visit to each of the five sites, we examined the educational experiences of two students with LD, one primary-grade student and one intermediate-grade student. The target students with LD were selected by district personnel, usually the building principal or the special education teacher. The district personnel arranged for permission to collect data and scheduled times to meet with parents and teachers of each target student.

We observed each student during reading, mathematics, science, social studies, and language arts instruction for 2 consecutive days. We took narrative notes on what the teacher was doing, what the class was doing, and what the target student with LD was doing at 5-minute intervals during each class period. Notes were entered onto a personal computer for data reduction and analysis.

We conducted semistructured interviews with each child, his or her parents, general education teachers and special education teachers who worked with the child, the principal, and the special education supervisor for the building. Teachers described the educational program for the target child, specifying any special aspects of the program. Parents described their child's program and their attitude toward that program. Each student described his or her daily experiences and highlighted his or her favorite activities in school. Administrators described the model of inclusion and explained how and why it had been developed. The interviews were audiotaped and transcribed for data reduction.

We reviewed students' records to obtain additional information about achievement levels, reasons for referral, and individualized education plans (IEPs). Finally, we collected permanent products that would help us to understand aspects of the model being implemented that we could not observe in our 2-day visit. We obtained copies of report cards, parent/student handbooks, IEP forms, and a local description of the inclusion model.

To reduce the data, all of the material was read and coded, highlighting information relevant to four areas: context for inclusion, model of inclusion, role of special education teachers, and educational experiences of students with LD. A comprehensive report of the study is in the *Journal of Special Education* (see Baker, 1995a, 1995b, 1995c; Zigmond, 1995a, 1995b).

Findings Related to Classroom Organization and Management

We had opted to visit schools that would differ in their approach to inclusion, and, indeed, the sites differed widely in who provided the leadership and motivation for the change in services, how school personnel were selected to participate in the new model, how students with LD were distributed into general education classes, and the nature of the *special* education that was provided. A complete discussion of these patterns can be found in Baker and Zigmond (1995) and Zigmond and Baker (1995). Nevertheless, all five models had in common their goal to have students with LD participate in the same lessons as nondisabled peers, and in our observation and interview data were examples of how classrooms were organized and instruction was managed to accommodate full inclusion and coteaching

Conspicuously absent, as we watched special education teachers and general education teachers teach students with LD (whether in large-group general class instruction, in small pull-aside groups, or in reinvented pull-out programs), were activities focused on assessing individual students or monitoring progress through the curriculum. Concern for the individual was replaced by concern for a group—the smooth functioning of the mainstream class, the progress of the reading group, the organization and management of cooperative learning groups or peer tutoring. No one seemed concerned about individual achievement, individual progress, or individual learning.

During the scheduled coteaching sessions, special education and general education teachers engaged in a wide variety of coteaching activities. Sometimes, the two teachers team-taught a whole-class lesson, with both teachers participating equally in the instructional activity. In this arrangement, there was no differentiation of teacher roles and, for the time that both teachers were present in the room, their background and designations were indistinguishable to an observer. An alternative approach to coteaching involved one of the two teachers teaching a whole-class lesson while the second teacher circulated, monitored, and prompted individual students as needed; the two teachers might alternate the role of teacher and monitor. More usually, when two teachers were present the class was divided into two groups and each teacher taught one of the groups. Sometimes each teacher would be teaching the same lesson, but having two teachers allowed each to work with a smaller group. Other times, the two teachers taught the same objective, but used different instructional strategies and/or materials. Or, the two teachers each taught a different lesson, but switched groups midway through the class period so that all students received both lessons.

The general education teachers we talked to seemed genuinely willing to make certain kinds of accommodations for the students with LD assigned to their classes—they would change their approach to instruction *for the whole class*, prompted by an attempt to meet the needs of the students with LD. As the special education teacher from Virginia put it, "Typically when we make modifications we make those modifications for the LD students, with them in mind, but for everyone at the same time. . . . You know, [it] helps everyone" (5/10/93).

Planning for instruction always occurred at the activity level (what reading assignment or worksheet would the group be given to do?), not at the individual student level (what unique assignment will be developed for a particular child?). When a special education teacher suggested an alternative assignment, or an adaptation to a proposed approach, it was at the level of LD stereotypes (e.g., "Students with LD are more likely to learn it if we use a graphic organizer") rather than at the level of meeting an individual student's needs (e.g., "Jason has difficulty remembering isolated facts so let's provide *him* with a weave on which to summarize the story"). Planning was also not data-based—teachers did not bring to the planning meeting assessment or monitoring data on individual students nor any formal or informal evaluations of how successful a previous lesson had been with a particular student or group of students. We did hear teachers saying, "This concept is hard, so let's try . . . " or "This worked really well last year, let's do it again," but data were not part of these discussions.

As a result, adaptations were very general—redesigned tests, more oral reading of textbooks during class time, allowing any student in the class to make use of a math matrix of multiplication or division facts, teaching the entire class some reading or composition strategy, or allowing choice and flexibility in the selection of part of the weekly spelling list. We rarely saw adaptations directed at a single student. When we did, the adaptations did not change the basic organization of the classroom and did not interfere with the teacher's management of instruction. For example, one teacher (Virginia, primary) made a particular effort with one student with LD assigned to her class: She repeated directions. "Day by day, talking her through it, reminding her of what needed to be done, and how to do it, and where it went" (5/10/93). But she did not change this student's assignments.

In every site we heard teachers, parents, and administrators acknowledging that some students with LD needed more than the in-class coteaching and the whole-class accommodations being provided in their model of services to students with LD. To give students more, the schools mobilized peers, paraprofessionals, and parents. Peer-mediated strategies were utilized in all sites to increase opportunities for individual student responding and to provide coaching for students who could not manage classroom work on their own. For example, in the Kansas school, each student with LD was paired with a classmate who helped him or her along, and that "study-buddy" provided the direct teaching and coaching for which neither the general education teacher nor the special education teacher(s) could find time. As one teacher noted:

In third grade I have some kids reading at first-grade level, however, we've put them on like *A Taste of Blackberries* and they keep up. We have them . . . working as study-buddies. They [the study-buddies] teach the vocabulary to the kids. They really are able to keep up with comprehension. (Kansas, primary teacher, 5/3/93)

In the Washington school, a cross-age peer tutoring program operated in the all-purpose room every day; intermediate-grades students were partnered with primary-grades students to work on reading fluency and comprehension. In their own classes, teachers also implemented cooperative learning groups for grade-level instructional activities in reading.

In several of the sites, the students with LD received their extra assistance, coaching, and direct instruction from paraprofessionals or volunteer parents, as well as from peers. Paraprofessionals and parents were generally asked to monitor practice tasks or listen to oral reading, but they were also regularly called on to teach small-group lessons to students who needed extra assistance.

OUTCOMES FOR STUDENTS WITH LD PLACED IN GENERAL EDUCATION CLASSROOMS

Our observations, our conversations with teachers, and our experiences in the schools convinced us that general education teachers can organize their classrooms and manage instruction so that students with LD can "fit in." In our MELD sites, in those social studies classrooms, and in the five elementary schools we visited across the nation, students with LD were being taught enthusiastically, not grudgingly, by general education teachers. Special education teachers, in the roles of consultant, coordinator, coplanner, or coteacher, had made it possible for these general education teachers to feel comfortable about the educational tasks with which they were confronted, and for the students with LD to feel comfortable about functioning in a general education setting. Accommodations that were made were generally directed to the entire class, so that from the student's perspective he or she was not singled out or made to feel different. Teachers, both general and special, were trying to teach everyone well and in that way meet the needs of the special education students who were present. Whatever "special" instruction or coaching was needed by the student was provided, unobtrusively, by peers, paraprofessionals, or parents, and provided to anyone who needed it, whether on an IEP or not. And if a student needed more than that, pull-out services were reinvented but, again, they were for anyone.

In our data, students were engaged and compliant; teachers believed that their instruction was working. Furthermore, there were some very positive outcomes of the inclusion experiments: Teachers felt the students assigned to their classrooms were teachable, and the teachers were not anxious to get rid of these students. Even in the MELD implementations, in which the coteacher spent only 30 minutes in each general education classroom 4 days per week, and coplanning was allocated only 30 minutes once a week, referrals to special education that would likely result in removal of students from the general education setting dropped to zero! The conclusion that might be drawn is that general education classrooms can be organized and managed to accommodate a diversity of students, including students with LD.

Indeed, if integration is the goal, what we have learned from our research is that it can be achieved successfully when the decision to change the venue of special education services is accompanied by building-based leadership, inservice training for general education teachers, and an energetic realignment of the time and energies of the special education personnel. If inclusion is seen as simply a school-level reorganization strategy, then it can be implemented with relatively minor changes in the organization and management of the general education classroom. The problem is that if one dares to look past the *rhetoric* of effectiveness to the *empirical data*, students with LD did not learn very much in the general education setting. Several of our data sets illustrate this point.

Outcomes in Social Studies

In a detailed analysis of student learning in two geography classes (Zigmond et al., 1993) and one history class (Zigmond et al., 1994), we showed that the students with LD just didn't "get it." In these studies, we documented the experiences and achievement of a small number of elementary-level students with LD. The students were those being taught by teachers who volunteered to participate in the research program; they are the teachers to whom we delivered the 1-week summer workshop designed to improve their social studies instruction, described earlier. Among the group of seven volunteers, three were assigned classrooms in the fall into which students with LD were integrated; two taught geography as the unit of instruction to be observed, and one taught history.

Audiotaping of the teachers and observations of the students provided us with detailed narratives of how teachers taught their units of social studies instruction and how the students with LD and classmates responded during the delivery of instruction. To complement these data, we administered a *pre-unit interview* to the students with LD and a designated high-achieving (HA) and low-achieving (LA) student in each class. The interview protocols were unique for each class and designed in collaboration with each teacher because they focused on the concepts and vocabulary to be taught in the upcoming unit of social studies. The information would provide a basis for determining students' background knowledge (prior knowledge) of the content of the unit. Then, each day the unit was taught, we identified one of the target students

(LD, HA, or LA) to be the focus of the narrative observation. Immediately following instruction, we conducted an *on-line interview* with that student to determine what specific content he or she had learned that particular day. We asked:

1. What did you learn about in Social Studies today?
2. Why do you think it might be important to learn [. . .]?
3. Is there anything more you would like to learn about after today's lesson?
4. What did you learn today that you didn't know before?
5. What did you like best about the lesson?
6. What new vocabulary words did you learn?
7. What does [new word] mean?
8. How did you use your text today?

We administered a *postunit interview* to assess what was learned by students by the end of the unit. The postunit interview was essentially the same as the preunit interview, adapted to reflect what had actually been taught. Finally, we administered a second postunit interview 4 months later in the school year. All interviews were tape recorded.

Geography: What Was Taught? What Was Learned?

Ms. P selected a unit on geography map skills to teach to her third-grade class. She covered the names and locations of the oceans, continents, prime meridian, equator, Tropic of Cancer, and Tropic of Capricorn. She introduced students to the compass rose, cardinal and intermediate directions, lines of longitude and latitude, and map keys. Students learned to read and construct maps of the classroom, the school, and the world.

Ms. J selected a unit on mountains for her fourth-grade class. She taught how mountains were formed and shaped, what they were made of, and the natural and renewable resources they provided. Students learned to identify three major mountain ranges in the United States and at least one famous peak in each range. Finally, students explored mountains as animal habitats.

For both teachers, more than half the lessons included whole-class instruction for at least some portion of the period, often related to a vocabulary review or student work with vocabulary words. Almost every lesson contained a teacher-directed activity to activate prior knowledge; a recitation-type question-and-answer session; and the teacher circulating about the room, monitoring students' completion of independent assignments. Rarely seen (in less than 25% of lessons) were reteaching, cooperative learning groups, higher-order questions, or paired reading.

Qualitative narrative notes revealed that both teachers did some very "neat" things: Ms. P was particularly conscientious about using concrete demonstrations to help students attach meaning to the new vocabulary words related to map skills. For example, to introduce the compass rose and cardinal directions, Ms. P showed her students a magnetized needle and explained to them that the needle always points north. Then she turned on an overhead projector, set a dish of water on the overhead, set the magnetized needle on top of a piece of Styrofoam floating in the water, and had the students see where in the classroom north was. In the lesson on latitude and longitude, she explained that "Latitude sounds like the word *ladder* and the latitude lines look like the rungs of a ladder going climbing up the ladder." To help students remember that the Tropic of Cancer was north of the equator and the Tropic of Capricorn was south of the equator, she invited one student to stand on her desk. Then she told the students to imagine that his knees were the equator. "Sometimes people get *corns* on their feet," she added, "so *south* of the equator we have the Tropic of Capri*corn*, *north* of the equator is Jerry's *can*," she said as she pointed to the student's backside, "so *north* of the equator is the Tropic of *Can*cer."

Ms. J also used concrete examples to help students learn the social studies content. She found a model of a volcano, constructed a second model using bricks and mud (to demonstrate fault-blocking), and made use of a telephone book (for folding) to illustrate how mountains were formed. Then she used bricks, mud, and tap water to demonstrate erosion. One day, Ms. J distributed apples cut in half to each student in the class for her lesson on the parts of a mountain: the core, the mantle, and the crust. She helped students draw the analogy before authorizing them to eat their apples.

Both teachers made a particular adaptation for the whole class that was designed to help the students with LD: They went through the important material several times. Ms. P taught *intermediate directions* in the first lesson (Activity 1), did a quick review on the second day (Activity 2.1), and a final review on day 10 (Activity 10.1). Longitude and latitude were introduced in Lesson 8 (Activities 8.4, 8.5, 8.6, 8.7, 8.12), reviewed again in Lesson 9 (Activities 9.1, 9.2, 9.3) and once more in Lesson 10 (Activities 10.2, 10.3).

Ms. J introduced her discussion of how mountains were formed and shaped in the demonstrations in Lesson 2 (Activity 2.6), reviewed it on Day 5 (Activity 5.1) and again on Day 6 in a class question-and-answer session (Activity 6.3), using a filmstrip (Activity 6.4), and another question-and-answer session (Activity 6.6). On Day 7, she had students insert the information on how mountains are formed and shaped into a study outline (Activity 7.1), and her final review of the information came on Day 12 (Activity 12.1). She introduced the names of the three mountain ranges she wanted students to remember on the first day of the unit (Activities 1.4, 1.6) and picked it up again in Lesson 2 (Activity 2.5). On Day 4, she had students locate the three mountain ranges again (Activity 4.2). The information on the three mountain ranges was embedded in application activities on Day 7 (Activity 7.3) and Day 9 (Activity 9.2), and reviewed one final time on Day 12 (Activity 12.2).

One source of evidence of what the students with LD learned was the on-line interview administered immediately after class. For example, on the day that Ms. P demonstrated north using the overhead projector, a container of water, and a floating magnetized needle, Bob was interviewed immediately after class.

Interviewer: How did your teacher help you use a compass today?
Bob: She got the thing down and put something in it and it pointed south and it moved in the water. There's this thing up there and it pointed south . . . or was it north?

On the day Ms P. defined and discussed the equator, her tape indicated that she said, "The equator is an imaginary line running across the earth. The equator is the hottest spot on the earth." After class that day, Bill defined the equator. "The equator goes around and takes pictures of the earth and stuff. No snow comes on it or nothing."

After the demonstration that would help students learn the location of the Tropic of Capricorn and the Tropic of Cancer, Bob was asked:

Interviewer: How did the teacher help you learn today?
Bob: She put Jerry on the table and turned him northwest and stuff.
Interviewer: Then what did she tell you?
Bob: His hips is the equator.
Interviewer: OK, but above the equator.
Bob: I don't know . . . something about his *butt!*

After the lesson on latitude in which Ms. P drew the analogy to a ladder, Chad was interviewed:

Interviewer: Latitude are lines that measure north and south of the equator. And your teacher helped you to remember this. The lines go like a what?
Chad: Like a *fence?*

The postunit interviews also revealed that the students with LD were very confused, even on topics that had been reviewed several times or had been demonstrated concretely. For example, in the fourth grade, the students with LD had a particularly difficult time with definitions for core and mantle, even after the apple analogy. Cal struggled to explain mantle: "It's like . . . not the middle . . . it's kinda like the outside . . . like an apple . . . or a peach. . . . "

History: What Gets Taught? What Gets Learned?

Our analysis of data from the fifth grade history class confirmed the impressions we drew from the geography analyses: Students with LD don't learn very much. But this time, we identified the likely culprit: *background knowledge*. Students with LD in this history class were so deficient in the knowledge they brought to the unit that the good instruction they experienced fell on sterile ground.

The teacher we observed was teaching a unit on the Revolutionary War. He covered events leading up to the war (French and Indian War, taxes, the Boston Massacre, Daughters/Sons of Liberty, Committees of Correspondence, the Boston Tea Party, punishment for colonists, and the First Continental Congress) and the war itself (famous battles such as those at Lexington and Concord, and famous people). To illustrate the problems of students with LD, I focus on two sections of the unit: the Boston Tea Party, and the battles of Lexington and Concord.

To teach about the Boston Tea Party, this teacher, like the two geography teachers, was deliberately iterative. Discussion of the Boston Tea Party was introduced in Lesson 1, and was reintroduced in Lesson 2 using a filmstrip followed by a discussion of the events leading up to the Boston Tea Party, the participants in the event, and the notion of "protesting." In Lesson 3, the teacher reviewed the concepts that had been provided on the filmstrip, and in Lesson 4 he had the students review the facts of the Boston Tea Party through a cause-and-effect writing activity. In Lesson 13, he reviewed the events of the Boston Tea Party one last time in preparation for the end-of-unit exam.

The teacher's treatment of the battles of Lexington and Concord was equally deliberate. In Lesson 5, he mediated the students' reading of that section of the textbook, explaining about "first shots fired" and Britain's poor fighting strategies. In Lesson 10, he reviewed the important role of Lexington and Concord in the Revolutionary War (first shots fired). Finally, in Lesson 13 he reviewed again in preparation for the end-of-unit exam.

The interview data provide striking evidence of how little the students with LD knew before the unit and how little they had to say about what they learned. To illustrate, the answers for the two students with LD are displayed in Tables 11.1, 11.2, and 11.3 next to the answers we received from a classmate selected by the teacher.

Based on our observations of these three teachers in action, we believe that all three were thoughtful and deliberate in their instruction, that they tried to vary the vehicles of instruction to accommodate a variety of learner capabilities, that they used concrete examples, that they paid close attention to activating prior knowledge and to introducing and developing vocabulary, and that they were iterative, repeating important concepts over and over again. We also observed that even such conscientious teachers treated social studies as a predominantly whole-class lesson, used small-group formats rarely, and did not differentiate assignments among students.

But this good social studies instruction did not expand the knowledge base

TABLE 11.1
Pre-unit Interview Responses

What do you know about the Boston Tea Party?

Classmate	LD1	LD2
People in Boston dressed up like Indians, and boarded ships. Some of the cargo was tea. They talked with them and the chests that were there and dumped them in the harbor.	The Boston Tea Party was they were going to try to— oh, what do you call it?— they were going to sit down and talk about signing a— I forget what you call it.	It was a fight . . . on a boat and they threw all the tea overboard.

What happened at Lexington and Concord?

Classmate	LD1	LD2
I think there was fighting between the British and us . . . and . . . the . . . but we were beating the British then reinforcements came in for the British.	This is difficult. No.	Uh . . . no.

TABLE 11.2
Postunit Interview Responses

Why did the American colonists take part in the Boston Tea Party?

Classmate	LD1	LD2
They didn't like the tax on tea. A ship didn't weigh its cargo for 20 days and couldn't sail back without doing that. The people in the city didn't like the tax on tea and opposed the tax. The colonist dressed up as Indians, boarded the ships and threw the tea into the harbor.	They were mad about the tax on the tea, so they dumped 300 chests of tea into the bay.	They didn't want to pay the tax.

What Happened at Lexington and Concord?

Classmate	LD1	LD2
The British soldiers camped in Lexington and there was a first battle and it wasn't very long. . . . After that they marched into Concord, had a fight on North Ridge on April 19, 1725, around noon. They won that battle but on the way back to Boston more people, lots of British soldiers got killed. The colonists would like hide behind trees and they would shoot once at the people and they would run.	Ah, well first Paul Revere rode there screaming, "The red coats are coming, the red coats are coming." And then we had a battle there.	It was like a war. The first shot was in Concord. Yes, the first shot.

TABLE 11.3
Interview Responses Four Months Later

Why did the American colonists take part in the Boston Tea Party?

Classmate	LD1	LD2
Well, they were really mad because they drank a lot of tea. So, when the British got to Boston Harbor, they had to unload all their cargo in 16 days. The government wouldn't let them unload their cargo. So, on the 16th day, they dressed up like Indians and went on and threw the tea overboard because they were mad at the British for putting the tax on something they used so much.	They were mad about the taxes on tea.	(not interviewed)

What happened at Lexington and Concord?

Classmate	LD1	LD2
Whenever the patriots found out that the British soldiers were going there, they told Paul Revere. They thought there was a whole ton of supplies like powders and guns. He went out and told the people at Lexington and Concord and then they went to Lexington and they won there. They went on to Concord and there was a battle the next day.	They fought a battle.	(not interviewed)

of students with LD; social studies information was not learned by the students with LD who were in these classes. The students with LD in the geography classes were selectively attentive, often focused on an extraneous part of a lesson or explanation, and were easily confused and very concrete. The students in the history class had so little prior knowledge, they had virtually nothing on which to "hook" the incoming facts and stories, and they learned little and retained less.

Outcomes in Reading

Our data on reading development in general education settings is just as discouraging. Three sets of data have been reported (see Zigmond et al., 1995): They represent reading achievement data for the MELD implementations in four elementary schools in Pennsylvania, and comparable reading achievement data for inclusion models implemented in Washington State and in Nashville. By prior agreement of the researchers, all three analyses utilized the Basic Academic Skills Samples (BASS) Reading Subtest developed by

Deno and colleagues (Espin, Deno, Maruyama, & Cohen, 1989) as the achievement measure, so that comparisons and aggregations of the data would be
possible. BASS Reading consists of silent reading passages written at approximately the second-grade reading level. Beginning with the second sentence
of each passage, every seventh word is deleted and replaced with three choices
for the correct insertion, one of which is to be circled. There are three such
reading maze (multiple choice cloze) probes and students are given 1 minute
for each. The BASS reading score is the average number correct across the
three passages. Although group-administered and brief, the BASS yields
scores that correlate well with longer, norm-referenced achievement tests
(Jenkins & Jewel, 1992).

The sample across these three data sets comprised all those for whom there
were fall and spring BASS data for a particular target year. This included 145
students with LD: 95 in the four schools in the Pittsburgh project (grades two
through 6), 13 in the Washington site (grades two through six), and 37 in the
Vanderbilt site (grades five through six).

We analyzed the data in three ways. First, we focused on the magnitude of
the reading gains registered by students with LD, specifically whether their
gains exceeded the standard error of measurement (SEM) of the reading test.
We judged gains that surpassed the SEM as indicative of material improvements in reading performance (i.e., indicative that students had made meaningful growth). Over the three projects, roughly half of the students with LD
(54%) achieved gains in excess of one SEM, ranging from 38% of the students
in Washington to 55% in Pennsylvania to 57% in Nashville. Of course this also
means that, in one academic year, approximately half of the target group
failed to register a gain in reading achievement that was larger than the standard error associated with the BASS test.

Typically, the achievement level of children with LD is far below that of
their peers. One goal, or hope, of special education is to prevent further widening of the achievement gap between students with LD and their peers. A
desired outcome is that students with LD, once they are diagnosed and assigned to special education services, will begin to hold their own. Typical IEP
goals for students with LD (e.g., "Johnny will make a year's growth in reading," "Suzy will make a year's growth in spelling") reflect an implicit acceptance of the idea that such students, with the help of special education, can
match the typical (or average) achievement growth rates, if not the levels, of
children without disabilities.

Consequently, in our second analysis of these three data sets we focused
on the extent to which education in general education classrooms prevented
further widening of the achievement gap between students with LD and their
peers. We first calculated mean achievement gains for each grade level within
each site. Then we compared the achievement gain of each student with LD
with the average gain of the relevant grade-level peer group. To maintain or nar-

row the gap, students with LD would have had to register gains that matched or exceeded the average gain of their grade-level peers. Results showed that the percentage of students with LD who made average or better gains varied by site (33% for Pennsylvania, 23% for Washington, and 54% for Nashville), with an average of 37% across sites. Thus, despite the school–university efforts and the teachers' perceptions of successful inclusion, a majority of students with LD (63%) did not register average-size achievement gains. Even more disconcerting, we found that 40% of the LD sample gained less than *half* as much as their classmates' grade-level average. In other words, 40% of students with LD educated in general education settings not only were failing to make average gains, but also were slipping behind at a disturbing rate.

In the previous analysis, we examined the relative progress of students with LD in relation to average grade-level progress, using the *magnitude* of achievement gains as the index for comparisons. The third way we analyzed these achievement data was to compare students' test *standing* relative to the peer group at the beginning and at the end of the school year, to determine whether students actually started to catch up to their average-achieving peers. Using reading test performance, we computed autumn and spring standard scores (z scores) for each grade level at each site separately, and then determined the percentage of students with LD whose achievement status (i.e., their relative standing in the grade-level peer group) had improved during the school year. Results revealed differences across the three projects, with 53% (Pennsylvania), 38% (Washington), and 62% (Nashville) of students with LD gaining ground on their peers. Overall, approximately half of the target group (54%) had moved up in relative standing; the other half had lost ground (i.e., their standard scores, derived from the reading measure, had fallen further from the mean of their respective population).

CONCLUDING COMMENTS ABOUT ORGANIZATION AND MANAGEMENT OF GENERAL EDUCATION CLASSROOMS AND INCLUSION

Of course, the data on progress of students with LD taught reading in resource room or self-contained special education settings is equally bleak. In fact, as a field, we have yet to demonstrate what instruction is needed to help students with LD who are far behind their peers make substantial progress in reading achievement, let alone whether this instruction can be incorporated into the organization and management framework (i.e., the ecology) of a general education setting.

But if what students with LD need is specially designed instruction, we have seen very little of that in general education classrooms. We have heard pragmatic talk about helping students manage the general education curriculum and providing extra help to anyone who needs it, but we have seen almost no specific, directed, individualized, intensive, remedial instruction of students who are clearly deficient academically and struggling with the schoolwork they are being given. If special education once meant a unique curriculum for a child with a disability, careful monitoring of student progress, instruction based on assessment data, or advocacy for an individual student's unique needs, it no longer held those meanings in the schools we have studied. Our impression is that general education classrooms in the real world are just not organized and managed to accommodate those concepts!

In our research to date, my colleagues and I have studied what is going on in general education classrooms, not what could be going on or what should be going on. We have discovered that students with LD in general education classrooms can get a good general education. We have also discovered both how functional the current organization of classrooms is for the sets of learners that populate them, and how resourceful general education teachers can be in accommodating diversity without changing the basic organization and structure of their classroom. But we have also noticed that within a general class setting there is more emphasis on accommodation than on learning, and there is more emphasis on order and quiet than on individual differences and student needs.

Perhaps before we go much further in teacher education, policy development, or research on service delivery models for students with LD, we, as a field, need to engage in a discussion of the goals of special education for our students. There is much to be said for the inclusive experience of a general education setting: Students with LD are exposed to an age-appropriate curriculum; when holidays and special events occur, they are included with their classmates. But based on my research findings, my goals of proficiency in literacy and numeracy and high levels of content knowledge cannot be achieved in the classrooms I have studied.

ACKNOWLEDGMENTS

Several colleagues at the University of Pittsburgh contributed significantly to the research reported in this chapter, and I wish acknowledge those efforts and express my thanks. Alphabetically, these individuals are Janice N. Baker (now at Vanderbilt University), Rita Bean, Barbara Colpo, Deborah Fulmer, Victoria Volonino, and Ruth Wolery.

Research described in this paper was funded, in part, by the Pennsylvania Department of Education, Bureau of Special Education through a Quality Education Initiatives grant, and the United States Department of Education/ Office of Special Education through Grant #G008730252, Educating Learning Disabled Students in Regular Education Classrooms: Mainstream Experiences for Learning Disabled (Project MELD), Grant #H023A0087, An Exploration of the Meaning and Practice of Special Education in the Context of Full-Time Mainstreaming for Students with LD, and Grant #H023D00003, An Analysis of Social Studies Curriculum and Instruction for Mainstreamed and Learning Disabled Students.

REFERENCES

Baker, J. M. (1995a). Inclusion in Minnesota: Educational experiences of students with learning disabilities in two elementary schools. *Journal of Special Education, 29,* 133–143.

Baker, J. M. (1995b). Inclusion in Virginia: Educational experiences of students with learning disabilities in one elementary school. *Journal of Special Education, 29,* 116–123.

Baker, J. M. (1995c). Inclusion in Washington: Educational experiences of students with learning disabilities in one elementary school. *Journal of Special Education, 29,* 155–162.

Baker, J., Colpo, B., Fulmer, D., & Zigmond, N. (1992, April). *Full time mainstreaming: Does it change the learning environment?* Paper presented at the annual meeting of the American Educational Research Association, San Francisco, CA.

Baker, J., Drylie-Quinn, D., Gaus, T., & Zigmond, N. (1988) Observer's codebook: Project MELD classroom observation system, Pittsburgh, PA: University of Pittsburgh.

Baker, J. M., & Zigmond, N. (1995). Themes and implications from these five cases. *Journal of Special Education, 29,* 163–180.

Bos, C. S., & Vaughn, S. (1988). *Strategies for teaching students with learning and behavior problems.* Boston: Allyn and Bacon.

Calfee, R. (1976). Sources of dependency in cognitive processes. In D. Klahr (Ed.), *Cognition and Instruction* (pp. 23–50). New York: Lawrence Erlbaum Associates.

Cooper, J. M. (1994) The teacher as decision maker. in J. M. Cooper (Ed.), *Classroom Teaching Skills* (pp. 1–18). Lexington, MA: Heath.

Donahoe, K., & Zigmond, N. (1990). High school grades of urban LD students and low achieving peers. *Exceptionality, 1,* 17–27.

Espin, C., Deno, S., Maruyama, G., & Cohen, C. (1989, April). *The basic academic skills samples (BASS): An instrument for the screening and identification of children at-risk for failure in regular education classrooms.* Paper presented at the annual American Educational Research Association Conference, San Francisco, CA.

Greenwood, C. R., Dinwiddie, D., Terry, B., Wade, L., Stanley, S. O., Thibadeau, S., & Delquadri, J. C. (1984). Teacher versus peer mediated instruction: An ecobehavioral analysis of achievement outcomes. *Journal of Applied Behavior Analysis, 17,* 521–538.

Jenkins, J. R., & Jewell, M. (1992) An examination of the concurrent validity of the Basic Academic Skills Samples (BASS). *Diagnostique, 17,* 273–288.

Johnson, D. W., & Johnson, R. T. (1986). Mainstreaming and cooperative learning strategies. *Exceptional Children, 52,* 553–561.

Kameenui, E. J., & Simmons, D. C. (1990) *Designing instructional strategies: The prevention of academic learning problems.* Columbus OH: Merrill.

Lemlech, J. K. (1994). *Curriculum and instructional methods for elementary and middle school.* New York: Macmillan.

National Association of State Boards of Education (NASBE). (1992). *Winners all: A call for inclusive schools.* Alexandria, VA: Author.

Schumm, J. S., & Strickler, K. (1991). Guidelines for adapting content area textbooks: Keeping teachers and students content. *Intervention in School and Clinic, 27,* 79–84.

Sharan, S. (1980). Cooperative learning in teams: Recent methods and effects on achievement, attitudes, and ethnic relations. *Review of Educational Research, 50,* 241–272.

Slavin, R. E. (1983). *Cooperative learning.* New York: Longman.

Slavin, R. E., Sharan, S., Kagan, S., Hertz-Lazarowitz, R., Webb, C. W., & Schmuck, R. (1985). *Learning to cooperate, cooperating to learn.* New York: Plenum.

Stainback, S., Stainback, W., & Forest, M. (Eds.). (1990). *Educating all students in the mainstream of regular education.* Baltimore: Brookes.

Zigmond, N. (1995a). Inclusion in Kansas: Educational experiences of students with learning disabilities in one elementary school. *Journal of Special Education, 29,* 144–154.

Zigmond, N. (1995b). Inclusion in Pennsylvania: Educational experiences of students with learning disabilities in one elementary school. *Journal of Special Education, 29,* 124–132.

Zigmond, N., & Baker, J. (1990). Project MELD: A preliminary report. *Exceptional Children, 57,* 176–185.

Zigmond, N., & Baker, J. N. (1995). Concluding comments: Current and future practices in inclusive schooling. *Journal of Special Education, 29,* 245–250.

Zigmond, N., Fulmer, D., Volonino, V., Wolery, R., & Bean, R. (1993, April). *Students in elementary mainstream social studies: What are they doing? What are they learning?* Poster presented at the annual meeting of the American Educational Research Association, Atlanta, GA.

Zigmond, N., Fulmer, D., Wolery, R., Meng, Y., & Bean, R. (1994, April). *Students with LD in elementary level mainstream history classes: What gets taught? What gets learned?* Poster presented at the annual meeting of the American Educational Research Association, New Orleans, LA.

Zigmond, N., Jenkins, J., Fuchs, L., Deno, S., Fuchs, D., Baker, J. N., Jenkins, L., & Coutinho, M. (1995): Special education in restructured schools: Findings from three multi-year studies. *KAPPAN, 76,* 531–535.

12

Order and Learning, Individuals and Groups: A Regular Education Teacher's Response

Marc Elrich
Montgomery Co. Public Schools, Maryland

Professors Zigmond and Cooper and Valli pose the following questions in their chapters in this volume: is the general education classroom an appropriate learning environment for the student with learning disabilities? How might a suitable classroom operate? Their commentary evokes a range of responses and provokes an even wider range of questions about the very nature of education for any student. I react pedagogically, politically, and emotionally to evidence they present, the issues that are raised run just that deep.

I begin with a personal story. When I was taking a course in mainstreaming the teacher posed this question, "How would we deal with it if a student with learning disabilities was placed in our classroom?" Most of my classmates had not begun to teach and the question was meant to be thought provoking. I had, on the other hand, taught in a classroom and I chuckled at the question. My teacher noticed this and proceeded to ask me what I found so amusing, to which I answered, "If you put a learning disabled child in my classroom, how would I know the difference?" I described the typical classrooms that I had seen where there were likely to be several children with learning disabilities, often *distinct* learning disabilities, in the class. Beyond these children were the uncoded students whose skill levels were virtually indistinguishable from those wearing learning disabled (LD) codes. I thought inclusion was the norm.

INDIVIDUAL RIGHTS AND GROUP CONCERNS

As an observer it appears that the debate about what constitutes an appropriate setting has gone full circle. Special education services developed and expanded as it became obvious that children with special needs were not having those needs adequately addressed in a regular classroom. Now, a perceived overuse of special education programs, the desire to mainstream (not segregate and categorize) children, and the poor performance that has persisted despite the differential treatment provided through special education services, have all converged to lead us back to the regular education classroom. And just as was determined many years ago, that setting still does not seem appropriate. What we seem to know now, that we did not know then, is that there are a whole lot of things that do not work well in a myriad of educational settings.

Zigmond, in her chapter, explores a variety of classroom settings throughout the country. The schools and their classrooms provided numerous models of how children with special needs are being integrated, successfully or not, into the regular education classroom. In some schools it appeared that individual accommodations have no place in the instructional setting, and the idea of accommodation is believed to be manifested by the mere presence of children with learning disabilities in an otherwise "normal" classroom. Other school districts seem to have actively embraced the idea of integration and participate in projects, such as MELD, in an effort to accommodate these students in a regular classroom setting.

It is fair to say, then, that children with learning disabilities are being exposed to a range of classroom settings, which ought to facilitate the study of what constitutes an effective learning environment. The evidence that Zigmond presents, and that Cooper and Valli corroborate, is that "students with LD did not learn very much in the general education setting" (Zigmond, p. 179, this volume). That is, despite a willingness to include students with learning disabilities and a desire to produce successful outcomes for those students, nothing really seems to work.

Is this a problem unique to the general education classroom? Is such a classroom an inappropriate setting when compared to the other alternatives? The reality appears to be that the success of a student with learning disabilities in a regular education classroom is likely to be no better, or no worse, than in a special education placement. "The data on progress of students with LD taught reading in resource room or self- contained special education settings is equally bleak . . . we have yet to demonstrate what instruction is needed to help students with LD . . . make substantial progress in reading achievement. . . . " (Zigmond, p. 187, this volume).

A number of problems have been identified with the structure and organization of the regular education classroom that warrant discussion. I offer my reactions to them as a classroom teacher and not necessarily in order of priority, save for two elements that I reserve for the end. Both authors assert that the orientation of the general education classroom is toward the group and not the individual. Instruction and supporting activities are designed to move the group. The curriculum itself is designed so that most average students can succeed in demonstrating that they have been exposed to the material (I hesitate to suggest that exposure should be equated with mastery). It is not hard to trace the forces behind this.

Teachers respond to the pressures that most directly affect their jobs. In the eyes of principals and school boards a class that performs poorly, either academically or behaviorally, is most likely to outweigh the achievements of a few individuals. These people want evidence of mass achievement, and parents increasingly look to school achievement scores to ascertain the worthiness of a school for their child. What is most often discussed with teachers, individually or collectively, is where the class or school stands, not where particular individuals place.

The task in the classroom is to move the group and to focus energy and resources on activities that keep the group controlled and moving forward. As a consequence, parents who feel that their child might be at either end of the achievement spectrum often argue that his or her needs are not being met. They may be rightly concerned, but the question concerning the claims of the individual vis-à-vis the claims of the group still remains. If most children make satisfactory progress on a given education diet, is it bad that some make less progress than they possibly otherwise might achieve? Could those students receive differentiated instruction without impacting the progress of the larger group? These are questions that teachers wrestle with. I only add that the more demanding the expectations placed on the teacher by parents and authorities, the less likely a teacher may be to experiment with alternative teaching styles.

THE COMPOSITION OF CLASSROOMS

I found myself wanting to know more about what these general education classrooms were like. Were they heterogeneous or homogeneous classrooms and, if they were heterogeneous, what constituted the range of abilities and behaviors of the so-called "normal" class before the introduction of children with learning disabilities? This goes back to my initial reaction regarding the mainstreaming instructor. If the child with learning disabilities is the only child who departs from the norm, whether academically or in terms of behavior, one kind of challenge is posed to the classroom teacher. An accommodation to one student in a classroom where the group, as a whole, possesses solid motivation, reasonable self-control, and adequate background knowledge, may not create much of a difficulty.

What if we are talking about a heterogeneous classroom where self-control is an issue for a third of the class and the majority of the class lacks the background knowledge that proved such an obstacle to learning even the "less rigorous" social studies curriculum described by Zigmond? If most of the class was below grade level in reading, though not identified as LD, and if their IQs ranged from 80 to 140, a teacher may view the introduction of a child with LD as pushing a difficult situation beyond the reasonable limit or, alternatively, may feel that the existing situation forces so many accommodations that the student will have to find a place among those existing accommodations.

The reality for many teachers, particularly in urban areas or even suburban rings, may well be approaching the latter case. Teachers of classrooms that approximate that description devote increasing amounts of time to behavior management. Creating an atmosphere so that teaching and learning can occur consumes inordinate amounts of the school day, devouring minutes that might otherwise be spent on a greater degree of differentiated instruction. Maintaining group order, so that group progress can be realized, becomes a priority.

In this light, every additional demand for special and differential accommodation reduces time and effort available to the whole group and introduces another competing priority into the teacher's planning and implementaton strategies. The difficulty of teaching under these conditions has not gone unnoticed by professional observers and parents. The observation that "teachers valued quiet and order" and that "students raised their hands to be recognized or to get permission to move around" (Zigmond, p. 165, this volume) does not say anything about the appropriateness of a classroom for a child with LD. Although my class does a lot of group work, specifically using the workshop approach for reading and writing and employing group activities for math and social studies, I absolutely value quiet and order, insist that whole class discussions be orderly, and expect that the conversations have, as their primary focus, the task at hand. I find these to be necessary conditions for the existence of a successful learning environment. There is no inherent contradiction between having a learning program that addresses individual differences and having a classroom where discipline and respect are a part of the environment. The observations about the structure of regular classrooms may have more to say about how teachers struggle to create a learning atmosphere under difficult conditions than about whether teachers are willing to accommodate children with learning disabilities in their classrooms.

BARRIERS TO CHANGE

Zigmond observed that, despite intensive training, willing teachers (as learners), support of administration, and extensive planning, the actual adoption of new and accommodating teaching techniques proved to be difficult. Good intentions and sincere efforts did not translate into great changes in teacher behavior. Why?

There are several reasons. Foremost may be that workshops are not real classroom settings, so that when the theory does not produce results and teachers look at the clock and see valuable instruction time being lost, they revert to methods in which they believe they have had previous success. Considering that the "new" methods were taught to facilitate the accommodation of the few, it is not hard to see why a teacher would abandon such a method if it appeared that the group would suffer. Following a path that has an uncertain outcome may be too risky for teachers who are under pressure to complete a set unit in a fixed time period. The group focus mitigates against experiments when benefits to the group are not obvious, or if impairment of group progress seems imminent.

Most teachers are not schooled in the pedagogical techniques of peer-assisted learning and cooperative groups, and curriculum is not typically designed for this approach. Teachers have years of experience teaching in a more didactic structure and have experienced their classrooms making adequate progress, at least by the standards of principals and school boards. This is not easily unlearned by attending a workshop. It is especially difficult to avoid reverting to practices that have a history of success attached to them, when confronted with a difficulty that threatens the ability to complete a task for which you may be held accountable.

In the end, we are left to conclude that the typical classroom, with its focus on group achievement, its lack of individual assessment, and its functional attributes modeled around a didactic model of instruction is no place for the child with learning disabilities. We are told that whether the effort be minimal (just placing them in a regular class) or maximal (providing training and support to willing teachers in an embracing system), the outcome is the same both in terms of how instruction is implemented (it remains largely didactic) and results in students with learning disabilities performing poorly, which widens the gap between them and their non-LD peers. Parenthetically, we are told that these are the same results achieved by specialists delivering instruction in settings that are more aligned with the needs of students with learning disabilities. What should we do?

PARADIGM SHIFT: GOOD NEWS, BAD NEWS

Professors Cooper and Valli suggest that we need to accomplish a profound change in how instruction is delivered to all students (chap. 10, this volume). Specifically, they embrace the movement toward content-based instruction in cooperative classrooms employing authentic assessments. Most importantly, the reason for supporting this is not to accommodate students with learning disabilities but to provide better instruction and to implement more meaningful methods of assessment for everyone. They see this as major paradigm shift that has positive implications for all learners.

To be certain, there are potential advantages implicit in this shift that address the problems that were so clearly enumerated in Zigmond's chapter. Not least important is the idea that change is presented as benefitting all students, not something done to fit a few misfits into the classroom. It becomes a way of teaching and not a way of accommodating and, therefore, can be more easily assimilated by all participants in the learning process into the realm of legitimacy. Introducing cooperative learning to facilitate the group process carries a different psychological weight than suggesting that a teacher adopt cooperative methods to accommodate the child with learning disabilities who will be coming into the classroom next week. It becomes a legitimate method of instruction. The downside is that it needs to be taught to teachers and is not something that can simply be accessed through a few days in a workshop or by scattering some in-service hours throughout the year. Also, teachers will need to be convinced that this is a genuine paradigm shift and not yet another effort to ride the latest trend.

Inherent in cooperative structures and the utilization of workshops is a greater emphasis on the progress of the individual. These structures provide greater opportunities to provide specific feedback on a continuing basis to all students. Mastery of a concept is assessed within the process of teaching it instead of being assessed solely at the conclusion of the unit, providing greater opportunities to adjust the pace of instruction to individual needs and to monitor progress and institute interventions when they are needed. It is, in theory, harder to fall behind and get lost. Moreover, instruction would not be solely dependent on the teacher because well-structured teams contain members with the skills and attitudes that allow them to act as peer coaches or student teachers. No student, including the student with learning disabilities, is left in a situation where the only information that is available comes from the teacher. Instead, all students are provided several points of support and more continuous reinforcement by their group than can be received from a single teacher trying to monitor, help, and reteach each student. Therefore, the possibility of students getting the information they need when they need it, from a source that is readily accessible, is greatly enhanced.

This paradigm shift, with its emphasis on authentic assessments, drives changes in curriculum and instruction. The pressures from the top may stay the same, but the incongruity between the demands of the curriculum that are based on memory and recall, and the expectation that the teachers adopt a style that emphasizes content and application to the real world begin to wither. It is certainly the case in Maryland that the change in state mandated assessments toward performance assessment is effecting changes in curriculum and, necessarily, in the methods for teaching that curriculum. Although none of these changes do anything to address the significant issue of adequate teacher training and support, they at least make clear that the expectations for desired outcomes is consistent with the instructional model needed to produce them. Ironically, teachers will have the same motivation to implement change as they had earlier to resist it, their superiors and the parents of their students will evaluate them on the basis of class performance on the new tests that required the changes to curriculum and instruction.

The net effect of this is to produce the classroom that eluded Zigmond's observations and which Cooper and Valli hold as the model most likely to result in the successful accommodation of students with learning disabilities. The question, "Will this address the alarming failure rate of students with learning disabilities?" still remains. If the thought is that this will replace special education services for the vast majority of students, then I remain pessimistic.

The new practices inherent in the cooperative classroom are not sufficient to significantly improve the rate of progress of students with learning disabilities. Monitoring group work and workshop activities is enormously time intensive. The fact that the teacher is no longer in the front of the room lecturing does not necessarily mean that there is now surplus time to attend leisurely to all students. In some cases the time pressures may increase. Consider the situation where the teacher hands out a worksheet and then walks about the class monitoring the work. Some students expect and need only a glance, there is no expectation of teacher interaction. The teacher can then focus time on a student or small group of students who seem to be having a difficulty.

Now picture a class with six heterogeneous groups engaged in group work. As the teacher circulates, the expectation by the students for a teacher interaction is far greater. If a student needs help, the teacher must be confident that someone in the group can provide adequate help if the teacher is to move on. This expectation of all students for their fair share of teacher time, not to mention that the kind of questioning that a teacher needs to engage in with each group, may result in little or no change in the amount of time available for reteaching to anyone, including students with learning disabilities.

A similar scenario can be applied to either writing or reading workshops. On the positive side, every student is assured of individual attention. On the negative side, because meaningful interaction with every student is expected, there may not be time for the kind of in-depth work that some students may need. Being able to conference for a minute or two does not mean that that is enough time to fill the gaps for a student with learning disabilities. As much as this approach requires individual attention and feedback, it does not guarantee adequate attention. And, it may not be possible to provide the level of attention needed, when there is a classroom full of children with equally legitimate claims on your time. In response to Zigmond's remark that "we have seen almost no specific, directed, individualized, intensive, remedial instruction of students who are clearly deficient academically . . . " (p. 188, this volume), I say that the adoption of a cooperative teaching style probably guarantees that this child would get specific, directed, and individualized instruction but, depending on the class size and overall make-up of the class, it may not change at all the amount of intensive, remedial instruction a student with learning disabilities receives. What is to be done for this child?

EFFECTIVE INSTRUCTION

Returning to Zigmond's observation that the effectiveness of instruction for children with learning disabilities is a failure regardless of where and how it is implemented, the starting point must be to develop a model of instruction that works. The cooperative setting that Cooper and Valli want is most closely approximated in the special education settings I have seen. If it does not work there, with low pupil-to-teacher ratios and specialists trained in the field, *how*, or more properly, *what* are we supposed to bring into the classroom? Personal observations and discussions with my peers confirm that children who are identified LD tend to stay LD, regardless of the level of intensity of the services they receive. This is a pretty bleak picture, but neither the critique of regular classrooms nor their didactic propensities seems to move toward a solution to the core problem which is, first and foremost, how to successfully educate children with learning disabilities. Focusing the discussion on what is wrong with regular instruction without saying what works in special education does not help me, a regular education teacher with several students possessing learning disabilities, behavior disorders, or both, conclude what, if anything, I might or should do differently.

I do not believe that students with learning disabilities, as a rule, need to be segregated in separate programs. In my classroom and classrooms throughout my school and the County, most students with learning disabilities are part of regular classroom settings. The most typical form of resource help they receive is through pull-out programs. When I, or other teachers, refer children who seem to be performing significantly below their potential to special education services, it is not to remove a child from the classroom but, rather, to get that child a more intensive and hopefully more individually focused form of intervention for a part of the school day. I believe that a student with learning disabilities can benefit academically from inclusion when instruction for everyone is more responsive to individual needs. At the same time, I think full-inclusion coupled with a removal of direct services constitutes a prescription for disaster. There are simply too many demands on teachers to expect them to provide effective special education services in a whole class setting without diminishing the time, attention, and quality of instruction given to the larger group. Cooperative groups and workshop learning situations are not panaceas, nor are they substitutes for the intensive instruction some children need.

ORDER VERSUS LEARNING
AND INDIVIDUAL VERSUS GROUP

I previously said there were two issues that warrant separate mention. I want to preface my comments by saying that there is no small amount of tension between competing players on the education field. Parents want to know why disruptive children are allowed to remain in regular classes, and why the lowest children receive the greatest resources, while average and above average children suffer high teacher–student ratios and receive little individualized attention. Regular education teachers are often suspicious of special education specialists who can seem too insensitive to the impact that a disruptive child can have on the learning of the vast majority of students.

Zigmond concludes that in most general education classrooms "there is more emphasis on order and quiet than on individual differences and student needs" (p. 188, this volume). Posed this way, it it hard to perceive it as doing anything but posing an either/or dichotomy. Either there is order, or individual needs are met. Either there is quiet, or individual differences are recognized. This translates roughly into saying that bringing students with learning disabilities into the classroom means that order and quiet must be sacrificed or, more directly, bringing children with learning disabilities into your classroom will tear it up. If this is what it truly means, then regular education teachers will continue to be wary of what inclusion will mean to their classroom and they will resist it. This phrasing intimates that there is something wrong with quiet and order and that they are, in fact, antithetical to genuine learning. I believe that you can have quiet and order, that they are not the same as silence and fear, and that the ability to attain quiet and order is essential even in the paradigm shift toward a cooperative pedagogy.

One goal of instruction ought to be to increase children's attention spans and abilities to focus on and evaluate information. Think for a moment about the transition to adulthood and consider that the information we are to grasp and evaluate comes increasingly from what we hear and not from what we read. Listening skills need to be developed; to do that, a learning environment must facilitate listening and responding. The choice is not between a classroom of still, silent zombies, nor of children whose mouths and bodies are in perpetual motion. What should be fostered is the development of children who can move between learning channels and accommodate a variety of different inputs and whose actions are appropriate to the learning situation they are in. I hope that if an observer enters that classroom during a time when the children are listening and reflecting on the information they are hearing (while sitting comfortably in their seats or on the floor), he or she will not write that the teacher values silence more than the growth of the individual student.

The second comment pertains to what special education ought to be. Is special education supposed to mean "a unique curriculum . . . careful monitoring of student progress, instruction based on assessment data, or advocacy for an individual student's unique needs"? (Zigmond, p. 188, this volume). It begs the question of what regular education means. I dare say that if you showed this to regular education teachers or to the parents of a child in the regular education progam they would both ask, "Why would you not strive to provide the same thing to a non-LD child? Isn't this a sensible way to educate all children?" The answer is that, of course it's sensible and every child would benefit, but stated this way it appears that these are the exclusive claims of children with learning disabilities on a school system and everyone else gets the over- crowded, under-suppplied classrooms. If the suggestion is that children with learning disabilities have a special right to a nurturing and supportive educational environment and a greater per pupil expense than is accorded a non-LD child, the making of the political and moral debate that surrounds special education service levels today results.

As educators, we need to provide this kind of nourishment to all students, recognizing that it has universal value. The specific activities that are provided under special education might necessarily be different, but the intention behind them should be the same as what is behind every pedagogical approach: to provide instruction in a way that allows each individual to realize his or her maximum potential.

SUGGESTIONS FOR FURTHER RESEARCH

I think that some directions for further research are needed. For one, we need to know what does work and what settings optimize the effectiveness of a particular remediation. The suggested lack of efficacy of any approach leads me to wonder if we need to get together with the researchers studying the structure, organization, and development of the brain itself and see if the insights might further our search for effective instructional techniques.

Related to this, we seem to proceed with the notion that everything can, in fact, be remediated. When the skill gap does not narrow, when students spend their academic lives in special education and end up as far, or farther, behind at the end of the process as they were at the beginning, we seek immediately to fault the school system while blaming the teacher, the methods, and the commitment of resources for the child's inability to flower intellectually. Perhaps the reality is that everything cannot be fixed. It is possible that some disabilities may have organic origins that no method of accommodation can overcome. Is special education a failure because it does not fix what cannot be fixed by instructional techniques alone? Do we imagine ourselves as gods, able to overcome any obstacle in our path? Such a view is both arrogant and destined to produce a record of failure.

I would extend this argument to the environmental factors shaping a child's development. To place the blame for all of our lost children on the door of the school house is nothing more than society's desire to escape responsibility for the larger social milieu. Are children with LD more or less likely to be products of environments that are typified by one or more of the following characteristics: low-income families, poorly educated parents, unstable families, experiences of violence, experiences of neglect, lack of adequate health care and nutrition, and substandard housing? I would guess that we would find a positive correlation between learning disabilities and environmental factors, which leads to the question, "Can we expect classroom accommodations to overcome all of the environmental forces at work in shaping a child's development? Do we have models to examine where interventions have been aggressively taken beyond the classroom and, if so, does more holistic intervention alter the impact of remedial programs?" I do not think it is possible to address instructional efficacy separate from the total learning environment of the child.

With such hope posited in the cooperative model, it would be interesting to examine systems that have had years of experience with the model and see whether they have had different experiences with their student population. For example, when children are in cooperative environments from kindergarten and upward, do as many of them appear to have learning disabilities? Do those children with identified disabilities appear to do better or worse than their counterparts in more traditional classrooms? What interventions are most effective in a cooperative setting? Most of the systems studied in the research reported here were based on more didactic approaches to instruction; therefore, it may be hard to make evaluations about the efficacy of cooperative classrooms when such classrooms have been the exception and not the norm of student experiences. My own experiences tell me that children with more long-term exposure to cooperative settings approach learning differently than students having less exposure to cooperative environments. It may be that a change to a cooperative setting is far more difficult to implement after students have spent years in more traditional settings, making the teachers' job more difficult than it might otherwise be and making the interventions less effective because students' previous experiences have significantly colored their relationship to the school setting.

Lastly, we need to find a way to more effectively give teachers alternative and effective instructional strategies. Workshops and a few half day in-services are not the answer. The real question is how we can give teachers authentic learning experiences so there can be a unity between theory and praxis. One idea would be to set up learning centers in typical schools and rotate teachers in these schools for a few weeks so they can see the implementation of effective instructional techniques. The issue of teacher training, however, begs the earlier question, "If special education settings are no more effective than regular classrooms, what is it that you are going to teach the teacher in a model school or any other training program?"

We need to go back to the root and ask why some children are not learning. Are the causes environmental, organic, or pedagogical? Do our remediations reflect what we know about the causes, or do they address only a limited aspect of the problem? Are we willing, as society, to acknowledge the complexity of some of these problems or do we prefer to keep the locus for the blame on our schools? I would suggest that, ultimately, where we are willing to look will determine what we are able to find.

13

Remediation and Inclusion: Can We Have It All?

Ann C. Schulte
North Carolina State University

The Zigmond and Cooper and Valli chapters offered two very different ways of looking at classroom management and organization. Cooper and Valli gave an historical view, mapping out how conceptions of management have changed as our conceptions of the teaching/learning process have changed. They ended on a hopeful note, suggesting that current reform efforts that reconceptualize learning as understanding will result in more effective classroom structures for all students, including those with learning disabilities. In contrast, Zigmond's chapter was a detailed snapshot, and a sobering one, of the limits of our current efforts at inclusion for students with learning disabilities. She suggested that, at least at present, we may have to choose between inclusion and high levels of literacy, numeracy, and content knowledge for students with learning disabilities. Thus, one chapter concluded with guarded optimism, and one with guarded pessimism. The focus of my chapter is whether we can have it all—inclusion and effective remediation—and what research strategies are needed to move us closer to this goal.

Perhaps the first step in answering this question is taking a close look at what we know about students with learning disabilities and how to remediate their academic deficits. One theme in the Zigmond chapter was the pervasive and cumulative deficits evidenced by students with learning disabilities. In her portraits of middle school classrooms, it was striking how little of the instruction these students took with them—even when it was creative, interesting instruction with mnemonic strategies embedded in it. Her vignettes seemed to be illustrations of Stanovich's (1986) "Matthew effect," in which students' learning problems become more broad and pervasive as their initial deficits limit their ability to profit from new learning opportunities. This same theme was echoed in the reading achievement data that Zigmond reported for the inclusion models in Pennsylvania, Washington State, and Tennessee. About 50% of the students with learning disabilities *lost ground* in reading with respect to peers during the course of the school year, even with mainstream remedial assistance.

But these discouraging outcomes aren't limited to inclusion programs. If achievement commensurate with peers is used to judge success, the longitudinal outcomes for students with learning disabilities, whether in inclusive or restrictive settings, are not positive (Kavale, 1988; Schonhaut & Satz, 1983). At present we do not have programs for students with learning disabilities that have demonstrated track records of producing high levels of literacy, numeracy, and content knowledge. We can document that several instructional and management practices improve outcomes for students with learning disabilities (Larrivee, 1989; Leinhardt & Pallay, 1982; Wang & Baker, 1986), but we have little information on what it would take to normalize the developmental trajectory for these students, and our research designs are generally geared toward showing superiority of one approach over another rather than assessing normalization.

An example of the type of study that would provide this information is a recent investigation of Reading Recovery by Iversen and Tunmer (1993). In this study, first-grade children identified as having reading difficulties were provided with either: (a) the standard Reading Recovery curriculum; (b) the Reading Recovery curriculum with a phonics component added; or (c) what they termed "standard intervention," small-group instruction in reading of the sort often provided through Chapter One funding. In addition to comparing outcomes across the three remedial approaches, intervention participants were also compared at endpoint with students whom teachers had identified as average readers in the regular classroom. Comparisons of the groups indicated that the two Reading Recovery groups outperformed the standard intervention group on measures of reading and component skills, and also equaled or outperformed average achievers.

This study is notable both in terms of its outcome (low achievers equaling or outperforming average students) and in the use of comparison groups that allowed assessment of how low achievers fared in three different remedial programs *and* compared to average achievers. Such a strategy allows comparisons among interventions, as well as an assessment of the extent to which the interventions normalized students' functioning. However, my citation of Iversen and Tunmer's impressive results shouldn't be interpreted as a suggestion that Reading Recovery would produce the same results if students with learning disabilities had been the participants. I believe that one of the reasons we've failed to produce impressive outcomes for students with learning disabilities is the number and severity of problems evidenced by these children. Students with learning disabilities have more severe academic deficits than do low achievers (Kavale, Fuchs, & Scruggs, 1994). In addition, recent research in comorbidity, or the extent to which two or more disorders tend to co-occur in the same individual, has shown that learning disabilities are linked with both internalizing and externalizing disorders as well as attentional disorders (Hinshaw, 1992; Holborow & Berry, 1986; Nieves, 1991; Rourke, 1988). Thus, students with learning disabilities often present management challenges to teachers in terms of their academic, behavioral, and social functioning. The management challenges presented by comorbidity are often ignored in planning for remediation, and few studies of learning disabilities interventions have screened for the presence/absence of co-occurring disorders in their subject population.

Given the severity of academic problems that students with learning disabilities often present, the likelihood that they will have other social and adjustment problems, and the poor track record of existing interventions for students with learning disabilities, I do not believe children with learning disabilities are well served by a research agenda that combines the questions about the impact of classroom environment on student learning with questions about effective interventions for severe academic deficits. My preference would be that our research agenda begin by asking what type and intensity of intervention is necessary to ensure that students with learning disabilities achieve commensurate with peers and, only when the limits of intervention have been determined, that we ask where high-quality services can be delivered.

In a sense, this research direction for special education is the backward mapping that Cooper and Valli called for in the reform of regular education. Rather than starting with a given classroom structure, we need to work backwards from student learning to the classroom and school organizational structures that support student progress, not just for regular education students, but for students with learning disabilities as well.

When one does this, one may end up rediscovering some of the basic tenets on which special education was founded. Zigmond noted that "If special education once meant a unique curriculum for a child with a disability, careful monitoring of student progress, instruction based on assessment data, or advocacy of an individual student's needs, it no longer held those meanings in the schools we have studied" (Zigmond, chap. 11, this volume). Yet, Reading Recovery (Clay, 1985), whose hallmarks are intensive, individual instruction based on assessment results and careful monitoring of student progress, is increasingly being used in regular education. At a time when special education has lost its specialness in some settings, it's interesting that regular education is rediscovering it!

Does a backward mapping approach mean that research on classroom ecology, inclusion, and learning disabilities is a waste of time? Certainly not. The quality of the regular education environment is linked to referral to special education (Skrtic, 1991) and reforms aimed at making the regular education classroom responsive to individual differences reduce special education referrals (Gutkin, Henning-Stout, & Piersel, 1988; Knoff & Batsche, 1993; Ritter, 1978; Slavin, 1990).

However, I maintain that the issue of accommodating students with learning disabilities is a special case, and an extreme case, of a broader question: How does one accommodate a wide range of learning needs and achievement levels in the classroom? This issue is central to much of the work presented at this conference, and the work of researchers trying to address this question has led to many innovations such as peer tutoring and cooperative learning that better accommodate the needs of all students in the regular classroom.

However, it is important to note that even when we have instructional and management techniques that succeed in accommodating a range of children in the classroom, we have little information on their specific impact on students with learning disabilities, and little guarantee that they will be used by schools. Both Vaughn and Schumm (chap. 7, this volume) and Zigmond (chap. 11, this volume) noted the widespread use of whole-group instruction in the classrooms they observed, with little use of differentiated instruction, or reteaching, and Cooper and Valli noted that knowing something and knowing it works doesn't ensure that teachers will do it. Understanding how and when schools adopt innovations that benefit low achievers and students with disabilities is an important area of research and one that is currently being supported through funding to 15 projects by the U.S. Department of Education's Office of Special Education Programs, including my own work examining adoption of special education/regular education collaborative teaching and curriculum-based measurement in two elementary schools (Schulte, 1992).

HAVING IT ALL: A RESEARCH AGENDA

As is evident from the previous discussion, I am not hopeful that we can presently offer students with severe learning disabilities both remediation and inclusion in the regular classroom. Even in the more innovative models presented at this conference we have not seen evidence that students with learning disabilities can make the kind of progress needed to achieve on par with peers. However, it is likely that they, and other low achievers, would fare better under the more innovative structures than in the traditional classroom.

My position is that we are most likely to have it all if we adopt a research strategy that aims toward developing effective interventions *first* and then examine the contexts in which they can be provided. To that end, the following suggestions for future research are offered.

Make the Development of Effective Academic Interventions a Research Priority

Current special education interventions are not powerful enough to close the achievement gap between students with learning disabilities and their peers (Kavale et al., 1994; Lombardi, Odell, & Novotny, 1990; Wagner, 1989). More research is needed that is focused on intense intervention packages that provide students with learning disabilities with the literacy, numeracy, thinking, and content skills they need in the regular education environment and beyond. Such research should take advantage of the strides in research methodology that have been made in the past few years, such as growth curve analysis (Bryk & Raudenbush, 1987) to provide finer grained analyses of what subgroups of students with learning disabilities benefit from what types of remediation at what age.

Use Research Designs and Measures That Permit In-Depth Understanding of the Processes Contributing to Change, as Well as the Outcomes for Students With Learning Disabilities

Zigmond's work used a combination of quantitative and qualitative methodology that clearly documented what students were taught, how they were taught, and what they learned after instruction. She also included comparisons with average achievers exposed to the same instruction. Similar research designs that included observation, qualitative measures, and authentic assessment of outcomes were described by other participants at this conference. Such research designs, and the longer time horizons they require, are essential to achieving an understanding of the needs of students with learning disabilities and how to help teachers successfully meet those needs.

Explicitly Examine the Extent to Which Students With Learning Disabilities Benefit From Regular Education Innovations

An implicit assumption in much of the work in regular education reported here has been that interventions for other low achievers will benefit students with learning disabilities. However, little research has explicitly tested this assumption, and that which has addressed this issue has not always yielded positive results (e.g., Cosden, Pearl, & Bryan, 1985). The extent to which educational innovations benefit students with learning disabilities should be explicitly tested in designs that compare the effects of the intervention on students who are average, those who are low achievers, and those who are identified as learning disabled. Such designs also should document how the intervention affects students with learning disabilities standing relative to age mates (e.g., Simmons, Fuchs, Fuchs, Hodge, & Mathes, 1994). Likewise, the preventive effects of such interventions in terms of the number of students referred for special education services should be examined. It may be that research focused on the question of accommodating a broader range of individual differences in the classroom holds more promise for the prevention of learning disabilities than their remediation.

Continue Research on the Adoption of Innovations at the School and Classroom Level

Zigmond documented that even when teachers had the knowledge and support to implement more individualized teaching, they did not do it. Why is this? This finding and the findings of many other researchers (e.g., Fullan & Miles, 1992; Huberman & Crandall, 1982; McLaughlin, 1991) suggest that meaningful change is not simply a matter of providing new technology and convincing others that it works. The creation of school environments responsive to the needs of children with learning disabilities will require that special educators have a better understanding of change in schools and the factors that impede and facilitate it.

In examining factors influencing change, teacher beliefs and assumptions about learning are both areas that should be explored. Cooper and Valli and Zigmond alluded to the importance of teachers' beliefs in determining what happens in the classroom, and the findings of several other researchers have supported this view (Smith & Shepard, 1988; Weinstein & Mignano, 1993; Winfield, 1986). This seems a promising area of research, particularly how teachers' beliefs about ability influence their instructional and management decisions. Nativist beliefs about the lack of malleability in intelligence and the extent to which ability rather than environmental variables account for individual differences in learning run deep in our culture and schools (Smith & Shepard, 1988; Stevenson, 1992). It may have been these beliefs that made teachers so resistant to changing their classroom structures in Zigmond's study, even when it was clear that some students were not learning. They likely account, in part, for why we have relatively little research on classroom process compared to the body of research on intelligence, and why there was a need for this conference on classroom ecology and learning disabilities rather than on the role of cognitive factors in learning disabilities.

In the opening of this chapter I commented that the Cooper and Valli and Zigmond chapters reflected guarded optimism and guarded pessimism respectively. The body of my chapter reflects both those sentiments. We have yet to demonstrate that we can meet the needs of students with learning disabilities, regardless of setting. However, the new classroom structures, richer conceptualizations of the teaching and learning processes, and new research tools described in this volume offer the promise of having it all to future generations of students with learning disabilities.

REFERENCES

Bryk, A. S., & Raudenbush, S. W. (1987). Application of hierarchical linear models to assessing change. *Psychological Bulletin, 101,* 147–158.

Clay, M. (1985). *The early detection of reading difficulties.* Auckland, New Zealand: Heinemann.

Cosden, M., Pearl, R., & Bryan, T. H. (1985). The effects of cooperative and individual goal structures on learning disabled and nondisabled students. *Exceptional Children, 52,* 103–114.

Fullan, M., & Miles, M. B. (1992). Getting reform right: What works and what doesn't. *Phi Delta Kappan, 74,* 745–752.

Gutkin, T. B., Henning-Stout, M., & Piersel, W. C. (1988). Impact of a district-wide behavioral consultation prereferral intervention service on patterns of school psychological service delivery. *Professional School Psychology, 3,* 301–308.

Hinshaw, S. P. (1992). Externalizing behavior problems and academic underachievement in childhood and adolescence: Causal relationships and underlying mechanisms. *Psychological Bulletin, 111,* 127–155.

Holborow, P. L., & Berry, P. S. (1986). Hyperactivity and learning difficulties. *Journal of Learning Disabilities, 19,* 426–431.

Huberman, A. M., & Crandall, D. P. (1982). *People, policies, and practices: Examining the chain of school improvement, Vol. IX, Implications for action.* Andover, MA: The Network.

Iversen, S., & Tunmer, W. (1993). Phonological processing skills and the Reading Recovery program. *Journal of Educational Psychology, 85,* 112–126.

Kavale, K. A. (1988). The long-term consequences of learning disabilities. In M. C. Wang, H. J. Walburg, & M. C. Reynolds (Eds.), *The handbook of special education: Research and practice* (pp. 303–344). New York: Pergamon.

Kavale, K. A., Fuchs, D., & Scruggs, T. E. (1994). Setting the record straight on learning disability and low achievement: Implications for policymaking. *Learning Disabilities Research and Practice, 9,* 70–77.

Knoff, H. M., & Batsche, G. M. (1993). A school reform process for at-risk students: Applying Caplan's organizational consultation principles to guide prevention, intervention, and home-school collaboration. In W. P. Erchul (Ed.), *Consultation in community, school, and organizational practice* (pp. 123–160). Washington, DC: Taylor & Francis.

Larrivee, B. (1989). Effective strategies for academically handicapped students in the regular classroom. In R. E. Slavin, N. L. Karweit, & N. A. Madden (Eds.), *Effective programs for students at risk* (pp. 291–319). Boston: Allyn & Bacon.

Leinhardt, G., & Pallay, A. (1982). Restrictive educational settings: Exile or haven? *Review of Educational Research, 52,* 557–578.

Lombardi, T. P., Odell, K. S., & Novotny, D. E. (1990). Special education and students at risk: Findings from a national study. *Remedial and Special Education, 12*(1), 56–62.

McLaughlin, M. W. (1991). The Rand change agent study: Ten years later. In A. R. Odden (Ed.), *Education policy implementation* (pp. 143–155). Albany, NY: State University of New York.

Nieves, N. (1991). Childhood psychopathology and learning disabilities: Neuropsychological relationships. In J. E. Obrzut & G. H. Hynd (Eds.), *Neuropsychological foundations of learning disabilities* (pp. 113–145). San Diego, CA: Academic Press.

Ritter, D. R. (1978). Effects of a school consultation program upon referral patterns of teachers. *Psychology in the Schools, 15,* 239–243.

Rourke, B. P. (1988). Socioemotional disturbances of learning disabled children. *Journal of Consulting and Clinical Psychology, 56,* 801–810.

Schonhaut, S., & Satz, P. (1983). Prognosis for children with learning disabilities: A review of follow-up studies. In M. Rutter (Ed.), *Developmental neuropsychiatry* (pp. 542–563). New York: Guilford.

Schulte, A. C. (1992). *Including children with disabilities in school-based change.* Grant funded by Division of Innovation and Development, Office of Special Education Programs, U.S. Department of Education.

Simmons, D. C., Fuchs, D., Fuchs, L. S., Hodge, J. P., & Mathes, P. G. (1994). Importance of instructional complexity and role reciprocity to classwide peer tutoring. *Learning Disabilities Research and Practice, 9,* 203–212.

Skrtic, T. M. (1991). The special education paradox: Equity as the way to excellence. *Harvard Educational Review, 61,* 49–58.

Slavin, R. E. (1990). General education under the Regular Education Initiative: How must it change? *Remedial and Special Education, 11*(3), 40–50.

Smith, M. L., & Shepard, L. A. (1988). Kindergarten readiness and retention: A qualitative study of teachers' beliefs and practices. *American Education Research Journal, 25,* 307–333.

Stanovich, K. E. (1986). Matthew effects in reading: Some consequences of individual differences in the acquisition of literacy. *Reading Research Quarterly, 21,* 360–406.

Stevenson, H. W. (1992). Learning from Asian schools. *Scientific American, 267*(6), 70–76.

Wagner, M. (1989, March). *The transition experiences of youth with disabilities: A report from the National Longitudinal Transition Study.* Paper presented at the meeting of the Council for Exceptional Children, San Francisco, CA.

Wang, M. C., & Baker, E. T. (1986). Mainstreaming programs: Design features and effects. *Journal of Special Education, 19,* 503–521.

Weinstein, C. S., & Mignano, A. J. (1993). *Elementary classroom management.* New York: McGraw-Hill.

Winfield, L. F. (1986). Teacher beliefs toward academically at risk students in inner urban schools. *Urban Review, 18,* 253–268.

PART IV

Research Perspectives

14

Methodological Issues and Strategies for Assessing Developmental Change and Evaluating Response to Intervention[1]

G. Reid Lyon
National Institute of Child Health and Human Development
National Institutes of Health
Bethesda, MD

This chapter discusses some conceptual and methodological issues that are typically associated with intervention research in classroom settings, and proposes the use of a longitudinal multivariate methodology that permits inferences about the nature of behavioral change and the factors associated with such change. At issue is the extent to which contextual (ecological) perspectives can be considered in conjunction with individual differences to help explain how children learn. By design, then, this chapter and the conference on which it is based seek to identify models, rules, and methodologies for the analysis of instructional environments and their relationships with school learning and school failure.

With this as background, one major goal of this chapter is to identify a number of critical conceptual and methodological features that have historically hindered both the conduct of intervention research and the interpretation of the results of intervention research. These methodological issues are particularly pertinent to intervention research that attempts to account for the influence of demographics, teaching environments, teacher characteristics, and classroom climates on student change. A second goal is to review methodological strategies for studying the effects of development and intervention over time so that inferences can be drawn about the nature of behavioral change *and* the factors associated with such change to include factors directly related to the intervention itself and factors related to contextual or ecological variables.

---

[1]This chapter is in the public domain.

SOME ISSUES THAT MAKE THE STUDY OF
CLASSROOM ECOLOGIES DIFFICULT

Before proceeding, it is worthwhile to note that accounting for the effects of ecological variables on development, in general, and on educational treatment response, in particular, is a challenging task. This is the case for a number of reasons. For instance, although instruction and learning are certainly not unidirectional and do not occur in a sociocultural vacuum, little is known about which multivariate ecological contexts (or specific variables) affect children's learning, how these interactions take place, and under what conditions. As Speece and Molloy (in review) stated, "The basic conundrum is specifying the processes by which context and cognition connect (p. 3). Moreover, the terms and definitions used in the literature on classroom ecologies are numerous and sometimes difficult to operationalize. Although investigators have created taxonomies that identify and describe components of an ecology construct in a relatively clear manner (i.e., setting, activity, activity structure, task/material, location, physical location, instructional grouping, disability), those employing belief systems and parental influences as ecological variables are less clear.

It is also not clear how terms such as *ecology, context* and *ecobehavioral systems*, as used in education and educational research, are related to classification systems used in other developmental sciences. For example, in developmental psychology there are frameworks that organize correlates of change into usually two broad environmental factor classes, which have been labeled by different investigators as risk and protective factors (DuBow & Luster, 1990), potentiating and compensatory factors (Cicchetti, 1989), vulnerability and protective factors (Werner, 1985), resilience and protective factors (Rutter, 1985), and risk and vulnerability factors (Barocas, Seifer, & Sameroff, 1985). The point to be made is that the use of these risk-oriented frameworks has proven valuable for identifying the cumulative, interactional, and transactional influences of environmental (ecological) factors that retard behavior and development (Dunst & Trivette, 1994). In addition, Gabarino (1982) developed a framework for ecological factors that places equal emphasis on factors that enhance and facilitate positive outcomes. Gabarino (1982) labeled these influences *sociocultural risk and opportunity factors*.

It also appears from a brief review of the educational literature that ecological studies conducted to date tend to assess different divergent aspects of the environment. As Speece and Molloy (in review) reported, the most frequent ecological features coded and analyzed are related to personnel and tasks/activities, followed by teacher scripts and student conduct, goals and purposes, and beliefs and values. The differential interest in these ecological variables across studies reflects the wide interest in understanding "extra-instructional" factors that influence learning, but such variability in what is studied may not bode favorably for replication and the description of ecological variables across settings, age groups, and curricula. Thus, it is difficult to understand if the field has achieved any degree of consensus related to those ecological factors that have the highest degree of influence on learning.

Finally, many of the studies attempting to study relationships between classroom ecological factors and children's learning have (a) not attended to, and/or controlled for, methodological factors that limit the conduct and interpretability of complex intervention research (Francis, Fletcher, Steubing, Davidson, & Thompson, 1991); (b) not employed methodological concepts and procedures that view change in learning as an ongoing and continuous process (rather than an incremental one) (Rogosa & Willett, 1985); and (c) have not provided a methodological context for the dynamic evaluation of individual change as a function of intervention *and* the ecological correlates of change (Dunst & Trivette, 1994; Torgesen & Davis, 1994). More specifically, we now have the capability to analyze data obtained from longitudinal intervention studies and from the measurement of ecological variables that permits an analysis of growth over time, that describes the change as a function of intervention for each individual separately and for groups of individuals collectively, and that accounts for the influence of demographic variables, teaching method, and teacher, student, and setting variables on learning (Berninger, 1994a, 1994b; Francis, Shaywitz, Steubing, Shaywitz, & Fletcher, 1994; Shaywitz & Shaywitz, 1994). Such capabilities do not appear to be used to their potential in educational intervention research at this time (Lyon, in press).

In the following section, a brief review of methodological factors that are troublesome to the conduct and interpretation of intervention studies is provided. Next, a review and analysis of the measurement and analysis of change as a function of multiple intervention and ecological factors is presented with an eye toward addressing many of the thorny methodological issues explicated in the first section. An emphasis is placed on the use of hierarchical linear modeling (HLM) to assess change, a description of the methodological underpinnings of the use of HLM to derive individual growth curves and to identify the variables that produce variations in individual growth over time, and a brief review of the assumptions, advantages, conditions, and limitations of growth curve modeling.

METHODOLOGICAL LIMITATIONS THAT REDUCE THE VALUE OF INTERVENTION RESEARCH WITH CHILDREN WITH LEARNING DISABILITIES

Review of the literature related to learning disabilities in general, and to reading disabilities in particular, indicates that no single teaching method, inter-

vention, or combination of methods has been found to yield clinically significant, long-term gains (Lyon, 1995, in press; Lyon & Flynn, 1991; Lyon &
Moats, 1988). This does not mean that such gains do not exist, it means only
that they are hard to identify for a variety of methodological reasons. More
specifically, there are several factors that contribute to limitations in documented treatment efficacy for underachieving children, including children
with LD, and these limiting factors should be considered in the design of intervention studies, including those incorporating an analysis of ecological
variables within the study design. These factors are reviewed next.

First, many studies addressing the efficacy of different intervention methods have studied heterogeneous groups of children with LD who are identified according to vague and inconsistent criteria and who demonstrate un-
accounted for differences in demographic features (i.e., SES, race, ethnicity,
number of parents, etc.), number and severity of behavioral and academic
disabilities, and a lack of information about the comorbidity of these disabilities (Keogh, 1993; Keogh & MacMillian, 1983; Morris et al., 1994). As such,
not only have replication efforts been negated, but it has been difficult to determine specific treatment effects and outcomes due to the influence of un-
controlled variables. Moreover, this lack of description with respect to children's demographic background, academic, and information processing
characteristics have made it difficult to identify which intervention methods
are most efficacious for which particular children and under what specific
ecological (contextual) conditions (Lyon, 1987, in press).

Second, a significant number of studies of LD children's response to teaching methods and approaches have employed procedures that are poorly described and defined (Johnson, 1981, 1987, 1994). For instance, few intervention studies critically describe how and why intervention/task stimuli are
represented to the child. In addition, the type of response that the procedure
requires of the child is rarely defined in detail. For example, in intervention
studies involving reading disorders, few studies (Johnson, 1994; Lovett, 1987;
Lyon, 1993; Moats, 1994) have provided sufficient detail with respect to the
following questions and issues: What is the nature of the structure of the spoken and written language used in the teaching methodology? What is the nature of the vocabulary? Is vocabulary controlled? Are the order of phonological representations controlled? On what basis were the words to be read in
the intervention phase selected? Do the word stimuli possess a consistent
phoneme–grapheme relationship? How many meaningful nouns and verbs
are used? Is the sentence structure similar to the child's language? What is
the nature of the content of the reading material used in the intervention? Are
the sound and word decoding strategies utilized in the method(s) analytic or
synthetic in nature? (See Johnson, 1987, for a comprehensive review of these
issues.) Unless sufficient descriptive data are available to answer these types

of questions, replication and an understanding of the critical conditions necessary for positive response to teaching methods will be difficult to ascertain. Third, intervention studies that use methods or approaches that consist of several components or procedures rarely report which component or procedure or which combination and sequence of procedures are most critical to promoting gains in learning (Lovett, 1984; Lyon, 1985, 1994; Zigmond, 1994). In addition, few studies address the interaction among teaching method, learning, stage of development, and learner characteristics. Likewise, intervention studies employing multimodal methods frequently fail to identify how and why different interventions are selected and the roles that different interventions play in achieving treatment gains. This information is critical, because some children with LD may require a more intense emphasis, a different sequence, or longer duration on particular components of an intervention program given their particular array of cognitive, linguistic, neuropsychological, behavioral, and attentional characteristics (Lyon, 1993; Lyon & Moats, 1988).

Fourth, the majority of intervention studies conducted with youngsters with LD have been relatively short term in duration (Berninger, 1994a, 1994b; Lyon, 1985; Lyon & Moats, 1988). As such, when limited effects of a method or intervention are reported, it is not clear whether the limited efficacy is due to the intervention itself, or to the fact that it was employed for a duration that was too short to promote long-term change, no matter how robust the intervention. Moreover, it is likely that even the most powerful interventions may not result in measurable effects if traditional pre- and posttest designs are employed and only two measurement points are sampled. Measurement methodologies must be able to assess rate and degree of change over time, and to be able to predict the slope and intercept of individual growth curves with multiple measures to include type of intervention, individual difference variables, ecological variables, and the like (Francis et al., 1994; Shaywitz & Shaywitz, 1994).

Fifth, many studies assessing the effectiveness of different interventions may have been confounded by the effects of previous and concurrent interventions (Lyon, 1985; Lyon & Flynn, 1989). It is unclear whether a history of a particular type of intervention significantly influences response to an ongoing intervention. Likewise, it is not well understood whether concurrent interventions or methods being used in general or special class settings influence response to ongoing experimental interventions. These issues must be addressed in order to separate specific treatment effects from additive practice or inhibitory effects produced by historical or concomitant interventions.

Sixth, a significant number of treatment studies involving children with LD have not separated specific intervention or program effects from clinician or teacher effects. That is, limited attention has been paid to delineating those teacher and contextual variables that can influence change within any treatment program (Lyon, 1993; Lyon & Moats, 1988).

Seventh, it is not clear from the existing intervention literature whether gains in academic skills developed under highly controlled intervention conditions generalize to less controlled naturalistic settings (Lyon, in press). As such, follow-up studies of treatment benefits have typically shown a decrease in intervention gains, particularly when measurements are taken in settings that are different from those employed in the original intervention trials (Lyon, 1993).

Eighth, it is rare that intervention studies analyze the degree of teacher fidelity with respect to the administration of the method or methods (Berninger, 1994a, 1994b). This is unfortunate given that even teachers who are trained in similar ways have been found to deviate significantly from their application of a method once in the experimental setting (Johnson, 1994; Lovett, 1991; Lovett, Ransby, & Barron, 1988; Lovett, Ransby, Hardwick, & Johns, 1989).

Taken individually or in combination, the methodological artifacts described here can limit significantly the power and interpretability of an intervention study. With respect to the interpretation of intervention studies, errors are typically made in judging the rate and amount of change that has taken place, and the effects of different types of intervention and nonintervention influences on growth. By nonintervention influences, I am referring to social, cultural, environmental, and ecological factors such as SES, parent education, bilingual language usage, pupil–teacher ratio, and so on. This is particularly true if changes take place at different times for different students during the intervention(s). During the past decade, a good deal of progress has been in both conceptualizing and measuring change in development such that errors in design and interpretation can be limited (Burchinal & Appelbaum, 1991; Foorman, 1994). A number of methodologies are available for describing quantitative change, and for studying the manner in which a variety of determinates, including ecological factors, influence rates and patterns of change. A longitudinal and multivariate methodology for estimating the key features of intraindividual and interindividual development is discussed next.

MEASURING AND ANALYZING CHANGE AS A FUNCTION OF DEVELOPMENT, INTERVENTION, AND ECOLOGICAL (CORRELATED) INFLUENCES

A good deal of research designed to assess the effect of an intervention has relied upon pretest–postest designs or on repeated measures analysis of variance for approximating the characteristics of developmental functions (Appelbaum & McCall, 1983; Dunst & Trivette, 1994). Such approaches have been criticized for being unreliable, indirect, and biased estimates of intraindividual change (Francis et al., 1994; McCall, 1977).

Hierarchical Linear Modeling

In contrast, a more powerful model and statistical method for estimating key features of prototypical and intraindividual development is embodied in hierarchical linear modeling (HLM). HLM is a highly flexible yet sophisticated technique for estimating linear, polynomial, and nonlinear growth curves for individuals and with groups (Burchinal & Appelbaum, 1991) and is particularly appealing to developmental psychologists and intervention researchers because of its special utility with developmental data collected over time. The appeal resides in the fact that the data may depict different forms and different patterns of growth at different stages of development or during treatment, and HLM methods are sensitive to such patterns and stages. Moreover, the analysis of individual growth curves via HLM provides the investigator with a new method for addressing the inevitable heterogeneity that will accompany any sample of children, no matter how carefully selected. For example, as Torgesen (1992) pointed out, even though one may intend to focus research on a group of children with specific phonologically related reading deficits, children in the sample will vary with respect to general intelligence, SES, general language skills, gender, race, and type and number of comorbid disorders. Thus, an additional strength of individual growth curve analyses to describe changes as a function of intervention is that one can study the way in which treatment factors influence response to treatment without having to depend on an a priori classification for assigning children to homogeneous subtypes. (For a discussion of detailed statistical and methodological procedures used to delineate individual and group growth curves via HLM, the reader is referred to Bryk & Raudenbush, 1987; Burchinal & Appelbaum, 1991; and Rogosa & Willitt, 1985.)

In general, HLM employs a two-stage model for assessing change (Burchinal & Appelbaum, 1991). At the first stage, termed the *within-subject stage,* data are first "formed-up" (analyzed) at the individual level before analyzing it for multiple individuals (Bryk & Raudenbush, 1987; Rogosa & Willett, 1985). Moreover, an individual's status on some trait (i.e., reading ability) is modeled as a function of an individual growth trajectory plus random error. At the second, or *between-subject stage,* the parameters (slope, intercept, plateau, etc.) of individual growth trajectories vary as a function of differences between subjects in treatment response and in the correlates of treatment response to include a child's background characteristics, a child's previous instructional history, the type and duration of instructional activities, the classroom climate, and the like (Dunst & Trivette, 1994). Thus, in Stage 1 both individual and group change are assessed, whereas in Stage 2 relationships between predictor and outcome variables are evaluated in conjunction with an analysis of the influence of correlated factors to include ecological variables, if so desired.

What is of significant conceptual and methodological significance is that the application of HLM and individual growth curve analysis to the study of change requires *longitudinal* data. This is because repeated observations of the same subjects over time allows study of intraindividual change across time in a manner that is uncontaminated by interindividual differences (Burchinal & Appelbaum, 1991). However, it is important to note that in using HLM, "Each subject's growth can be measured at different ages and a number of different times. Thus, the within-subject model does not assume a uniform data collection design across subjects" (Bryk & Raudenbush, 1987, p. 148).

SOME BASIC ASSUMPTIONS THAT UNDERLIE INDIVIDUAL GROWTH MODELS

First, in assessing any trait or behavior, it is assumed that the rate of growth and development of the behavior varies across students (Shaywitz & Shaywitz, 1994). A second assumption is that this variation will affect both the final level of behavioral performance (plateau) and the age at which children reach this level of performance. Moreover, patterns of development may differ according to the rate of accelerations/decelerations; the level of behavioral or skill performance achieved; and the pattern of growth (e.g., whether growth is linear or, more logically, whether it conforms to a nonlinear pattern such as quadratic growth to a plateau) (Dunst & Trivette, 1994).

ADVANTAGES, CONDITIONS, AND LIMITATIONS OF USING GROWTH CURVE MODELING

As has been mentioned previously, using growth curve modeling is particularly relevant to longitudinal studies that attempt to map the course of development of a particular trait and to identify factors that modify or influence such development. Individual growth curve models provide a dynamic view of learning that emphasizes individual change *and* correlates of change (Francis et al., 1994). Individual growth curve models offer a number of practical advantages, which include the ability to accommodate multiple waves of data, to include cases with incomplete data, and to estimate the reliability of the measurement of change (Shaywitz & Shaywitz, 1994).

Given these advantages it is important to note that growth curve modeling requires specific conditions and has several limitations. First, it should be noted that the within-subject stage of the analysis (as in using HLM) can measure only quantitative, not qualitative, change. The development of growth curve models is based on the assumption that the skills measured are qualitatively constant over time and that only quantitative change is taking place (Shaywitz & Shaywitz, 1994). The factors used to measure the developmental trait or behavior must be reliable, without floor or ceiling effects, and must use interval scaling (on the outcome measures) where the scale properties remain constant across the entire response range and the age span of the children being studied (Francis et al., 1994). Finally, individual growth curve methodology requires that subjects be assessed at multiple time points (preferably four), although three time points are appropriate given high reliability of measurement.

CORRELATES OF CHANGE IN DEVELOPMENT

Two goals of the application of growth curve analysis and the use of HLM methods are to generate developmental functions *and* to identify factors that are associated with variations in intraindividual change. As Dunst and Trivette (1994) pointed out, terms such as *mediators, determinants, moderators,* and *predictors* fall under the broad term of *correlate*. Thus, the methodology provides a context for studying how a variety of correlates influence the rate and shape of a growth curve depicting change. Such correlates may be causal or noncausal, distal or proximal, experimental or nonexperimental, conditional or unconditional, and interventive or noninterventive (Achenbach, 1987). In assessing the correlates of change, the focus is on the relationship between the correlates as independent variables, and developmental functions (rate, intercept) as dependent variables.

As mentioned earlier in this chapter, correlates of change have been classified in several different ways using frameworks that have been organized into environmental or ecological classes. Specific to the study of classroom interventions, such correlates (i.e., predictors) of growth rate and shape could include factors related to class size, pupil–teacher ratio, independent work time, teacher's expertise with the content of the intervention, teacher's expertise with the method of intervention, student's beliefs and goals, general intelligence of the teacher, general intelligence of the student, and so on. What is important to consider when designing and conducting intervention research is that a host of nonteaching factors as well as instructional factors will have a direct bearing on the child's response to the intervention programs(s). A powerful way to disentangle the critical instructional conditions from the more nebulous historical and contextual conditions is to conduct longitudinal studies that allow for the measurement and prediction of change over time as a function of the total ecology.

APPLICATION OF GROWTH CURVE ANALYSIS TO THE STUDY OF DEVELOPMENT OF READING AND READING DISABILITIES

In this section the use of HLM is illustrated via discussion of a study designed to evaluate the developmental lag versus deficit hypothesis in reading disability. In addition, the investigation provided a context to determine the validity of the use of aptitude (IQ)–achievement discrepancies in the definition and diagnosis of reading disability.

Developmental Lag Versus Deficit in Reading Disability (RD)

In an effort to determine whether children identified in the first grade as RD continued to manifest deficits in word recognition and decoding skills through the sixth grade, Francis and his associates (Francis et al., 1994; Francis, Shaywitz, Steubing, Shaywitz, & Fletcher, 1995) applied individual growth curve analysis via HLM to the reading scores of 407 students. Of specific interest was whether the development of children with RD is best characterized by a developmental lag model or a developmental deficit model. If the developmental lag model is valid, one would expect that RD children would demonstrate initial deficits in reading skills but would catch up to their normal reading counterparts over time. In contrast, the deficit model argues that the initial reading deficits are actually maintained over time with little observed improvement.

To evaluate whether readers with and without RD differed in a manner consistent with the lag or deficit model, students were administered a kindergarten screening and were assessed for progress in reading achievement every academic year from the first through the sixth grade. Because of the large size of the longitudinal sample, Francis and his colleagues also had the opportunity to determine whether RD children with a discrepancy between their intelligence and their reading achievement differed in the development of component reading skills from RD children without a discrepancy, thus addressing a critical policy question inherent to the field of learning disabilities.

With this as background, Francis et al. (1994) identified three groups within their longitudinal, epidemiological sample: (a) a reading achievement-aptitude discrepant group (RD) (N = 32) made up of children with IQ scores of 80 or higher, who showed a regression-based achievement–IQ discrepancy of at least 1.5 standard deviation units at grade 3; (b) a low achievement group (LA) (N = 12), composed of youngsters who did not meet the criterion for the RD group but who scored at least 1.5 standard deviation units below average in reading achievement at grade 3; and (c) a normal reading group (N = 352). Eleven children could not be assigned to any of the three groups. Reading

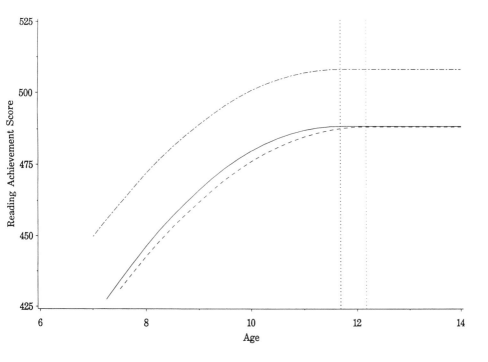

FIG. 14.1.   Mean achievement curves of three groups.

achievement data derived from each of the six assessments are presented as growth curves for each of the three groups in Fig. 14.1.

A number of features associated with the growth curves are worth noting. First, it is clear that children who manifest deficits in basic reading skills continue to display these deficits over time. Thus, disabilities in basic reading skills appears to reflect a deficit rather than a developmental lag. In addition, Fig. 14.1 shows that the RD and the LA poor reading groups did not differ from one another with respect to rate of learning or plateau of learning. These findings obviously raise important questions about the validity of aptitude–achievement discrepancies in the definition and identification of LD children who have primary deficits in basic reading skills. It should be pointed out that in this study no attempt was made to assess the responsiveness of basic reading skills to well-defined intervention approaches. Historical data on the sample clearly show that a majority of the children with reading difficulties did receive either special education services and/or Chapter 1 services. However, intervention data were not collected systematically due to the number of different approaches employed by the schools.

The Francis et al. (1994) study shows the utility of conducting longitudinal studies with unselected samples of normal and disabled readers. The application of growth curve analysis to the data allows for an unbiased picture of how children develop over time. In addition, the rate of growth and the plateau of growth depicted in Fig. 14.1 can be further analyzed by inspecting the correlates of the change observed over time. That is, one may be interested in whether these group curves are related to a number of background factors including SES, parental education, teacher–pupil ratios, and the like, and to information processing variables such as phonological awareness, rapid naming ability, language comprehension, visual perception, and so on. Within this context, factors associated with the child's ecology and cognitive abilities can be factored into the growth curve solution to provide ideas related to causal and correlated events.

SUMMARY

This chapter has identified a number of methodological features that hinder the conduct and interpretation of developmental and intervention research. Given these methodological limitations, alternative procedures for studying and interpreting the effects of interventions within the child, setting, and demographic contexts were discussed. Specifically, hierarchical linear modeling (HLM) was described as a two-stage methodology for assessing change that can be attributed to development, intervention, or other ecological factors. HLM is applied within the context of longitudinal studies where the same individuals are measured repeatedly on outcome measures of interest. HLM is particularly applicable to the conduct of intervention studies with children with learning disabilities, because the effects of intervention on academic and behavioral growth over time can be isolated from other correlated factors. On the other hand, HLM allows the investigator to identify multiple determinates of change and to measure their relative influences. With this as background, the application of growth curve models to the study of learning and learning disability represents a new frontier characterized by a shift from static measurement of achievement to the measurement of the underlying process of change.

The use of longitudinal assessments, in contrast to cross-sectional analyses, was also emphasized given the number of advantages that longitudinal data provide. First, longitudinal studies place the emphasis on learning and change over time rather than a focus on static achievement outcomes. In addition, as Francis et al. (1994) demonstrated, the use of longitudinal assessments to measure learning rates provides an excellent strategy for the early identification of learning problems. Early identification and intervention take on particular significance given the recent findings that 74% of reading disabled children continue to manifest difficulties throughout school if they are not identified and provided with appropriate interventions before the third grade (Shaywitz & Shaywitz, 1994). Growth curve models also have the capacity to track the effects of intervention on well-defined academic skills and to identify which intervention approach or approaches have the highest probability of success with a given deficit at a given developmental period (Foorman, Francis, Novy, & Liberman, 1991). Studies of this nature will be critical to the education that children with learning disabilities will receive in the future.

In sum, the use of growth curve models has demonstrated utility in addressing a number of significant problems related to the definition, conceptualization, and assessment of development and interventions for learning differences and disorders. As Shaywitz and Shaywitz (1994) have expressed, "Learning and learning disability, at their most elemental level, reflect change; growth curve models explicitly focus on describing the ongoing process of change and thus represent a natural expression of the process of change underlying the conceptualization of learning and learning disability. . . . " (p. 67).

REFERENCES

Achenbach, T. M. (1987). *Research in developmental psychology concepts, strategies, methods.* New York: Free Press

Appelbaum, M. I., & McCall, R. B. (1983). Design and analysis in developmental psychology. In P. Mussen (Ed.), *Handbook of child psychology* (Vol. 1, pp. 415–476). New York: Wiley.

Barocas, R., Seifer, R., & Sameroff, A. J. (1985). Defining environmental risk: Multiple dimensions of psychological vulnerability. *American Journal of Community Psychology, 13,* 433–447.

Berninger, V. W. (1994a). Future directions for research on writing disabilities: Integrating endogenous and exogenous variables. In G. R. Lyon (Ed.), *Frames of reference for the assessment of learning disabilities: New views on measurement issues* (pp. 419–439). Baltimore, MD: Brookes.

Berninger, V. W. (1994b). *Reading and writing acquisition: A developmental neuropsychological perspective.* Madison, WI: Brown and Benchmark.

Bryk, A. S., & Raudenbush, S. W. (1987). Application of heirarchical models to assessing change. *Psychological Bulletin, 101,* 147–158.

Burchinal, M., & Appelbaum, M. I. (1991). Estimating individual developmental functions: Methods and their assumptions. *Child Development, 62,* 23–43.

Cicchetti, D. (1989). How researching child maltreatment has informed the study of child development: Perspectives from developmental psychopathology. In D. Cicchetti & V. Carlson (Eds.), *Child maltreatment: Theory and research on the cause and consequences of child abuse and neglect* (pp. 377–431). Cambridge, England: Cambridge University Press.

DuBow, E. F., & Luster, T. (1990). Adjustment of children born to teenage mothers: The contribution of risk and protective factors. *Journal of Marriage and the Family, 52,* 393–404.

Dunst, C. J., & Trivette, C. M. (1994). Methodological considerations and strategies for studying the long-term effects of early intervention. In S. L. Friedman & H. Carl Haywood (Eds.), *Developmental follow-up: Concepts, domains, and methods* (pp. 277–313). New York: Academic Press.

Foorman, B. (1994, August). *Review of the University of Houston Project: Objectives, progress, and problems.* Paper presented at the NICHD Conference on Interventions for Children With Reading and Related Language Disorders, Rockville, MD.

Foorman, B., Francis, D., Novy, D., & Liberman, D. (1991). How letter–sound instruction mediates progress in first-grade reading and spelling. *Journal of Educational Psychology, 83,* 456–469.

Francis, D. J., Fletcher, J. M., Steubing, K., Davidson, K., & Thompson, N. (1991). Analysis of change: Modeling individual growth. *Journal of Consulting and Clinical Psychology, 59,* 27–37.

Francis, D. J., Shaywitz, S. E., Steubing, K., Shaywitz, B. A., & Fletcher, J. M. (1994). Measurement of change: Assessing behavior over time and within a developmental framework. In G. R. Lyon (Ed.), *Frames of reference for the assessment of learning disabilities: New views on measurement issues* (pp. 29–58). Baltimore, MD: Brookes.

Francis, D. J., Shaywitz, S. E., Steubing, K., Shaywitz, B. A., & Fletcher, J. M. (1995, March). *Developmental lag versus deficit models of reading disability: A longitudinal, individual growth curve analysis.* Paper presented at the 1995 Society for Research in Child Development Conference, Indianapolis, IN.

Gabarino, J. (1982). *Children and families in the social environment.* New York: Aldine.

Johnson, D. J. (1981). Factors to consider in programming for children with language disorders. *Topics in Language Disorders, 2,* 13–27.

Johnson, D. J. (1987). Assessment issues in learning disabilities research. In S. Vaughn & C. Bos (Eds.), *Reseach in learning disabilities: Issues and future directions* (pp. 141–151). San Diego, CA: College-Hill.

Johnson, D. J. (1994). Measurement of listening and speaking. In G. R. Lyon (Ed.), *Frames of reference for the assessment of learning disabilities: New views on measurement issues* (pp. 201–227). Baltimore, MD: Brookes.

Keogh, B. K. (1993). Linking purpose and practice: Social–political and developmental perspectives on classification. In G. R. Lyon, D. Gray, J. Kavanagh, & N. Krasnegor (Eds.), *Better understanding learning disabilities: New views from research and their implications for education and public policies* (pp. 311–323). Baltimore, MD: Brookes.

Keogh, B. K., & MacMillan, D. L. (1983). The logic of sample selection: Who represents what? *Exceptional Education Quarterly, 4,* 84–96.

Lovett, M. W. (1984). A developmental perspective on reading dysfunction: Accuracy and rate criteria in the subtyping of dyslexic children. *Brain and Language, 22,* 67–91.

Lovett, M. W. (1987). A developmental approach to reading disability: Accuracy and speed criteria of normal and eficient reading skill. *Child Development, 58,* 234–260.

Lovett, M. W. (1991). Reading, writing, and remediation: Perspectives on the dyslexic learning disability from remedial outcome data. *Learning and Individual Differences, 3,* 295–305.

Lovett, M. W., Ransby, M. J., & Barron, R. W. (1988). Treatment, subtype, and word type effects in dyslexic children's response to remediation. *Brain and Language, 34,* 328–349.

Lovett, M. W., Ransby, M. J., Hardwick, N., & Johns, M. S. (1989). Can dyslexia be treated? Treatment-specific and generalized treatment effects in dyslexic children's response to remediation. *Brain and Language, 37,* 90–121.

Lyon, G. R. (1985). Identification and remediation of learning disability subtypes. *Learning Disability Focus, 1,* 21–35.

Lyon, G. R. (1987). Learning disabilities research: False starts and broken promises. In S. Vaughn & C. Bos (Eds.), *Research in learning disabilities: Issues and future directions* (pp. 69–85). San Diego, CA: College-Hill.

Lyon, G. R. (1993). *Treatment effectiveness for the learning disabled.* Request for Applications (93-009). Bethesda, MD: The National Institute of Child Health and Human Development.

Lyon, G. R. (1994). Critical issues in the measurement of learning disabilities. In G. R. Lyon

(Ed.), *Frames of reference for the assessment of learning disabilities: New views on measurement issues* (pp. 3–13). Baltimore, MD: Brookes.

Lyon, G. R. (1995). Research initiatives in learning disabilities: Contributions from scientists supported by the National Institute of Child Health and Human Development. *Journal of Child Neurology, 10,* 120–126.

Lyon, G. R. (in press). Learning disabilities. In E. Marsh & R. Barkley (Eds.), *Childhood psychopathology.* New York: Guilford Press.

Lyon, G. R., & Flynn, J. M. (1989). Educational validation studies with subtypes of learning disabled readers. In B. P. Rourke (Ed.), *Neuropsychological validation of learning disability subtypes* (pp. 203–242). New York: Guilford.

Lyon, G. R., & Flynn, J. M. (1991). Assessing subtypes of learning disabilities. In H. L. Swanson (Ed.), *Handbook on the assessment of learning disabilities: Theory, research, and practice* (pp. 59–74). Austin, TX: Pro-ed.

Lyon, G. R., & Moats, L. C. (1988). Critical isssues in the instruction of the learning disabled. *Journal of Consulting and Clinical Psychology, 56,* 830–835.

McCall, R. B. (1977). Challanges to a science of developmental psychology. *Child Development, 48,* 333–334.

Moats, L. C. (1994). Honing the concepts of listening and speaking: A prerequisite to the valid measurement of language behavior in children. In G. R. Lyon (Ed.), *Frames of reference for the assessment of learning disabilities: New views on measurement issues* (pp. 229–241). Baltimore, MD: Brookes.

Moats, L. C., & Lyon, G. R. (1993). Learning disabilities in the United States: Advocacy, science, and the future of the field. *Journal of Learning Disabilites, 26,* 282–294.

Morris, R., Lyon, G. R., Alexander, D., Gray, D., Kavanagh, J., Rourke, B., & Swanson, H. (1994). Proposed guidelines and criteria for describing samples of persons with learning disabilities. *Learning Disability Quarterly, 17,* 106–109.

Rogosa, D. R., & Willett, J. B. (1985). Understanding correlates of change by modeling individual differences in growth. *Psychometrica, 50,* 203–228.

Rutter, M. (1985). Resilience in the face of adversity. Protective factors and resistence to psychiatric disorder. *British Journal of Psychiatry, 147,* 598–611.

Shaywitz, B. A., & Shaywitz, S. E. (1994). Measuring and analyzing change. In G. R. Lyon (Ed.), *Frames of reference for the assessment of learning disabilities: New views on measurement issues* (pp. 29–58). Baltimore, MD: Brookes.

Speece, D. L., & Molloy, D. E. *Viewing classroom contexts of young children with learning problems: A case for activity settings.* Manuscript submitted for review.

Torgesen, J. K. (1992). Learning disabilities: Historical and conceptual issues. In B. Y. L. Wong (Ed.), *Learning about learning disabilities* (pp. 3–38). San Diego, CA: Academic Press.

Torgesen, J. K., & Davis, C. (1994). *Individual difference variables that predict response to training in phonological awareness.* Unpublished manuscript, Florida State University, Tallahassee.

Werner, E. E. (1985). Stress and protective factors in children's lives. In A. R. Nicol (Ed.), *Longitudinal studies in child psychology and psychiatry* (pp. 335–355). New York: Wiley.

Zigmond, N. (1994). *Acquisition of reading in children with severe LD.* PHS/NICHD R01 Application submitted, July 1994.

15

Classrooms are Just Another Cultural Activity

Ronald Gallimore
Department of Psychiatry & Graduate School of Education
University of California, Los Angeles

Empirical classroom research began in the United States at the beginning of the 20th century. There was optimism that emerging methodologies would produce results that transformed educational practice. For example, one investigator's use of stenographic recordings to study classrooms (Stevens, 1910) initiated a methodology used for several decades (Hoetker & Ahlbrand, 1969) and anticipated electronic technologies in use today. Yet for all the optimism generated by such methodological advances, 20 years later Barr's (1929) examination of stenographic records revealed that good teachers, as in Stevens' time, were just as likely as poor teachers to be relying on "fact" rather than "thought" questions. Two decades of original empirical research seemingly had no impact on the much criticized recitation teaching that had been the focus of research and reform since Stevens' pioneering studies.

Sixty years and more after Barr's report, empirical research has still produced much less change in classroom practices than our intellectual grandmothers and grandfathers had expected (Heckman, 1984; Hoetker & Ahlbrand, 1969). In fact, classroom innovation guided by empirical studies has proven remarkably frustrating and slow, leading some extreme critics to dismiss educational research in general (Finn, 1988). Certainly, despite all the advances in research, reforming America's classroom practices has provided "steady work" for a long time (Elmore & McLaughlin, 1988). Today's reform efforts are only the latest in a series of waves flowing around the same issues. Even the latest and vigorous national effort has yet to achieve a major shift in practices, if we believe most observers. Cuban (1990) said current efforts

"bring new meaning to Yogi Berra's observation: 'It's déjà vu all over again'"
(p. 4).

With this history, it's hard to argue that a century of classroom research
has had the impact most believe it should, or can. It's not that researchers
have failed to identify important alternatives to traditional practice or ineffective teaching/learning strategies. The problem is that in spite of these findings, certain features of classroom practice persist, decade after decade.

The persistence of classroom practices is not a new discovery (Sarason,
1971). More is now understood about this hard resistance to change, but the
basic facts remains the same: We know many developmentally significant and
effective classroom practices that ought to be implemented. Most change efforts either don't work, don't work well, or don't survive very long. Once the
implementing scaffolds are taken down, in most cases there is a flow back to
the classroom practices that prompted a wave of reform in the first place.

For some segments of the research community the resistance phenomenon may seem discouraging but only tangential to their theoretical and empirical work. I disagree. I believe it is a key and unrecognized finding directly
relevant to many lines of contemporary classroom research. The resistance
of classroom practices is one of those phenomena that undergo an evolutionary change in how they are perceived. I believe it is approaching the last
of McGuire's three stages (McGuire, 1969).

First, like the placebo effect, the immutability of classroom practices was
not recognized for a long time as a phenomenon worthy of investigation in its
own right. Once recognized, again like placebo, in the second stage it was
treated as a methodological nuisance to be eliminated. For example, in Stage
2 the difficulties of getting teachers to use and sustain a new practice was relegated to a few lines in the Methods section. The fact it was hard to get teachers to change even for a short time was not perceived as theoretically or empirically relevant. "Resistance of classrooms to change" was considered the
province of policymakers and school administrators, or someone, but was not
perceived as part of the investigator's brief.

Finally, according to McGuire, in the third stage some phenomena are recognized as more than a target of methodological controls and become central
to theorizing and the formation of research questions. Sometimes in the third
stage what was once not recognized or considered a methodological nuisance
or limitation is reclassified as a missing conceptual link in theories in use.
Sometimes theories incorporate what was once treated as an artifact.

The immutability of practice is one of those that, in the third of McGuire's
stages, has become recognized as central to many lines of classroom research.
It is not just a problem of dissemination of results, or the uncertain and loose
coupling of research, policy, and practice. The enduring nature of classroom
practices is an indication that we are dealing not just with psychological and
pedagogical issues. We are dealing with cultural matters.

Policy researchers Fuller and Clarke (1994) made a similar argument. They challenged the assumption that researchers can ignore cultural matters and identify universal classroom inputs. They based their challenge on a review of achievement effects of specific classroom inputs in Third World schools. Fuller and Clarke (1994) distinguished between policy mechanics and classroom culturalists. Policy mechanics "have tried to empirically isolate those instructional inputs and uniform teaching practices that yield higher achievement" (p. 120). The goal of the mechanics is a list of discrete classroom practices to guide policymakers and central administrations. Their review of evidence indicated that effects of discrete inputs are conditioned by local factors and the culturally constructed meaning of classroom practices. Treating classrooms as black boxes into which inputs are channeled and outputs observed is likely to lead, as Fuller and Clarke argued, to potentially wasteful top-down reforms that are ill suited to at least a large minority of communities, schools, and classrooms.

We had an earlier wake-up call on this point by one of the deans of research methodology. Cronbach (1975) warned that by reducing complex psychological and cultural phenomena to discrete inputs it's assumed that, with enough evidence, it will be possible to put them back together into a dynamic whole that accomplishes specific goals. Cronbach argued that the discrete main effects we identify in our experimental studies are, when taken into real settings, transformed by higher-order interactions into a "hall of mirrors" (Cronbach, 1975, p. 119). Vygotsky (1986) made a similar point: Reducing complex psychological and behavior phenomena runs a risk equivalent to reducing water to its constituent elements and never realizing that although oxygen and hydrogen each fuel a flame, when combined they quench it.

If we take up Fuller and Clarke's challenge, Cronbach's warning is the good news—we won't lose our jobs as classroom researchers. There'll still be plenty of work. The bad news is, like many other citizens in this era, we'll have to work harder and smarter once we begin to see classrooms as cultural activities. It does not spell the end to the study of discrete variables. It does mean the end of the illusion that we can reform every classroom practice by the steady accretion of robust, discrete "inputs" that will have predictable effects once they are all assembled.

The idea that the context is a powerful influence is a long-standing one for many areas of social and behavioral science. In recent years, the explicit argument that classrooms are bundles of cultural activity has been made by sociocultural theorists, for example: Erickson (chap. 6, this volume); Rogoff (1990); Moll (1990); Forman, Minick, and Stone (1993); among others. The problem is that many of us don't quite know what to do with some of the more recent versions of this idea, however plausible we may find it. One problem I think is rooted in the traditions of psychological research that interpreted "cultural or contextual factors" to refer to the objective features. The solution in this tradition was to add some controlling variables such as socioeconomic status, or culture-group membership.

Classrooms have objective features. However, their reality is defined by more than their objective ecology—the culture of the classroom is also in part socially constructed from the "meaning" classroom activity has in the minds of participants and stakeholders. The meaning of a classroom and its activities is a mix of personal construction and the objective reality. The subjective and objective are intertwined; together they are the cultural context for the individual and some of its features we cannot directly observe. Objective and subjective features are never sharply separated. What's in the head of participants in a particular setting contributes to the "reality" that is perceived and responded to. Not only is reality composed of the personnel present and the task operations carried out, but activities are cultural because they have meaning in terms of participants' conception of its purpose and the proper and acceptable scripts for conduct (Weisner, 1984). Reading a text can be for fun, learning, a gateway to upward mobility, or a sacred path to heaven. A child may be assigned to feed an animal by the family because the labor contributed helps survival, or because parents believe that care of another living thing teaches empathy. The task itself and who does it may be less significant than the cultural meaning it is given by the participants in a particular context (Gallimore, Goldenberg, & Weisner, 1993).

As a result, cultural activities are so familiar and mundane that their functions and effects are often unseen, invisible, and unnoticed. They are the architecture of everyday life in schools just as they are in communities, homes, workplaces, and play yards. Some cultural activities that are part of the classroom routine, like recitation teaching, stretch back to the 19th century. Circle time in kindergarten is so familiar in terms of the personnel, operations, purposes, and scripts that it need not be described. Finals week is so pervasive a cultural activity that many long removed from student days dream the same dreams of forgotten deadlines and exams. It is little wonder that even the most robust of findings, (e.g., in cognitive science) makes no headway in the nation's classrooms.

Cultural activities in classrooms and elsewhere are historically evolved solutions to adaptive challenges. They were constructed over time through collaborative human effort to achieve a stable daily routine of life in families, schools, and workplaces. Cultural activities and daily routines are neither static nor rigid. As our proximal and distal environments change, cultural activities are modified and changed to meet new challenges.

Typically, changes in cultural activity are made slowly, gradually, and are built on existing routines. For example, research shows that teachers trained to use innovations gradually alter the new practices to fit into current classroom routines, so that their well-worked-out and deeply instantiated activities remain unchanged (McLaughlin, 1990; Tharp & Gallimore, 1988). The same is true of experimenting families who, despite often extreme countercultural aspirations, in fact are able to make only modest adjustments in childrearing practices (Weisner, 1986). For example, some families seek to fundamentally alter the gender beliefs and practices of their children, but the press of the cultural surround is such that their achievements fall far short of their aspirations (Weisner & Wilson-Mitchell, 1990). Although they achieve some changes on the margins that they value, they are better classified as secular trend leaders than counterculture revolutionaries.

Changing cultural activities means reconsidering some enduring challenges as well as adapting to new ones. The dilemma is how to keep the good parts of our activities intact when we are forced to make changes. The strategy of most individuals and groups is to make changes mostly through small experiments on the margins. We change activities just enough to make things work—we are satisficers (to use Herbert Simon's term) rather than maximizers, happy with just good enough (Edgerton, 1992). The more our environments change, the more we try to keep our routines the same. The more we try to keep them same, the more we have to change. Ask anyone—ask yourself—how often you've said in recent months "I really ought to stop doing that, and start doing this," and then kept right on doing what you had been doing. Little wonder, then, that classroom practices have been so slow to change.

One fatality of this point of view is the prevailing and unexamined assumption that individualistic units of analysis adequately capture teaching and learning in classrooms. Although the cultural nature of activities such as classrooms is easy to acknowledge at one level, many assume that its analysis "can somehow be appended onto a preexisting 'basic' account of the individual" learner (Wertsch, Tulviste, & Hagstrom, 1993, p. 337). Not so—the very idea that a context is a joint, social construction of two or more participants means that more than an individual unit of analysis is required. This is an idea that takes some getting used to.

The purpose of an activity, why it's valued, the rules governing the activity, and how it's understood by students and teachers alike are part of the reality that shapes reaction to reformers' inputs. These social constructions in the heads of participants matter for learning and achievement, and for this reason alone we can't go back to a simpler conception. There is something in the classroom black box that actively responds to reform efforts, and one of its clearest manifestations is the resistance to change that reformers encounter. The classroom is a cultural system that does not passively react to reformers or researchers.

Next I illustrate some of these ideas by looking at examples of how teachers, children, and researchers socially construct the meaning of classroom activities. A final section offers some general methodological implications.

CULTURE IN THE HEADS OF TEACHERS:
A CASE STUDY

Lots of colleagues tell me that they've tried again and again to present to teachers research findings that could improve classroom practice. Many are frustrated that teachers do not share their enthusiasm. Even if told that other schools successfully tried new research-based practices, teachers may still reject what's offered. "It's different at our school," they'll say. "Maybe it worked at those other schools, but your findings are not relevant to our situation, in our school, with our students."

This insistence on the distinctiveness of the local situation is a tipoff that cultural processes are at work. The local routine of classroom activities and how they are perceived are taken for granted as reality itself. They are the way things are, they way they are supposed to be. They are not recognized as evolved adaptations to the challenges of teaching at a particular school. They are not seen as local variations on broadly universal patterns found in many American schools. If pressed, teachers defend them as unique, essential, and rational. Otherwise, they are so taken for granted they are seldom noticed and almost never examined. Asking that they be given up raise questions in the minds of teachers about the researcher's grasp on reality.

One example of how teachers' local perceptions affected their interpretation of research information was documented in a case study that Claude Goldenberg and I conducted in Southern California. During postdoctoral studies at UCLA, Claude taught first grade half-time. At the same time, he led our research team's effort to improve the literacy program in a school serving a largely Latino population. Working first with one individual and then with a group of teachers, eventually a number of significant changes were made in the language arts program of the school. The full description of this effort and documentation of significant gains in average reading levels are presented elsewhere (Goldenberg & Gallimore, 1991).

When the project began, the curricular emphasis in kindergarten at Benson Elementary (and often on into first grade) was mainly on child development and academic readiness. Despite a certain ambivalence, most of the teachers at Benson believed that reading instruction did not belong in kindergarten. For them, the best environment for kindergartners (and possibly also for many first graders) deemphasized instruction and concentrated instead on developmental learning, discovery, socialization, language development, self-concept, motivation, play, and readiness skills such as auditory and visual discrimination.

What the teachers held to be true for children in general was seen as especially true for Benson's population of low-income, mostly Spanish-speaking children. As evidence, teachers cited parents' low level of education, and an assumed absence of developmentally appropriate learning opportunities for children at home (which underestimated how much in fact was present). These assumptions about the children and their families reinforced the teachers' view that learning to read did not belong in the school's kindergarten program. Given teachers' academic, preservice, and professional experiences, this was not an exceptional view at least in Southern California. But at Benson, it naturally led to minimizing literacy learning in kindergarten and, often, even on into first grade.

Compounding the picture was a third factor—the teachers' definition of beginning reading instruction. The basic model consisted of teaching children letters and sounds and how they combine to form syllables and words. Although teachers read to children and provided them with opportunities to develop their oral language, the focus was learning letters and sounds and how they combine to form ever-larger units. Even then, letter sounds were not taught until at least halfway through kindergarten and later in some cases.

This emphasis on reading readiness and letter sound instruction in kindergarten was so limited that it virtually assured that children would not make much progress in their early literacy development. The lack of progress reinforced the local assumption of teachers that children in this community were not yet ready to begin learning something about becoming literate.

Over the course of two school years, however, a gradual shift took place in the role that teachers accorded to literacy instruction and learning in kindergarten. As might be expected, early attempts to introduce new ideas based on contemporary research were controversial. For example, the idea of adding a richer array of literacy activities to kindergarten conflicted with the local commitment to a readiness and developmental approach.

Eventually, there emerged a gradual acceptance among teachers that literacy learning can—in fact, should—begin in kindergarten. There were at least three reasons for this shift.

First, Claude helped organize numerous discussions with and presentations about early literacy research and programs. This included consideration of the conditions under which children, although not necessarily learning to read conventionally, can nonetheless make significant progress in learning about literacy. Second, promising results from changes made by two pioneering kindergarten teachers led some skeptics to accept their plausibility as one way of helping children acquire literacy. Perhaps more important, it gave credence to the theory that under the right circumstances even "these kids" can learn some valuable lessons about literacy. Third, teacher turnover, and the arrival of new kindergarten faculty and other personnel with a stronger "academic" orientation, led to significant shift in staff composition. A critical mass of academically oriented teachers and administrators was assembled, all of whom shared at least some commitment to bringing an early literacy emphasis to Benson.

For all of these reasons, learning about print and early exposure to meaningful texts came to occupy a far more prominent place in the school's kindergarten curriculum than ever before. There was still controversy over the content of the early reading curriculum. The debates at Benson mirrored the controversies that exist in the field as a whole between code- and meaning-oriented approaches. The issue at Benson was no longer whether literacy learning should form a part of kindergarten. Rather than asking, "Should we be teaching children to read in kindergarten?" the teachers were now asking, "What kinds of opportunities for learning about literacy should we be providing our kindergartners?"

It was a significant shift, one that was made possible by both research findings about early literacy in general and local findings about the local school population. In particular, those who led the trend toward more early literacy were obtaining impressive results that were persuasive enough to affect local opinion. The shift signaled a widespread acceptance by teachers at the school that kindergarten children in the district were more capable and ready than most people realized; under the right circumstances, they can learn a great deal about print and how it functions; and that the school should make a major and direct contribution to the process of early literacy development. Moreover, the successful involvement of parents began to shift the terms of discussion regarding their potential contributions.

What happened locally once the kindergarten program began to change? Subsequent test results suggested gains in standardized test scores, as well as highly favorable teacher evaluations of what children were able to do when they had richer early literacy instruction (Goldenberg & Gallimore, 1991).

Some changes at Benson were invisible, and not quickly noticed. A few years after the project ended and the test results were in, Claude talked to one of the reading specialists who was new to the school. The new specialist was asked what was considered grade level in first-grade Spanish reading at Benson. Unlike her predecessor, the new coordinator said first graders should finish the third preprimer. When told that five years earlier first graders had been considered on grade level if they had only completed the second book, she expressed considerable surprise. The local culture had changed and, even if it was noticed, it was seldom noted.

Classrooms, like politics, are experienced as local phenomena. A significant portion of this local orientation arises from the invisibility of the everyday routine of cultural practices and activities. The assumptions and practices at Benson tended to reinforce each other in ways that were internally consistent. These internally consistent perceptions reveal some workings of classroom culture as defined from a sociocultural perspective. These local constructions of reality are one of the factors that makes inputs from central authority fail to have their intended impact or fail altogether (Fuller & Clarke, 1994). Such local perceptions and interpretations are what make classroom practices so hard to change, and research so often have so little impact. But it is not only teachers' perceptions about which researchers need to worry.

CULTURE IN THE HEADS OF STUDENTS: SOME EXAMPLES

Teachers are not the only contributors to the socially constructed classroom reality that resists change. Students also contribute. The meaning of contexts and how they are responded to is accordingly as complex from the perspective of the students and it was in the case of the Benson teachers.

A compelling example of student interpretations of context comes from Piagetian studies of conservation. This illustration might be most analogous to assessment situations, but it also parallels many classroom situations in which student cognitive functions are implicated.

Originally, Piagetian theory was an essentially maturational view of cognitive development that relegated social context factors to a secondary role. About 20 years ago, the role of social factors began to be reconsidered. In Switzerland, Ann-Nelly Perret-Clermont and others began to examine the impact of peer interaction. In Britain, Margaret Donaldson and others explored the conversational rules in the social interaction of adult and child in testing situations. Both lines of investigation used the traditional Piagetian conservation test as a "useful microcosm" for the study of social factors and, in so doing, provided a bridge between these new efforts and traditional Piagetian studies (Light & Perret-Clermont, 1989). This testing of 4- to 7-year-olds' capacity to conserve, for example, the conservation of liquids, involves the following kind of materials transformation task. A child is asked if two identical glasses, filled to the same level, contain the same amount of liquid. When he or she agree that they do, the contents of one are poured into a different size and shape of glass. The child is then asked whether the two different-sized glasses still have the same amount. Justifications are requested from the child for the answer given. If the child says the quantities are different now that they are in different sized and shaped containers, he or she has failed to conserve once the materials were transformed by being put into different containers. Nonconservation is interpreted to mean the child's maturation has not yet progressed to an expectable stage.

Determining just when a child displays conservation has proven a vexing problem. The lessons learned are relevant to our concerns in this conference. For example, if another adult enters the room on some pretext, tells the first experimenter there is a phone call, and volunteers to continue, the percentage of 5- and 6-year-olds conserving rises dramatically. Conservation also increases among young children ages 5 and 6 when the task is converted into a "game" in which equality of amounts become a fairness issue. The "game" condition produced 50% conservation compared to 20% in the control group, and if a second adult "interrupted" the figure rose to 70%. Other investigators have used a variety of "incidental" transformations, for example, using a badly chipped beaker as the reason for pouring the contents from one container to another, or having a naughty puppet disrupt the display before asking the crucial conservation question. The beaker variation produced 70% conservation in a sample of 5- and 6-year-olds, compared to 5% in a control group tested in the usual manner.

These results have been replicated enough times that now the focus is on the features of the interaction that produce differential outcomes. As exciting as this work is, there is no consensus on what it means for Piaget's theory. Some argue that it means younger children really can conserve if you ask them properly, whereas others argue that the social context is enabling performance beyond true competence (Light & Perret-Clermont, 1989).

A child brings to any encounter with an adult—parent, researcher, or teacher—some understanding of the meaning and purpose of an activity, a set of normative interaction rules or conduct scripts, and some capacity to construct an interpretation of the unexpected. The Piagetian experiments suggest that cultural norms are affecting some children's response to the conservation problem (Light & Perret-Clermont, 1989). For young children, this kind of examination question is a departure from the normative interactions to which they are accustomed. For a young child who is still mastering the "subtle, culturally elaborated abstractions" encoded in talk about conservation, who asks the second question may be more important than the palpable equalities being asked about.

> The child [is] immersed in a language and a culture which are themselves grounded in practical and social human purposes. The concepts of amount, number, area, volume, weight, and so on exist in that language and culture because they have long served just such practical purposes, associated with sharing, distributing, and transacting various commodities. . . . Conservation concepts can thus be thought of not as transcendent logical entities but as historically elaborated products of certain practical and social purposes. (Light & Perret-Clermont, 1989, p. 109)

Young children in the conservation experiments bring whatever pieces of that heritage they have thus far appropriated. The variability in results as a function of subtle changes in the testing context indicate that they use these appropriations to construct an understanding of what the task is and what the experimenter wants to know. This complicates the experimenter's task but again alerts us to the workings of culture. The experimental dilemmas of the Piagetians are analogous to problems we confront in classroom research. Two areas of study offer useful parallels: motivational studies and the search for challenging, authentic classroom activities.

An intriguing analog was suggested in a recent review of motivation research and learning. Phyllis Blumenfeld (1992) noted a paradox. Many students resist or avoid challenging and complex tasks. For example, given difficult and ambiguous tasks students try to negotiate a lower requirement or fail to cooperate with the teacher, thus slowing down the lesson. In response to student resistance, teachers often reduce the level of difficulty and challenge. This common response is dismaying because of the abundant evidence that students who take up the challenge of difficult tasks display more intrinsic motivation for learning as opposed to performance motivation (e.g., get praise or good grades).

One take on Blumenfeld's paradox is that resistance to challenging tasks reflects students' social constructions. Blumenfeld suggested that prior educational history, conventional classroom practices, or prevailing peer norms form the basis of student resistance. In other words, students may resist challenging tasks for sociocultural reasons.

For another example, consider Saunders' study of student writing that examined the interactions of classroom context and teacher and student perceptions (Saunders, 1993). Saunders studied the writings of an advanced middle school classroom. These students were taught in a combined two-period English and social studies class by a teacher who was also the advisor to the school newspaper. Part of class time was devoted to production of the newspaper, which was sometimes used as vehicle for writing instruction. In addition, the students wrote essays and journals. This provided an opportunity to examine how writing was approached, and what was produced, in three contexts that seemed at first to vary in authenticity. The essays were written only for the teacher's eyes. The journals were read by the teacher, but also could be shared and were to include whatever the author wished. The newspaper, potentially the most authentic writing task, was distributed schoolwide several times a year. Saunders expected, based on a review of the literature, that the newspaper was a more authentic writing task because of the intended audience. Because of the "real" nature of the task, he expected that newspaper writing would motivate more effort and better products, for example, more frequent revisions, improved drafts from revision, and so on.

The newspaper tasks (context) did produce higher levels of effort than did other more conventional classroom writing tasks (i.e., students worked longer on pieces, pursued more drafts, and were more inclined to say they wanted to produce high-quality work). Yet the students' more extensive efforts were limited by their novice understanding of the newspaper genre. They worked harder to do well what they knew how to do, but increased effort did not lead them to discover more effective approaches to their newspaper articles. In some cases, students simply bypassed the potential challenges of the writing tasks (e.g., justifying their opinions in a movie review) because they did not recognize them as potential avenues to pursue. They avoided more sophisticated topics, and kept their articles short and cursory, noticeably under-developed, based on their perceptions of their peers' taste in journalism. Audience did not function simply as a motivator per se; it also influenced the students' perceptions of the writing task itself. In turn, those perceptions shaped the nature of the challenges the students undertook, or, in many cases, failed to undertake.

The teacher in Saunders' study did not consistently provide the kind of instruction that maximized the challenging nature of newspaper writing. Most of the year she confined herself to organizing and managing the activity flow. When she did teach there were detectable improvements in the quality of newspaper writing. But her conception of the activity did not place a premium on instruction, but rather on the organization and flow of assignments. Clearly, the seemingly more authentic tasks did not operate as expected, and suggest some skepticism about how easily one can manipulate students into accepting the teacher's or curriculum developer's definition of authenticity.

In Saunders' study, the motivation experiments reviewed by Blumenfeld, and the subjects of Swiss researchers, the objective features of the experimental situation, the classroom, or any other context were not the only factors shaping children's responses. Likewise, the teachers' interpretations were not the only subjective features of classroom reality. The dimensions under the "vague term of 'social context' are not simply external variables which influence the child's cognitive activity. The child's cognitive activity is . . . always an answer to the [local] staging [or activity setting] and what he interprets about its sense and aims" (Grossen & Perret-Clermont, in press, p. 4). The child brings into the classroom or assessment situation a sociocultural heritage of interpretations, scripts, and purposes. The classroom and its activity structure has cultural history and meaning for the child. These social constructions are part of the mix that can override "objective inputs," according to Fuller and Clarke (1994). They are part of the cultural processes that make classroom practices so resistant to change.

CULTURE IN THE HEADS OF RESEARCHERS: THEIR SOCIAL CONSTRUCTION OF TEACHERS' PROFESSIONAL DEVELOPMENT

As if dealing with the cultural constructions of teachers and students were not enough, a sociocultural perspective invites us to consider two other groups of stakeholders in the design of our research: reformers and researchers. We also bring cultural baggage to classrooms, which shapes the reality we see and gives a particular slant to the work we undertake.

Consider the case of traditional classroom discourse patterns (Cazden, 1988). Cuban (1988) noted that discourse patterns have been the subject of reform efforts as often as any other teaching practice. They have also been the focus of much research. Yet, as far as we know, the everyday forms of teacher discourse in U.S. classrooms remain essentially unchanged (see, e.g., Goodlad, 1984).

One reason why teacher discourse is so stable and unchanging is how the issue is approached by reformers and researchers—their social constructions of them. Mostly, the focus is on the interactions of teacher and students, and on what students are doing in and getting from a lesson. The overriding view is that if one gives students access to more varieties of discourse in the classroom, they will prosper. The focus is on the learning experiences of the students.

But what about the experiences of teachers? Are their experiences, work environments, and local culture congruent with practices they are expected to learn and use? Consider the following observation of Sarason about teachers' development in general:

> I have spent thousands of hours in schools and one of the first things I sensed was that the longer the person had been a teacher the less excited, or alive, or stimulated he seemed to be about his role . . . *schools are not created to foster the intellectual and professional growth of teachers. The assumption that teachers can create and maintain those conditions which make school . . . stimulating for children, without those same conditions existing for teachers, has no warrant in the history of man[kind].* That the different efforts to [change teaching practices have failed] is in part a consequence of the implicit value that schools are primarily for children, a value which gives rise to ways of thinking, to a view of technology, to ways of training, and to modes of organization which make for one grand error of misplaced emphasis. . . . (Sarason, 1983, pp. 123–124, emphasis added)

Ironically, many reform-minded trainers of teachers have not noticed what Sarason described so forcefully. Often, reformers who want teachers to develop more "conversational" styles of teaching have relied on the reviled discourse patterns that they want teachers to stop using. They have often resorted to telling teachers how to interact in new ways. Although we want teachers to adopt different discourse styles such as fewer restrictions on student opportunities to talk, we haven't reformed our own teaching practices. In lots of research reports on alternative classroom discourse, the means by which the participating teachers are introduced to experimental teaching forms are reduced to a few lines in the method section.

The radical claim of a sociocultural perspective insists we examine both the broad and narrow contexts of teacher discourse—including the community of discourse of which they (and we temporarily) are a part, and the local activities that create and sustain existing patterns of discourse, and which must be bent to sustain a new form. This is another way to put the point: We need to think about the development of teachers in *terms as least as broad and deep as we do of students.* Everything that is claimed about cultural and contextual effects on student development and performance is also true of teachers.

I'll illustrate this idea with some studies at UCLA that attempted to alter teacher–student classroom discourse patterns. In general, teachers in these studies, as is common, tended to control classroom discourse in ways that greatly restricted students' participation. They joined our research effort because they wanted to loosen up and provide more conversationlike opportunities for students to discuss the texts they were reading. They met weekly to plan lessons, view videotapes, and help each other work toward this goal.

Four teachers met regularly with a researcher (C. Goldenberg) over the course of a school year. Saunders, Goldenberg, and Hamann (1992) analyzed transcripts of 28 of these sessions. Transcript analyses indicated that working toward a common objective (becoming more conversational in their teaching) created interactions and discussions that mirrored how they wanted to teach their students. The teachers talked about getting students talking about what they were reading and writing. Teachers were not trained or taught how to conduct conversational lessons. Conversations that instruct are not only an end, but a means to that end. Gradually, over the course of the year, the teachers appropriated the discourse style of their weekly meetings and began to transfer this into their classrooms.

To provide for and sustain other professional development opportunities, a more ambitious project was begun. The school community was restructured to provide "opportunity slots" for more teachers to participate in small peer groups such as instructional conversation and other innovations. They developed through the new community of activities an integrated set of learning goals for each grade level, and a set of user-friendly, diversified assessments as benchmarks of quarterly progress. The data these benchmarks generated helped focus subsequent activity (Goldenberg & Sullivan, in press).

During the first year of the project, the school had the lowest test scores in the district. Four years later it had the highest scores, and approached the state average (Goldenberg & Sullivan, in press). In interviews with selected teachers and administrators, changes in individual teachers' practices were credited in varying degrees to changes in the interpersonal and community life of the school.

Individual teachers became more proficient at and confident about their classroom work, partly through their contacts with peers in a school context that supported such interactions and provided effective leadership and assistance. These features reflected a principle claim of a sociocultural perspective: To understand and assist the behavior of a teacher and what goes on in his or her classroom, one must keep in perspective three planes of development. In this case, the *personal* development of individual teachers was fostered by the creation of an *interpersonal* context, which was sustained by changes in the school *community* (Rogoff, in press; Rogoff, Baker-Sennett, Lacasa, & Goldsmith, in press). The following passage illustrates this:

> The *community plane of analysis* focuses on people participating with others in culturally organized activity, with institutional practices and development extending from historical events into the present, guided by cultural values and goals. The *interpersonal plane of analysis* focuses on how people communicate and coordinate efforts in face-to-face and side-by-side interactions as well as more distal arrangements of people's activities . . . , e.g., choices of where and with whom. . . . The *personal plane of analysis* focuses on how individuals change through their involvement in one or another activity. . . . (Rogoff et al., in press, ms pp. 2–3).

METHODOLOGICAL IMPLICATIONS
FOR CLASSROOM RESEARCHERS

A sociocultural perspective invites investigators to spend lots of time in classrooms. Time is needed to understand the local culture, and for researchers to discover their own limiting constructions. These understandings are essential knowledge for those who want to change classroom practices. Our world may be pragmatically divided into those who study classrooms, those who want to reform them, those who work there, and those who go there to be taught. But all are confronted with the problem of understanding how the cultural processes play out. For researchers, the task is to spend enough time studying this culture so that they can discover how it will accommodate and assimilate the phenomena they study.

Not everyone is optimistic that more time spent with teachers and students will give us broadly applicable principles to make changes happen. Shavelson (1988) argued that translating scientific knowledge into practice will always require substantial local fitting. The set of potential applications of any piece of research knowledge is indefinitely large, and so is the set of novel situations encountered by practitioners. Practice will always include "the art of translating scientific knowledge into actions applied to novel situations, even constructing new knowledge on the spot from experience when surprising situations arise" (p. 6).

Shavelson was right about the enduring need for artful fitting of new knowledge and practices to local context. Anyone who has operated a program for any length of time realizes that, like any bundle of cultural activity, adaptation is never finished. Adapting research findings to local conditions never ends, because new findings keep emerging, conditions change, populations change, and so on. Shavelson's point can be rephrased into empirical questions: Can we reduce some of the ambiguities that practitioners face by researching artful implementations? Can we approach classroom research in ways that narrow the gap between findings and practice? Can we develop some principles of cultural change in classrooms so that classroom research has a better chance of having an effect on practice? I think so.

Happily, fate has been kind. A great opportunity has been given to researchers of this era by the historic impulse to reform American schools. It is being pushed by many elements of society, including some of the most powerful parts of the economic and political establishment. For the first time in a hundred years, there are signs that a genuine restructuring of the educational system is under way. It will take several more decades to determine what happened, but if current evidence predicts the future, changes are being made that will alter the cultural activity we call "classroom." In that historical process lies many opportunities to observe, explore, experiment, and change.

Many researchers are taking advantage of reform efforts now under way in many communities. Such efforts offer historically unmatched opportunities for long-term, sustained collaborations between researchers and practitioners. Many involve researchers in new practices of investigation, such as mixes of quantitative and qualitative methods that just a decade ago would have been unseemly in some disciplines.

Practitioner–researcher collaborations offer unique advantages from a sociocultural perspective. They allow us to work long enough to produce significant changes in classroom practices, for example, the instantiation of forms of teacher discourse that truly depart from the ones that have dominated U.S. schools. In this way, we open up research opportunities that are not now possible because of the restricted range of teacher discourse. If we are limited to the study of current practices, we never discover what's possible, and because the lack of reliable instantiations in real classrooms researchers cannot observe and experiment with the new forms. In our own work with conversational teaching, a major problem is instantiation by enough practitioners to allow for evaluation of specific effects on student learning (Saunders & Goldenberg, 1992). To get enough teachers reliably engaging in instructional conversations requires an elaborate, long-term professional development program. To establish such a program requires a long-term, sustained involvement in many schools that cannot be limited narrowly to teacher discourse. The complexities multiply quickly, which is both a curse and an opportunity. They are an opportunity because they force attention to the three planes of analysis—community, interpersonal, and personal experiences of teachers (Rogoff et al., in press)—on which reliable instantiations of altered teaching discourse depend.

A key dynamic in sustained collaborations, and an example of a culture change for researchers, is the nature of the shared goals. McLaughlin (1990) warned that efforts focused narrowly on some approach, for example, cooperative learning or thematic teaching, are susceptible to a reversal of means and ends. Many of the efforts that she and others examined became so preoccupied with implementing a narrow approach that the ends were lost in the details of implementation. Keeping student learning and achievement as the shared goal of the researcher–practitioner collaborative is one helpful corrective. This necessarily complicates investigations, but it also prevents researchers from assuming that once they have demonstrated the efficacy of a variable that the major work is finished—that there is no need to attend to effectiveness. As Cronbach (1975) warned, and as Fuller and Clarke (1994) demonstrated, moving a robust effect from the laboratory creates interaction effects that can only be observed and understood in the cultural context of the classroom.

This is analogous to the distinction between efficacy and effectiveness studies in clinical research (Sechrest & Figueredo, 1996, in press). Efficacy studies are typically carried out under carefully controlled situations to show that an input can be made to work and have some effect on a dependent variable of interest. Some of these may be in laboratory settings removed from actual classrooms. Some may be in classrooms that are temporary laboratories, but with so many special resources that they are far from typical.

Effectiveness studies are conducted under less well-controlled conditions. The purpose of effectiveness studies is to determine if an intervention that has been shown to be efficacious can work in more ordinary settings—in the real sociocultural world in which practice is conducted. The most useful effectiveness studies help identify what is local and universal, and by contributing to universal generalizations increases the generality of efficacy study results.

Sometimes, a clinical intervention that is efficacious turns out to be ineffective because it cannot be reliably instantiated long enough to achieve an effect. Often there are so many local variations in implementation of the independent variables that only clouded effectiveness results are obtained. In such outcomes, we are reminded of Shavelson's principle that artful implementation can never be eliminated in the translation of research to practice.

Local effects are not mere nuisances—they create valuable research opportunities. Case study, qualitative investigation, small-scale experimentation, and moderate to long clinical trials are all ways of studying culture as it affects and transforms our attempts to make practice more efficacious. Many of the researcher–practitioner collaboratives in the current wave of reform are exploitations of such opportunities. They provide investigators with research angles that keep in focus the sociocultural context of the classroom (Rogoff, 1990). As Rogoff stated:

> Rather than viewing individuals, their social partners, and the sociocultural context as independent "influences" or factors . . . [in a sociocultural perspective] they represent differing angles of analysis of an integrated process. Although researchers and scholars find it convenient to focus their investigation in a spe-

cific angle, looking at the complex process . . . through a particularly interesting window, the different angles or windows may artificially divide a unified, whole . . . process. For convenience of study or discussion, we may focus on one or another, but we must remember the integrated nature of the . . . process. (Rogoff, 1990, p. 27)

The sociocultural invitation to spend time in real settings means sharing the evaluation pressures confronting practitioner–collaborators. Although not all collaborations must be problem- or outcome-driven, such projects can create opportunities that investigators cannot otherwise find. In the history of science, many such collaborations produced great scientific advances because of the discovery opportunities they created. To exploit these opportunities takes some methodological diversity and inclusiveness: We need a balanced mix efficacy/effectiveness, theory-driven, and outcome-driven investigations. Because so many features of schools and classrooms are constrained by history and custom, it is only through multimethod, problem-driven investigations (e.g., raising achievement test scores) that truly experimental changes can be investigated. It's the researcher willing to share the risks with the practitioners as well as the potential rewards that will be able to carry out bold experiments.

In collaboratives that attempt to translate research findings into program elements, the succession of steps from uncertain beginnings to climatic endings can be likened to stages in the evolution of a mature forest (Tharp & Gallimore, 1979, 1982). Like the many elements of the climax forest that emerged over some time through an evolutionary succession of life forms, only some research findings will survive the evaluation pressure of classroom culture.

At each stage of an investigation, different methods of research and evaluation are relatively more useful. In the beginning and when threats arise to an immature system of newly emerging classroom practice, the methods of ethnography, systematic observation, personal knowing, and short-term quasi-experimental tinkering are often the most valuable. At later, more stable, and mature stages, the methods of random assignment to treated and untreated conditions and full-blown summative evaluation come into play. Do we look at the trees or the forest? The questions dictate the method. The stage of program succession shapes the questions.

Forests and classrooms are complex, viable, and interacting element bundles. Like the forest, classrooms grow, change, evolve over time, and must be adapted to the local environment (although universal qualities are always detectable). Every classroom and forest displays local feature, because both often begin not in virgin soil but in burned-out or plowed-over places. If environmental conditions remain constant, if resources are sufficient and not changed too much, the more enduring, longer-lived elements prosper and weather evaluation pressures, and the climax stage of the succession is reached —a tall timber forest, or a classroom that works. Too often both new forests and program elements are cut before the evolutionary process has run its course, and we never learn which elements would have survived and prospered. The cycle may begin anew, but the legacies of the dead forest and program, their storehouses of adaptations, must evolve all over again.

By diversifying our approach to classroom research we will find ourselves in good company. Sechrest and Figueredo offered this metaphorical description of perspective change that classrooms researchers might adopt as they contemplate the study of this complex cultural activity:

[For most of this century, social, behavioral, and developmental science was governed by a Newtonian (Sir Issac Newton) metaphor. It was a] social physics . . . patterned on that of celestial mechanics and the dynamics of non living material particles. The resultant image [was] a mechanical universe governed by absolute and unalterable laws, made of indivisible and identical units, of a finite number of specifiable types, majestically floating along predetermined pathways in a limitless void. . . . [We researchers watched in cool detachment inside our space suits.]

[This Newtonian metaphor mentally prepared us] for a bold exploration of the icy depths of interplanetary space. Instead, [we] found [ourselves] completely unprepared for the tropical nightmare of a Darwinian jungle: A steaming green Hell, where everything is alive and keenly aware of you, . . . and nothing waits passively to be acted upon by an external force. . . . The Darwinian jungle manipulates and deceives the unwary wanderer into serving myriads of contrary and conflicting ends. [The] sweltering space suits . . . had to come off. (Sechrest & Figueredo, 1993, pp. 647–648).

Generations of researchers imagined their subjects passively letting themselves be manipulated in the service of a social physics. They never noticed that their subjects, skilled in social camouflage, were also observers and experimental manipulators and constructors of reality.

There's a lesson in this metaphor for classroom researchers too. Treating classrooms as if they were culture-free is the equivalent of studying human behavior in an air-conditioned space suit. You may get statistically significant effects, but you never understand very well what's going on, and you certainly never figure out how to make changes that are sustainable and effective.

The teachers and students we study are more clever and aware than we have thought, and the classrooms they inhabit represent more than bits and pieces of structure and process that can be conveniently dissected by air-conditioned study. Classrooms are just another cultural activity. They are evolved solutions to complex adaptive challenges. Taking a bit or piece from here or there to study in isolated detachment is an indispensable research paradigm, but it's not sufficient. At some point, the bits or pieces under study must be seen as part of a culturally adapted whole that perpetuates the sturdy resistance to change of classroom practices. It also perpetuates the unhappy history of a century of educational research that has had little effect on the nation's classrooms. In 2095 our intellectual great-grandchildren may credit us for connecting educational research to practice, because we changed our cultural activity.

ACKNOWLEDGMENTS

The research reported was supported by grants from the Spencer Foundation, the National Institute of Child Health and Human Development, the Linguistic Minority Research Program of the University of California, and the Center for Cultural Diversity and Second Language, University of California, Santa Cruz. Continuing support has been provided at UCLA by the Sociobehavioral Research Group (Mental Retardation Research Center), the Division of Social Psychiatry, Department of Psychiatry and Biobehavioral Sciences, and the Urban Education Studies Center, Graduate School of Education, UCLA. I am grateful to the parents, children, teachers, and administrators of the school districts where we conducted our research. Thanks also to colleagues who generously read and commented on earlier versions of this chapter: Lindsay Clare, Claude Goldenberg, Bill Saunders, and Barbara Keogh for helpful criticisms and conversations.

REFERENCES

Barr, A. S. (1929). *Characteristic differences in the teaching performance of good and poor teachers of social studies*. Bloomington, IL: Public School Publishing Co.
Blumenfeld, P. C. (1992). Classroom learning and motivation: Clarifying and expanding goal theory. *Journal of Educational Psychology, 84*(3), 272–281.
Cazden, C. (1988). *Classroom discourse: The language of teaching and learning*. Portsmouth, NH: Heinemann.
Cronbach, L. J. (1975). Beyond the two disciplines of scientific psychology. *American Psychologist, 30*, 116–127.
Cuban, L. (1988). A fundamental puzzle of school reform. *Phi Delta Kappan, 69*(5), 341–344.
Cuban, L. (1990). Reforming again, again, and again. *Educational Researcher, 19*(1), 3–13.
Edgerton, R. B. (1992). *Sick societies: Challenging the myth of primitive harmony*. New York: Free Press.
Elmore, R. F., & McLaughlin, M. W. (1988). *Steady work: Policy, practice, and the reform of education*. Santa Monica, CA: The RAND Corporation.
Finn, C. E., Jr. (1988). What ails educational research. *Educational Researcher, 17*(1), 5–8.
Forman, E., Minick, N., & Stone, C. A. (1993). *Contexts for learning: Sociocultural dynamics in children's development*. Oxford, England: Oxford University Press.
Fuller, B., & Clarke, P. (1994). Raising school effects while ignoring culture? Local conditions

and the influence of classroom tools, rules, and pedagogy. *Review of Educational Research, 64*(1), 119–157.

Gallimore, R., Goldenberg, C., & Weisner, T. (1993). The social construction and subjective reality of activity settings: Implications for community psychology. *American Journal of Community Psychology, 21*(44), 537–559.

Goldenberg, C. N., & Gallimore, R. (1991). Local knowledge, research knowledge, and educational change: A case study of early Spanish reading improvement . *Educational Researcher, 20*(8), 2–14.

Goldenberg, C. N., & Sullivan, J. (1994). *Making change happen in a language-minority school: A search for coherence* (Educational Practice Rep. No. 13). Santa Cruz, CA: The National Center for Research on Cultural Diversity and Second Language Learning.

Goodlad, J. (1984). *A place called school.* New York: McGraw-Hill.

Grossen, M., & Perret-Clermont, A-N. (in press). Psych-social perspective on cognitive development: Construction of adult–child intersubjectivity in logic tasks. In W. de Graaf and R. Maier (Eds.), *Processes of sociogenesis.* New York: Springer-Verlag.

Heckman, P. (1984). On the corruption of teacher education by psychology. *Teacher Education Quarterly, 11*(1), 1–13.

Hoetker, J., & Ahlbrand, W. (1969). The persistence of recitation. *American Educational Research Journal, 6*, 145–167.

Light, P., & Perret-Clermont, A-N. (1989). Social context effects in learning and testing. In A. Gellatly, D. Rogers, & J. A. Sloboda (Eds.), *Cognition and social worlds* (pp. 99–112). Oxford: Oxford Science Publications, University Press.

McGuire, W. J. (1969). Suspiciousness of experimenter's intent. In R. Rosenthal & R. L. Rosnow (Eds.), *Artifacts in behavioral research* (pp. 13–57). New York: Academic.

McLaughlin, M. W. (1990). The RAND change agent study: Macro perspectives and micro realities. *Educational Researcher, 9*, 11–16.

Moll, L. C. (Ed.). (1990). *Vygotsky and education: Instructional implications and applications of sociohistorical psychology.* Cambridge, England: Cambridge University Press.

Rogoff, B. (1990). *Apprenticeship in thinking: Cognitive development in social context.* Oxford, England: Oxford University Press.

Rogoff, B. (1995). Observing sociocultural activity on three planes: Participatory appropriation, guided participation, apprenticeship. In J. V. Wertsch, P. del Rio, & A. Alvarez (Eds.), *Sociocultural studies of mind* (pp. 139–164). Cambridge, UK: Cambridge University Press.

Rogoff, B., Baker-Sennett, J., Lacasa, P., & Goldsmith, D. (1995). Development through participation in sociocultural activity. In J. J. Goodnow, P. J. Miller, & F. Kessel (Eds.), *Cultural practices as contexts for development* (pp. 45–65). San Francisco, CA: Jossey-Bass.

Sarason, S. B. (1971). *The culture of the school and the problem of change.* Boston: Allyn & Bacon.

Sarason, S. B. (1983). *Schooling in America: Scapegoat and salvation.* New York: Free Press.

Saunders, W. M. (1993). *The influence of three different school contexts on the writing and learning of four seventh graders.* Unpublished doctoral dissertation, Graduate School of Education, University of California, Los Angeles.

Saunders, W., & Goldenberg, C. (1992, April). *Effects of instructional conversations on transition students' concepts of "friendship": An experimental study.* Paper presented at the annual meeting of the American Educational Research Association, San Francisco, CA.

Saunders, W., Goldenberg, C., and Hamann, J. (1992). Instructional conversations beget instructional conversations. *Teaching and Teacher Education, 8*, 199–218.

Sechrest, L., & Figueredo, A. J. (1993). Program evaluation. *Annual Review of Psychology, 44*, 645–674.

Sechrest, L., & Figueredo, A. J. (1996). *Approaches used in conducting outcomes and effec-*

tiveness research: Evaluation and program planning. Department of Psychology, University of Arizona, Tucson.

Shavelson, R. J. (1988). Contributions of educational research to policy and practice: Constructing, challenging, changing cognition. *Educational Researcher, 17*(7), 4–11, 22.

Stevens, R. (1910). Stenographic reports of high school lessons. *Teachers College Record, 11*, entire issue.

Tharp, R. G., & Gallimore, R. (1979). The ecology of program research and evaluation: A model of evaluation succession. In L. B. Sechrest (Ed.), *Evaluation studies annual review* (vol. 4, pp. 39–60). Beverly Hills, CA: Sage.

Tharp, R. G., & Gallimore, R. (1982). Inquiry processes in program development. *Journal of Community Psychology, 10*, 103–118.

Tharp, R. G., & Gallimore, R. (1988). *Rousing minds to life: Teaching, learning, and schooling in social context.* Cambridge, England: Cambridge University Press.

Vygotsky, L. (1986). *Thought and Language.* Cambridge: MIT Press.

Weisner, T. (1986). Implementing new relationship styles in conventional and nonconventional American families. In W. Hartup & Z. Rubin (Eds.), *Relationships and development* (pp. 185–206). Hillsdale, NJ: Lawrence Erlbaum Associates.

Weisner, T. S. (1984). Ecocultural niches of middle childhood: A cross-cultural perspective. In W. A. Collins (Ed.), *Development during middle childhood: The years from six to twelve* (pp. 335–369). Washington, DC: National Academy of Sciences.

Weisner, T., & Wilson-Mitchell, J. (1990). Nonconventional family lifestyles and sex typing in six year olds. *Child Development, 61*(6), 1915–1933.

Wertsch, J. V., Tulviste, P., & Hagstrom, F. (1993). A sociocultural approach to agency. In E. Forman, N. Minick, & C. A. Stone (Eds.), *Contexts for learning: Sociocultural dynamics in children's development* (pp. 336–356). Oxford, England: Oxford University Press.

16

Bridging the Gap Between Qualitative and Quantitative Approaches to the Analysis of Instructional Innovations for Students With Learning Disabilities: A Commentary on Gallimore and Lyon

C. Addison Stone
Northwestern University

One of the central questions posed by the chapters in the present volume is whether the "regular" educational classroom can become a successful learning environment for children with learning disabilities. Although the authors of these chapters vary in their optimism regarding this issue, most share, either explicitly or implicitly, a common perspective. This perspective is that although there are many current barriers to learning in the mainstream for students with learning disabilities, there is also much promise for such students associated with attempts to optimize instructional contingencies in the mainstream. The challenge, of course, is to identify those aspects of the classroom that can be changed in order to improve the opportunities for learning in the specific case of the child with learning disabilities.

Although several of the earlier chapters in this book touched indirectly on issues of engineering and assessing change—both in the classroom and in the student—this set of issues is the central focus of the chapters by Gallimore (chap. 15) and Lyon (chap. 14). The two authors focused on different aspects of educational change—Gallimore on classroom or institutional change, and Lyon on instructional change; however, both authors were in agreement that the identification and engineering of effective instructional contingencies for atypical learners will involve thoughtful conceptual and methodological decisions. Despite this common theme, however, the two discussions represented very different perspectives on educational research, and thus the authors arrived at very different recommendations. In the present chapter, I discuss the gap between these two different perspectives and the importance of bridging this gap. In doing so, I comment on the recommendations of each author, and I make some suggestions for how to incorporate their insights into a unified approach to research on instruction and learning in children with learning disabilities.

TWO APPROACHES TO THE STUDY OF LEARNING AND INSTRUCTION

As mentioned previously, Gallimore and Lyon presented two seemingly incompatible perspectives on the important methodological issues involved in studying instructional innovations. At the risk of some distortion, I provide a brief summary of each argument as a basis for the discussion to follow.

Gallimore's main focus was on the child and the teacher as participants in a school community. His emphasis was that instruction is, in essence, a cultural activity, even when it takes place in relatively scripted lessons. Likewise, he argued that children's responses to instruction are filtered through a set of cultural assumptions, assumptions that mediate the impact of instructional innovations. One conclusion that he drew from this perspective is that it is unwise to study instruction and learning without capturing this set of cultural issues and casting one's constructs in contextual terms. An even stronger point was that instructional change that is not sensitive to cultural values both within and around the school setting, and that does not emphasize systemic change, is doomed to fail. The strategy of choice for the study of instructional impact from this perspective is the qualitative analysis of teacher and student activity, with an eye to understanding the perceptions and motivations of the participants.

Lyon, in contrast, argued for a quasi-experimental approach in which carefully scripted interventions are applied in settings allowing for rigorous control. He assumed that student and teacher behaviors can be profitably studied by objective observers, and he put emphasis on the need to collect rich objective data regarding student characteristics and outcomes. His strategy for studying instructional impact was a rigorous analysis of rate of learning at both the individual and group levels, with quantitative analyses of the student and teacher behaviors that predict rate of change.

In the course of his discussion, Gallimore captured one important aspect of the difference between the two perspectives embodied in his chapter and Lyon's chapter. Following Sechrest and Figueredo (1993), he drew a distinction between what these authors referred to as "efficacy" and "effectiveness" studies. Efficacy studies are those that emphasize the documentation of the impact of an intervention under highly controlled conditions. Effectiveness studies, on the other hand, are focused on the evaluation of an intervention's impact under real-world conditions. The distinction at issue here is very similar to that referred to by Rossi and Freeman (1993) as "reproducibility" versus "generalizability." In the context of discussions of program evaluations, a given intervention is reproducible if it is replicated under the same conditions (i.e., highly similar procedures and context). However, such an intervention may not retain any power in new settings with more real-world conditions, and hence it may lack generalizability. Rossi and Freeman (1993) also linked this distinction to that between basic science models versus policy-oriented models.

Although Lyon does mention a need for what Gallimore termed *effectiveness studies*, his preference appeared to be for efficacy studies. That is, he emphasized studies that make use of carefully controlled small-group intervention designs in which every effort is made to create an optimal (if necessarily specialized and separate) learning environment. Such an approach emphasizes measurement objectivity, reliability, and sensitivity. Gallimore's preference, in contrast, was for context-sensitive analyses of classroom dynamics and participant goals. Lyon wanted to know whether a given "treatment" *can* work under optimal conditions, whereas Gallimore wanted to know how to make things work (or what prevents their working) in naturalistic (and realistic) settings. To some extent, this is a matter of choosing tactics for a given stage of knowledge development within a larger time scale of investigation, as both authors pointed out (see also Rossi & Freeman, 1993). However, I believe that there is more at work here than differing opinions about where we are in our knowledge development with respect to the identification of effective instructional tools. There are two reasons for this belief.

First, when one considers the relative merits of these two approaches in the context of the current policy scene in the field of special education, one is struck by the need to take into consideration not just the current scene, but also a vision of the future. In essence, the real-world context within which we must judge these issues is not, or need not be, static. In their discussion of how evaluation research interfaces with the real world, Rossi and Freeman (1993) referred to the "volatility of policy space." In their discussion of this issue, these authors began with the largely implicit assumption that evaluation researchers work in the service of policymakers and must therefore confront the reality of the "moving target" [my term] of policy zeitgeist, a target that is not under their control but that must nonetheless be heeded. Implicit in both Lyon's and Gallimore's chapters was a somewhat more activist stance. In essence, they were both interested in changing instructional environments and educational policy with respect to children with special learning needs, and *not* in optimizing instruction under current constraints. However, their visions for what the future should hold were different, which leads to the second reason why their respective positions with respect to research strategy are not just different moments in a common long-term plan of attack.

The distinction between the two approaches advocated by Gallimore and

Lyon can also be cast in other terms, ones that highlight meta-theoretical differences rather than strategic differences. Carlson (1991), for example, drew a distinction between what he called the "sociolinguistic" and "process–product" approaches to the study of classroom dynamics. The process–product tradition includes both correlational and intervention studies in which attempts are made to identify causal links between specific quantifiable aspects of teacher behavior (e.g., number of questions asked, amount of "wait time") and student outcome measures. In contrast, the sociolinguistic tradition emphasizes the interdependency of (indeed, the constitutive relation between) language and context. Thus, workers in this tradition tend to engage in context-sensitive analyses of the functions served by teacher questions, rather than their objective structure or frequency. These two traditions do not represent specific moments in an overall research agenda as much as differing assumptions regarding the nature of human behavior and learning. There is a very real sense in which the arguments made by Lyon and Gallimore came from such differing perspectives. Indeed, Gallimore alluded to this meta-theoretical gulf in his discussion of the work of Cronbach (1975) and Fuller and Clarke (1994).

The reality of this gulf can be seen by means of a quick comparison of the two chapters. First, although both authors are focused on the issue of how to improve children's learning, they focus at different levels of analysis. Lyon emphasized the need to focus on the individual child; Gallimore focused on the classroom as a whole, what he calls the "culture" of the classroom. The issue here is not, however, whether or not it is valuable to study individual children. Although Gallimore did not do so in his chapter, he would not be adverse to individual case studies. However, he *would* be uncomfortable with a focus on objective (i.e., decontextualized) measures of the individual. Lyon, on the other hand, stressed the importance of objectivity and consistency in measurement and was uncomfortable with inadequately operationalized constructs. This is an important difference.

A second and related difference between the two perspectives centers on the conceptualization of the instructional context of the child. Here, again, Lyon chose to focus on objective features of the learning setting (student–teacher ratio, independent work time, teacher's declarative and procedural knowledge). In contrast, Gallimore emphasized the need to study teacher perceptions of instructional goals and procedures, the activity setting within which instruction is embedded, or student interpretations of the instructional context. For Gallimore, objective features, such as those emphasized by Lyon, represent decontextualized and potentially distorted windows into the actual dynamics of the instructional setting. For Lyon, a focus on interpretations, perceptions, and "culture" is inherently subjective and unreliable. Here, again, we see a large gap.

Although there is no inherent reason in their respective perspectives that they should do so, the two authors agreed that it is important for the field to move beyond the traditional pre–post design in its search for effective instructional procedures. Lyon was quite explicit about this issue, emphasizing the need for multiple measurement points in an ongoing instructional process. He was interested in capturing the pace and pattern of learning, and in identifying changes in the rate of learning as a function of specific instructional contingencies. Gallimore did not address this design issue directly, but he did emphasize the need to study changes in perceptions and patterns of interactions. The studies that he described take place over months or years, not days or weeks, and they involve the continual collection of data regarding classroom process. Despite this similar emphasis on the assessment of change across time, the two authors differed dramatically in the methods they would employ. Lyon called for repeated use of the same observations or probes, whereas Gallimore emphasized a sensitivity to changes with time in perceptions and practices.

Another issue that separates these two perspectives relates to the identification of barriers to change. Both authors were interested in the isolation of those factors that stand in the way of meaningful learning for children. However, they tended to look in different places, or with different lenses. Lyon argued for the isolation of specific teacher behaviors (e.g., poor implementation of an instructional approach) or child characteristics (e.g., deficient language skills) that stand in the way of effective learning. Gallimore, in contrast, focused on entrenched patterns of acting and ways of seeing, on the part of teachers or children.

One final point of comparison between the two chapters relates to their openness to other perspectives. Here, there is some similarity, but it lies in a shared skepticism about the perspective embodied in the other's discussion. Although he did not single out Gallimore in particular, Lyon had little patience for the subjectivity involved in conceptual and methodological systems that cannot be analytically decomposed. Gallimore, on the other hand, had concerns about approaches that "reduc[e] complex psychological and cultural phenomena to discrete inputs."

There is, indeed, a gap between these two perspectives. This gap is not a specific issue of two individuals, however. The perspectives they each embody are shared by significant numbers of educational researchers interested in atypical learners. Indeed, they are represented by the authors of the various chapters of this volume. At an even broader level, they are represented by the various participants in the debate in the general and special educational literature regarding the merits of qualitative and quantitative research (e.g., Bogdan & Lutfiyya, 1992; Simpson, 1992; Smith, 1983). Thus, our response to this gap should not be one of bemused neglect. Both perspectives have many adherents and much merit. Indeed, I would argue that the insights afforded by these two perspectives are *both* necessary if we are to make progress in understanding how to improve the learning of atypical children. The real challenge posed by these chapters is how to integrate the two perspectives without losing what is valuable in each.

HOW CAN WE BRIDGE THE GAP?

Whenever one attempts to combine two divergent perspectives, the risk is that the essential features of both will be distorted. Thus, the key question in the present case is: How can we combine the insights of both perspectives, but in a principled more than an eclectic way, one that preserves key insights from each perspective? From the sociocultural approach represented by Gallimore, we gain the insight that both child and teacher behavior must be viewed, and indeed defined, in the context of the past and current learning activities in the classroom. From the more individualistic psychological approach represented by Lyon, we gain the insight that individuals can be characterized in terms of relatively stable processes, skills, and knowledge bases through which new inputs are filtered. Both perspectives are necessary for a comprehensive picture of instructional dynamics.

One approach to integrating these perspectives is to identify individual behavioral units, as Lyon would want, but ones that are defined, not objectively, but in terms of the interpersonal context of the instructional setting. This can be accomplished if we can identify an appropriate unit for analysis. The individual will not work as the unit, because this approach ignores the context (or adds it as a secondary, modulating variable). The classroom culture or the activity setting will not work, because it does not provide a natural means of incorporating individual cognitive functioning, except as a series of situationally determined perceptions.

My own preference for solving this dilemma would be to choose as our basic unit for analysis in instructional research the communicative exchange constituting any instructional activity. When a teacher interacts with one or more students in the context of a lesson, the dyad or group engages in an ongoing exchange, one that can be conceptualized as a communicative inference (Stone, 1993; Stone & Reid, 1994). In such a perspective, the behaviors of each participant (e.g., questions, statements, gestures, demonstrations) are conceptualized as communicative moves. As these moves unfold, each participant must strive, consciously or unconsciously, to make sense of the moves made by the other. In the process, each participant must infer the goals and intents of the other and integrate that insight into his or her own evolving conception of the situation. This process of inference engages the cognitive and linguistic capabilities of the student (as well as the teacher). That is, a thorough analysis of the communicative exchanges involved in teaching and learning involves a single conceptual framework that incorporates both individual or psychological and interpersonal or cultural issues.

Viewed from this perspective, an analysis of any instructional exchange involves careful attention to the cognitive and linguistic activity of the student (and, ideally, the teacher), but it also requires that these activities be defined, not in the abstract, but in terms of the goal structure of the exchange. An example should help to make this point a little clearer. Let's assume for the moment that we are conducting an intervention study in the area of written language, in which the goal is the assessment of a specific approach for teaching students how to write well-formed, simple declarative sentences. The instructional approach might center on helping students to master a simple multistep strategy for generating and checking a sentence. In the individualistic approach, we would focus primarily on repeated assessments of the key outcome variable: the accuracy of sentence productions. In order to understand factors influencing the students' progress, we might also assess such factors as the fidelity of the teacher to an instructional script, students' verbal ability (as indexed perhaps by a standardized measure of grammatical sophistication in oral language), and a measure of spelling and/or visual–motor skills. In the contextualist approach, we might engage in a descriptive analysis of the lessons, in which we focused on the teacher's assumptions regarding the purpose of writing and the students' awareness of the future value of the current exercise. In the communicative-exchange perspective, we might focus on the cycles of teacher–student exchange to derive repeating indices of the match between teacher and student assumptions about the task, as indexed in word choice and cohesiveness of exchange sequences. This approach would also motivate associated measures of linguistic sophistication, verbal short-term memory, and reasoning—not as isolated indices of ability, but as crucial determinants of communicational "uptake" in the present situation. Thus, a perspective sensitive to the communicational dimensions of instruction provides a motivation for an integrated assessment of both contextual and individual factors.

It should be noted that there are some potentially important limitations to the value of an integrated perspective such as that previously suggested. This is particularly true in the case of a study of objective skills, such as the speed of access to mental representations. Let's assume, for example, that one were interested in studying the effectiveness of a specific approach to increasing the automaticity of word recognition skills. One important outcome measure here would undoubtedly be reaction time to pronounce a series of visually presented words. The key instructional intervention might involve repeated presentations, perhaps in a gamelike computer-based format, of words sequenced carefully in terms of orthographic frequency and phonological and morphological complexity, using performance contingencies to determine progression through the sequence, and so on. In such a situation, many of the interpersonal/contextual features stressed by Gallimore would not apply, and the research design might be structured much as Lyon proposed. It is still the case, however, that one would ignore certain situational issues at peril. For example, such a study would include a focus on measuring and explaining rate of change in decoding automaticity. In doing so, one would need to conceptualize the possibly related factors not just in terms of objective features (e.g., word-list structure, prior measures of rapid automatized naming or vocabulary knowledge, or student responses to a self-concept scale), but also in terms of contextually determined features, such as the student's conceptualization of the instructor's goals. In the case of issues such as these, a contextually sensitive perspective provides some advantage over a purely individual perspective, particularly when one considers issues of rate of learning and ease of generalization; however, it is clear that the individual perspective is at its strength in cases such as this one, where one is focusing on lower-level skills.

PUTTING METHODOLOGY TO USE

Whether or not we opt for the individual/psychological approach advocated by Lyon, the cultural/contextual approach advocated by Gallimore, or some hybrid such as the communicational approach sketched in this chapter, the question that remains is how we should be applying the methodology to improve the education of students with learning disabilities. Lyon would seem to argue for a traditional experimental approach, one in which we use theory to devise experimental procedures and then test them in the laboratory (or in carefully controlled experimental classrooms). Gallimore would seem to argue for the creation of alternative classroom environments in which teachers engage students in meaningful, goal-based learning activities linked to real-world objectives. In essence, both of these approaches would pull us away from the reality of current-day classrooms. This is both a strength and a weakness. Such approaches have the advantage of freeing us from the "drag" of current practices, ones that have, in the eyes of many, failed to serve the needs of students with learning disabilities (e.g., Baker & Zigmond, 1990; Fuchs & Fuchs, 1990; Kauffman, 1989). They also have the advantage of freeing us from the constraints embodied in current-day school structure.

However, these advantages come at some cost. One drawback is that we will miss the opportunity to study the often-powerful instructional approaches already embodied in the activities of gifted clinicians or teachers. Although many such individuals have written about teaching, there are very few, if any, systematic observational studies of such individuals at work. Although their own writings do provide some insight into the techniques they use, I would expect that careful study of successful lessons would lead to the identification of key instructional contingencies of which the practitioners are not fully aware. Why should we ignore such insights?

A second drawback of a purely theory-driven, ivory-tower approach is the creation of instructional approaches that are not feasibly implemented in our school systems. Here, both Gallimore and Lyon would probably dismiss this concern. Both authors would undoubtedly argue that we should not take the current educational system as a given when it comes to the case of atypical learners (or, in Gallimore's case, *any* students). This is the activism in each author's discussion that I mentioned earlier. Gallimore would cheer the reorganization of schools in general. Lyon would argue that the specialized instruction found most efficacious for students with learning disabilities might well have to be provided in special classrooms, if only for a brief portion of a given student's career. Thus, neither author is concerned about the fit of their experimental instructional activities into a school system as it is currently constituted, although Gallimore in particular would emphasize the need to consider carefully the reality of the surrounding community's values in planning educational change that will "take root" (Goldenberg & Gallimore, 1991). There is, of course, a good deal of truth in what they would advocate. However, we should bear in mind that educational change tends to be evolutionary, not revolutionary, and advocates of specialized instruction for atypical learners can ignore potential clashes in educational philosophy and technology at the peril of losing policy battles down the road.

Again, I would return to my initial refrain. The wisest approach to developing effective instructional approaches for children with learning disabilities may lie down the road of principled eclecticism. We cannot afford to ignore current practices or policies in framing our search. We also cannot afford to ignore either the sociocultural realities of teaching and learning, or the psychological realities of cognitive processing. We need both contextually sensitive units of measurement *and* careful experimental designs. Without such a multipronged approach, we may move no faster or farther than we have moved over the last 30 years.

ACKNOWLEDGMENTS

I would like to thank Joanne Carlisle and Barbara Keogh for their comments on earlier drafts of this chapter. I would also like to thank Ron Gallimore and Reid Lyon for providing thoughtful grist for the mill. Hopefully, I have not grossly distorted their perspectives on the issues at hand.

REFERENCES

Baker, J. M., & Zigmond, N. (1990). Are regular education classes equipped to accommodate students with learning disabilities? *Exceptional Children, 56,* 515–526.

Bogdan, R., & Lutfiyya, Z. M. (1992). Standing on its own: Qualitative research in special education. In W. Stainback & S. Stainback (Eds.), *Controversial issues confronting special education: Divergent perspectives* (pp. 243–251). Needham Heights, MA: Allyn & Bacon.

Carlson, W. S. (1991). Questioning in classrooms: A sociolinguistic perspective. *Review of Educational Research, 61,* 157–178.

Cronbach, L. J. (1975). Beyond the two disciplines of scientific psychology. *American Psychologist, 30,* 116–127.

Fuchs, D., & Fuchs, L. (1990). Enhancing the education of difficult-to-teach students in the mainstream: Federally sponsored research. *Exceptional Children, 57,* 102–190.

Fuller, B., & Clarke, P. (1994). Raising school effects while ignoring culture? Local conditions and the influence of classroom tools, rules, and pedagogy. *Review of Educational Research, 64,* 119–157.

Goldenberg, C., & Gallimore, R. (1991). Local knowledge, research knowledge, and educational change: A case study of early Spanish reading improvement. *Educational Researcher, 20*(8), 2–14.

Kauffman, J. M. (1989). The regular education initiative as Reagan–Bush education policy: A trickle-down theory of education of the hard-to-teach. *Journal of Special Education, 23,* 256–278.

Rossi, P. H., & Freeman, H. E. (1993). *Evaluation: A systematic approach* (5th ed.). Newbury Park, CA: Sage.

Sechrest, L., & Figueredo, A. J. (1993). Program evaluation. *Annual Review of Psychology, 44,* 645–674.

Simpson, R. G. (1992). Quantitative research as the method of choice within a continuum model. In W. Stainback & S. Stainback (Eds.), *Controversial issues confronting special education: Divergent perspectives* (pp. 235–242). Needham Heights, MA: Allyn & Bacon.

Smith, J. K. (1983). Quantitative versus qualitative research : An attempt to clarify the issue. *Educational Researcher, 12,* 6–13.

Stone, C. A. (1993). What's missing in the metaphor of scaffolding? In E. A. Forman, N. Minick, & C. A. Stone (Eds.), *Contexts for learning: Sociocultural dynamics of children's development* (pp. 169–183). New York: Oxford University Press.

Stone, C. A., & Reid, D. K. (1994). Social and individual forces in children's learning: Implications for the instruction of children with learning difficulties. *Learning Disability Quarterly, 17,* 72–86.

Epilogue

Classroom Ecologies and Learning Disabilities: What We Learned and What We Need to Know

Deborah L. Speece
University of Maryland at College Park

Barbara K. Keogh
University of California, Los Angeles

Cuban (1990) observed that the reason we continue to witness wave after wave of school reform is that reform never begins in the place where change is most likely to have its greatest impact: the classroom. Teachers and their daily work with children are almost afterthoughts in educational blueprints for change. In this volume we have sought to understand the classroom from multiple perspectives. Our goals were to identify what we know and what still needs to be examined with respect to the development of children with learning disabilities. Simple, and likely accurate, responses to these two goals would be "not enough" and "a whole lot." However, the substance and breadth of content in the chapters suggest that we do have considerable understanding of the complexities of classroom life, and there are clearly defined directions for a research agenda addressing classroom influences.

In this closing commentary we delineate some of the themes across the chapters and propose directions for further study. There is no attempt to summarize the authors' work, because we could not do justice to the scope of the ideas presented. Rather, we present issues that appeared with some consistency across the chapters and chart research questions that may advance our knowledge of the complexities of classrooms, teachers, children, and learning.

ATTEND TO INSTRUCTIONAL INTERACTIONS (OR LACK THEREOF)

We know that children must be actively involved in their learning and that when they are given opportunities to participate in meaningful ways, their achievement increases. A demand to participate actively, particularly verbal participation, may be difficult for children with learning disabilities as many are not facile with the rigors of academic discourse, a considerably more difficult task than conversational language. Peer-mediated learning may be one avenue to assist students in appropriating academic language in the pursuit of active participation. However, these techniques may not be enough for children with severely deficient language skills who require intense and long-term instruction.

We emphasize that instructional practices that promote the active involvement of learners are critical in all subject matter areas. Erickson's (chap. 6, this volume) metaphor of the "phantom woodworker" aptly captures the role of too many children who learn that by fading into the woodwork they'll get by. This lesson is often supported by teachers who enter into their own "don't ask, don't tell" pact with students that gets played out by moving through the day with few if any academic challenges. Finding ways to break this covenant between teachers and children and move toward active roles for all participants is a critical task for teachers and researchers.

DESIGN PROXIMAL ASSESSMENTS

A second major theme had to do with assessment. Whether one chooses curriculum-based assessments, portfolios, or some other index of learning, it is essential that we keep better track of children's progress. Assessment procedures that tap "online" learning by being closer to instruction provide essential information that should be the basis of subsequent instructional decisions. Published, norm-referenced tests still have their place, but were not designed to provide the type of feedback teachers need to evaluate instruction or that students need to evaluate progress. As underscored by several authors, it is imperative that we not confuse activity and positive affect with learning. Instead, instructional decisions need to be guided by evidence, and compliance and surveillance must be replaced by learning and assessment.

ORGANIZE CLASSROOMS FOR LEARNING

A third point of consensus had to do with how the organization of classrooms affected instruction. The authors who contributed to this volume made it clear that business as usual will not suffice, especially for children with learning disabilities. However, sustained and innovative modifications were seldom observed. A dramatic example was the continued reliance on group instruction. Despite educators' best intentions, and despite many efforts to bring about change, we have seen that classrooms are dominated by whole-class instruction with little opportunity for participation by children with learning disabilities. Whole-class instruction, the initiation-response-evaluation script, end point assessment, single file participation, and accommodations that do not promote learning are simply inadequate to meet the needs of many children. There is considerable evidence that educators agree that individualization is a key to good teaching, yet group lessons continue to dominate. We suggest that whole-class instruction is evidence of a powerful cultural tradition, and that innovation, no matter how sound, must address the culture and routines that determine life in the classroom.

The problem, of course, is organizing classrooms in ways that address real-life management issues of time, behavior, and curriculum that are consistent with teachers' beliefs and that promote learning. Regardless of shifting theoretical orientations, these management issues will not go away. There is the sobering suggestion in these pages that inclusion of children with special needs comes at a high price—a price we may not be willing to pay. That is, if inclusion accomplishes social goals but not academic goals, then the needs of children with learning disabilities will not be met.

In this vein, it is also critical to examine the organization of special education settings. Currently, the concept of the continuum of services is still viable, yet little research attention has been directed to improving outcomes for children who participate in resource or self-contained classroom settings or in identifying the important influences on learning. Special education classes, like their general education counterparts, differ in goals, curricular emphasis, instructional methods, and how and in what ways time and space are organized. It is erroneous to talk about special education as a unitary program. Similarly, it is a mistake to assume that the problems of and solutions for educating children with learning disabilities will be found only in the general education classroom. It would seem reasonable, then, to devote more effort to understanding all the classroom settings experienced by children with learning disabilities.

PROVIDE PROFESSIONAL DEVELOPMENT THAT WORKS

Underlying the data, arguments, and discussion is the recognition that teachers are key players in the ecology of the classroom and, thus, need ongoing support if any type of meaningful change is to occur. This is not a novel observation. However, the frequency with which the statement was made suggests that past efforts have had little impact on practice. Our authors noted that children may resist learning and may find active participation in lessons too risky a venture to pursue. The corollary is that the same is true for teachers: Traditional instructional and management methods will not be forsaken based on administrative mandates or researchers' theories. A clear generalization from the authors' discussions in this volume is that whatever the specifics, change in educational practices is slow, often painful, and frequently resisted. Change that is not calibrated to existing beliefs and conditions will be resisted, and the risk will not be taken. There will be little change in classrooms until teachers are comfortable with alternative instructional and assessment methods and held accountable for children's progress. By the same token, there will be little change in the knowledge base on teaching and learning until researchers examine their beliefs about what constitutes appropriate research questions.

INTEGRATE MODELS OF INDIVIDUAL DIFFERENCES AND ECOLOGICAL FACTORS

As we noted in the opening chapter to this volume, research in learning disabilities has been ruled by individual difference perspectives, with scant attention paid to the influences of ecological factors on development. It is a fair criticism that research on classroom factors lacks an organizing framework, making study difficult. However, it is also fair to point out that research that treats factors external to the child as nuisance variables misses a valuable opportunity to explain child variance. The work in this volume suggests that an organizing framework is possible and needed. That is, individual classrooms, like children, have unique features but are not so variable as to defy description. We simply have not put much effort into understanding classroom ecological effects. One thing we have learned from the work herein is that behaviorism and social constructivism may not be as disparate as some would suggest, and that mutual adoption of variables and methods may pay larger dividends than would either one alone. Although neither approach is associated with an individual difference perspective, we argue that incorporation of individual differences with contextually relevant variables is a powerful approach for addressing the schooling problems of children with learning disabilities.

We conclude with the reminder that schools and classrooms are embedded in a larger ecology that sometimes constricts and sometimes directs educational practice. *Goals 2000: Educate America Act* reflects national concerns for raising standards and improving the educational achievement of American students. The policy of inclusion argues for the delivery of educational services to children in regular educational programs. These policies influence the delivery of educational services at the school and district level and affect directly the educational experiences of children with learning disabilities. In some instances, these value-driven policies may be in conflict and work to the detriment rather than the benefit of children with special educational needs. We suggest that educational programs for children with learning disabilities must be evaluated with the test of evidence. This is not an easy task and will require time, given the heterogeneity of characteristics of children identified as learning disabled and the range of programs that serve them. However, the authors of the chapters in this volume provide an optimistic view of the future through their thorough analyses of important classroom ecological elements and their thoughtful recommendations for research and practice.

REFERENCES

Cuban, L. (1990). Reforming again, again, and again. *Educational Researcher, 19*(1), 3–13.

Author Index

Subject Index